THE DEF

THE
DEFENDER

THE BATTLE TO PROTECT THE RIGHTS
OF THE ACCUSED IN PHILADELPHIA

EDWARD W. MADEIRA JR.
AND MICHAEL D. SCHAFFER

TEMPLE UNIVERSITY PRESS
Philadelphia | *Rome* | *Tokyo*

TEMPLE UNIVERSITY PRESS
Philadelphia, Pennsylvania 19122
tupress.temple.edu

Library of Congress Cataloging-in-Publication Data

Names: Madeira, Edward W., Jr., 1928–2020 author. | Schaffer, Michael D.,
    1947– author.
Title: The Defender : the battle to protect the rights of the accused in Philadelphia /
    Edward W. Madeira, Jr. and Michael D. Schaffer.
Description: Philadelphia : Temple University Press, 2020. | Includes index. |
    Summary: "A history of the Defender Association of Philadelphia, from a
    two-lawyer volunteer office to an integral part of Philadelphia's court and prison
    system. Each era finds new challenges as the burdens on the justice system expand
    and the Defender remakes itself to rigorously defend the indigent people of
    Philadelphia"—Provided by publisher.
Identifiers: LCCN 2019057879 (print) | LCCN 2019057880 (ebook) | ISBN
    9781439918524 (cloth) | ISBN 9781439918548 (pdf)
Subjects: LCSH: Defender Association of Philadelphia—History. | Public
    defenders—Pennsylvania—Philadelphia—History. | Legal assistance
    to the poor—Pennsylvania—Philadelphia—History.
Classification: LCC KFX2137.4.P8 M33 2020 (print) | LCC KFX2137.4.P8 (ebook)
    | DDC 345.748/01423630974811—dc23
LC record available at https://lccn.loc.gov/2019057879
LC ebook record available at https://lccn.loc.gov/2019057880

Printed in the United States of America

9 8 7 6 5 4 3 2 1

To the thousands

of Philadelphia public defenders

and their staffs,

who have fought for the constitutional rights

of their indigent clients and

for a more just criminal justice system

CONTENTS

Illustrations begin after page 104

Acknowledgments

WITH OUR DEEPEST GRATITUDE, we acknowledge those whose valuable contributions made this book possible, including former chief defenders the Honorable Benjamin Lerner, judge of the Philadelphia Court of Common Pleas, and Ellen Greenlee; the current chief defender, Keir Bradford-Grey, and her executive assistant, Christine Noble; former first assistant defenders Charles A. Cunningham, David Rudovsky, and Louis M. Natali Jr.; longtime Defender Board of Directors member David Richman and Mary DeFusco, director of training and recruitment at the Defender, for providing an introduction to Municipal Court. They have given liberally of their time in helping us put together the history of this great institution. Our thanks also go to Temple University executive vice president, provost, and law professor JoAnne Epps, former chair of the Defender board, whose support and encouragement got us started. We are also grateful to Ryan Mulligan, our editor at Temple University Press, who saw the promise in our book proposal and helped us shape and sharpen the finished work. Ryan pushed us to explore the Defender's impact on Philadelphia and on criminal justice in Pennsylvania.

Special thanks go to the twenty-six people we interviewed, named elsewhere herein, who provided background information and a variety of perspectives on the growth and strength of the Defender Association.

We are especially grateful to the late chief defender Vincent Ziccardi, who had the foresight in the early 1970s to provide the Temple University library with Defender annual reports and related documents from the association's establishment in 1934. Those documents were essential in writing the Defender's early history, and we are indebted to the library for maintaining the records and making them available to us.

We are grateful to Joanne Stoner, legal secretary at Pepper Hamilton LLP, for her assistance and to the Pepper Hamilton firm for its hospitality in providing a place for us to meet.

Thanks go to Bill Marimow, former editor of the *Philadelphia Inquirer*, for suggesting that Mike Schaffer would be a good choice to help Ned Madeira fulfill his long-standing ambition of writing the story of the Defender.

Finally, we thank Ben Lerner, David Rudovsky, Ellen Greenlee, and David Richman for all their input and encouragement. They kept us on the right path; any errors or omissions are ours alone.

THE DEFENDER

INTRODUCTION

"There Is Need of a Defender"

ON MAY 8, 1787, just a few weeks before the delegates to the Constitutional Convention met in Philadelphia to remake the government of the young United States, thirty-seven of the city's leading citizens gathered at the German School on Cherry Street with another kind of change in mind. Led by Dr. Benjamin Rush, a pioneer in the treatment of mental illness, and Episcopal bishop William White, they created the Philadelphia Society for Alleviating the Miseries of Public Prisons. Their aim was to get better treatment for prisoners at the Walnut Street Jail, which was filthy, crowded, and dangerous. Prodded by the society, the state legislature ordered the construction of a new building—called a penitentiary—to be added to the jail. Prisoners would be housed in cells instead of in large rooms where young and old, male and female, hardened criminals, and people who just could not pay their bills were thrown together.[1]

The society, which changed its name to the Pennsylvania Prison Society in 1887 and remains active to this day, has been a consistent advocate throughout its history for the fair and humane treatment of prisoners. Early in the twentieth century, the society began to take an interest not just in what was happening to inmates behind bars but in how they got there. Members of the Prison Society found in talking to inmates that many criminal defendants in Philadelphia were facing the justice system without legal counsel because they could not afford to hire a lawyer and were being held in custody awaiting trial because they could not make bail.[2]

In 1926, Albert G. Fraser, superintendent of the Prison Society's Department of Released Prisoners, reported to the society's Acting Committee about the plight of prisoners without lawyers. Fraser based his report on his own visits with prisoners, but the society soon backed him up with hard numbers. Two members of the Prison Society's staff examined one thousand Philadelphia court cases over a three-month period in 1928 and found that 68 percent of the defendants were not represented by counsel.[3]

The scene in a Philadelphia courtroom in those days was dreary and oppressive, like something out of Franz Kafka. Defendants were taken to court the day after indictment to be arraigned and tried. One by one, they would be hauled out of a holding cell that was packed with more than twenty prisoners to face a judge, hear the charges, and enter a plea—all in the space of a few minutes and almost always without counsel. The accused were left to represent themselves as best they could. If an indigent defendant did ask for an attorney or the judge decided for some reason that a defendant needed a lawyer, counsel would be appointed on the spot from lawyers in the courtroom and the trial would proceed, without any chance for the lawyer to prepare a case.[4]

Fraser suggested that Philadelphia needed a group of lawyers, similar to the Voluntary Defenders Committee of New York County (Manhattan), willing to provide free representation to impoverished defendants.[5] Fraser's report stunned a new member of the Acting Committee, Philadelphia lawyer Francis Fisher Kane, who joined the Prison Society in 1926 and would go on to become its president in 1934. Kane, a frail-looking man with a robust sense of justice, proved to be a kindred spirit to Dr. Rush and Bishop White. He already had a long record as a champion of social justice and progressive causes. Born in Philadelphia in 1866, the son and grandson of Quaker lawyers, Kane graduated from Princeton University in 1886 and from the University of Pennsylvania Law School in 1889. He ran for mayor as a Democrat in 1903, when a Democrat in Philadelphia stood almost no chance of winning. President Woodrow Wilson appointed him U.S. attorney for the Eastern District of Pennsylvania in 1913, but he resigned in 1920 to protest the series of politically motivated raids on supposed communists ordered by U.S. attorney general A. Mitchell Palmer.[6]

Kane was an experienced prosecutor, but on the federal level. When Fraser's report led him to look at the local courts in Philadelphia, he was horrified. He found that five thousand defendants were passing through Philadelphia's Court of Quarter Sessions each year without a lawyer. Not all of them required legal representation, Kane said, but if even half did, that meant there were twenty-five hundred "who needed counsel if their cases were properly to be considered by the court . . . and who didn't get it because they were too poor. Wasn't that a monstrous thought, a nightmarish thought?"[7]

Kane rallied his colleagues on the Prison Society's Acting Committee: "There appear cases where legal assistance is much needed and often the arrested person has no means to employ counsel. Hence, there is need of a Defender."[8] Filling that need was going to be an uphill battle. Indigent defense was not unheard of in the United States before 1926, but it was not common either. New Jersey enacted a law in 1795 requiring compulsory assignment of a lawyer to any defendant unable to hire one.[9] The Indiana Supreme Court ruled in an 1854 case, *Webb v. Baird*, that "it is not to be thought of in a civilized community for a moment that any citizen put in jeopardy of life or liberty should be debarred because he is too poor to employ such aid. . . . It seems eminently proper and just that the treasury of the county should be chargeable with his defense." The Indiana court also held that "defense of the poor in [felony] cases is a duty which will at once be conceded as essential to the accused, to the court and to the public."[10] Farther west and a decade later, the first Montana Territorial Legislature declared in 1864 that an indigent defendant charged with a felony had the right to free counsel.[11] In 1893, Clara Shortridge Foltz, California's first female lawyer, argued powerfully for the creation of public defender offices in a half-hour speech to the Congress of Jurisprudence and Law Reform, held at the Chicago World's Fair. Foltz declared that for every public prosecutor, there also should be a public defender whose work would be supported by taxes, not by charity.[12] In 1914, Los Angeles County opened the first government-funded public defender office in the United States.[13]

The idea of a tax-supported public defender caught on in the Midwest and West, but not in the East, where the private bar preferred that indigent defense be voluntary, not government supported. In the big cities of the East, with their entrenched legal establishments, criminal lawyers feared that public defenders would cut into their business, and elite corporate lawyers opposed what they viewed as government intrusion into the independence of the bar.[14] As Fraser suggested, Kane and other Philadelphia advocates of a public defender looked to New York as a model. The courts there had been empowered since 1788 to appoint counsel for indigent defendants, and the Legal Aid Society began representing impoverished clients in 1879, more than a decade before Foltz made her case at the Chicago World's Fair for public defenders. In 1881, the New York state legislature required that poor defendants in felony cases be provided pro bono counsel. In 1917, the Voluntary Defenders Committee of New York began its work with the blessing of the New York Bar Association, which had opposed the idea of a public defender as a government intrusion but enthusiastically supported the idea of a voluntary defender supported by private philanthropy. "New York has a viable claim to inventing public defense in America," wrote Geoff Burkhart, deputy director of the American Bar Association Center for Innovation.[15]

Unlike New York (or New Jersey, Indiana, or Montana), Pennsylvania law had no tradition of providing free counsel to indigent defendants, although the state constitution adopted in 1776 did declare, "In all prosecutions for criminal offences, a man hath a right to be heard by himself and his council [sic]."[16] Creating a government office for defending the indigent would be a hard sell in Philadelphia. As Fraser told delegates to a gathering called the Philadelphia Conference on City Government in 1928, "It may take some time to awaken public interest sufficiently to bring about the appointment of an official public defender."[17] Fraser thought that Philadelphia should have a public defender, just as it had a public prosecutor. Otherwise, there would be "one law for the rich and another for the poor," he warned.[18] The Prison Society tried to allay any fear the public might have that a defender would help the guilty go free. The society's 1929 annual report declared that the aim of having a public defender was not "to minimize the guilt of the accused party, but to produce extenuating circumstances, if any could be found, which would have a weight in the determination of the penalty that should be imposed upon the defendant."[19]

Since the public was not ready to act, Fraser said, the Pennsylvania Prison Society was advocating appointment of a voluntary public defender: "His services will be paid for by organizations interested in the movement and he will be available to all who are too poor to pay for legal defense."[20] In 1927, following New York's example, Kane and the Prison Society began to organize the Voluntary Defender Committee. "A committee of this kind might discover a process of selection of suitable cases out of this flotsam and jetsam which flows through our courts of justice annually," Fraser remarked in the Prison Society's January 1927 annual report.[21]

Kane set to work convincing Philadelphia's legal community—bench and bar—that the city needed an organization, supported by charity and free from political interference, to represent poor people accused of crime. He evangelized tirelessly for the cause: lecturing, writing, buttonholing lawyers, going on the radio.[22] The Prison Society helped the effort by holding a large luncheon at the Bellevue-Stratford in May 1928 and bringing in New York district attorney Joab Banton to talk about creating a defender organization. The event served as the launch for a three-year campaign by the Prison Society to raise forty-five thousand dollars for the support of the Voluntary Defender Committee.[23] By 1929, Kane had convinced sixteen stars of the Philadelphia bar to become members of the committee, including Henry S. Drinker Jr., Frederic L. Ballard, Morris Wolf, Maurice Saul, Robert Dechert, and Owen J. Roberts, who would be named an associate justice of the U.S. Supreme Court in 1930.[24]

Kane's efforts paid off when Judge Eugene V. Alessandroni of Philadelphia's Court of Common Pleas approved the Voluntary Defender Committee's incorporation as the Voluntary Defender Association on April 14, 1934, "to provide for the representation in the courts of poor persons accused of crime, who by reason of their poverty, are unable to pay counsel fees, and of persons accused of crime in cases which are referred to the Association by charitable agencies and which may be assigned to it by the Judges of the several courts."[25] The incorporators not only lent the new association the luster of their names but also agreed to raise funds to support the work.[26]

With Kane leading the decision, the association quickly hired a defender, Thomas E. Cogan, and an assistant defender, Harry Steinbrook, who went to work on April 2, 1934, with a staff of one investigator, an assistant investigator, and two stenographers.[27] Kane made clear what he expected of Cogan and Steinbrook: "The Defender's responsibility in turning down a case is heavier than rests upon private counsel for he deals with a helpless defendant who, if he be turned down, will probably have no other attorney to represent him." Defendants, he emphasized, had a right to legal counsel and should not have to make themselves paupers to get it: "Neither good morals nor good sense demands that a defendant should part with his tools or pawn his clothes in order to obtain counsel." Kane also left an admonition for those who would come after him: "Generation after generation must see to it that the courts dispense an even justice—even to rich and poor alike."[28]

Kane kept a careful watch on the association until his death in 1955, serving in various capacities on the Board of Directors, first as secretary, later as secretary/treasurer and honorary president. When he received the Philadelphia Award in 1936 for his work in establishing the association, he tried to deflect praise, claiming he had done "such a tiny, little thing."[29] More than eighty years later, the "tiny, little thing" Kane helped create has long since dropped "Voluntary" from its name and is supported not by charity but by tax dollars. Free representation for indigent defense is no longer a charitable option but a constitutional requirement, thanks to the U.S. Supreme Court's landmark 1963 decision in *Gideon v. Wainwright*.

The Defender Association has grown into a major law firm, recognized as one of the best public defender offices in the United States. In 2016, the Defender took on forty-seven thousand new criminal cases and another fourteen thousand juvenile cases. The staff has grown from its original 2 lawyers in 1934 to about 230 in 2017, with another 70 working in the federal courts, and a total staff of about 480, including social workers, investigators, and office support.[30] Many Defender alumni have gone on to success in private practice, law school professorships, and judgeships.

In the twenty-first century, the Defender is still acting as counsel for the poor, although in ways that even Kane might not have imagined, not only going to trial frequently on behalf of its clients but also placing ever more emphasis on trying to keep its clients out of jail by diverting them into rehabilitation or training programs. "We want more community engagement" to help identify and address community problems that foster crime, said Keir Bradford-Grey, who became the chief defender in 2015. "I call it twenty-first-century defending."[31] Francis Fisher Kane would have approved.

1

THE EARLY YEARS

I T HAD TAKEN Francis Fisher Kane's outraged sense of justice and the Prison Society's tireless advocacy on behalf of the imprisoned to awaken Philadelphia to the need for a defender of indigents accused of crime—a need that even Kane did not know existed until inmates began telling the Prison Society that they had been rushed through the court system without a lawyer. Now that Kane and his supporters had incorporated the Voluntary Defender Association, they faced the challenge of getting it organized and integrating it into the complicated legal landscape of one of America's largest cities. From a list of more than fifty attorneys, the association's Board of Directors, carefully steered by Kane, chose Thomas E. Cogan as the chief defender and Harry Steinbrook as his assistant. Both had extensive experience in criminal law and had earned the respect of the criminal defense bar.[1] Cogan had worked with prominent defense attorney William A. Gray, who would later be named by the Philadelphia Bar Association as one of its "Legends of the Bar," a legal Hall of Fame.[2]

The genial Cogan and the soft-spoken, scholarly Steinbrook set up shop in Room 409 of the Harrison Building at Fifteenth and Market Streets and plunged into the work. There was plenty to do; two-thirds of criminal cases in Philadelphia had been going to trial without counsel because the defendants could not afford it. Cogan and Steinbrook were no sooner installed in office than applications for free counsel came flooding in, mostly through the prison agent, the Prison Society worker charged with tending to the welfare of defendants who had to wait in jail for their court date. Each application for help involved a personal interview at the prison, since almost all of the Defender's potential clients were held in jail awaiting trial because they could not make bail. The association's rules required a face-to-face meeting between defender and defendant before the Defender could take a case. Defendants answered a set of routine questions from a printed form, including whether they could afford a lawyer, before they were allowed to tell the lawyer their stories. In that way, "the truth is best elicited," according to the first annual report of the association's directors.[3]

It took less than a month for Cogan to show Philadelphia what the Defender could do. "Philadelphia's public defender proved the value of his office yesterday when he unearthed evidence showing that an innocent man has been serving time for a robbery in which he had no part as a result of a grudge against him by the real criminal," the *Inquirer* reported.[4] Cogan had become interested in the case while interviewing prisoners at the old Moyamensing Prison in South Philadelphia. His curiosity led him to Nathan Zubarsky, who was serving time for holding up a South Street jewelry store in 1932. Zubarsky pleaded guilty but claimed that another man, Herman Pasha, had been an accomplice. Pasha was convicted on Zubarsky's testimony, but Cogan got Zubarsky to admit that he had concocted the story to get back at Pasha for beating him up seven years earlier.[5] Pasha, who had served sixteen months of a seven- to fourteen-year sentence, got a new trial and was acquitted.[6] A news photo showed a triumphant Cogan—victory cigar in hand, derby hat at a jaunty angle—outside a courtroom with Pasha.[7]

The Voluntary Defender Association got a warm welcome from its courtroom rivals, the district attorney's office. "The District Attorney has from the first been sympathetic, and we desire to express our gratitude for the assistance and cooperation which we have received from the public prosecutor and his staff," the Defender directors wrote in their 1934 annual report. The board even acknowledged "the assistance received from the Police Department" and from Philadelphia prison officials, "without whose cooperation it would have been most difficult to carry on the work."[8]

The new association garnered praise from the press, quickly earning the label "the poor man's lawyer." *Inquirer* columnist Eleanor Morton wrote eight months after the Defender began operation, "Already, hundreds of cases, in which tragic injustice might have been worked, have been brought to a just decision." Newspaper stories portrayed the Defender's clients as uneducated, bewildered by the complexities of the legal system, and "unable . . . to tell [their] story and make [themselves] believed in court."[9] Nearly two years later, Morton's enthusiasm for the Defender had not dimmed. She wrote of the Defender, "Here is something new and very fine, something which could not have existed in a time before our own. Here is equality before the law. It is to the great honor of the law that leading lawyers themselves have created this beneficence for the forlorn, the friendless, the penniless."[10] A 1936 series in the *Inquirer* by Herman A. Lowe, one of the paper's top reporters, described the Defender's triumphs, including how Cogan saved one Philadelphia man from being sent to Virginia to face trial for a murder he could not have committed and intervened to keep a runaway teenager from Maine from being charged with a weapons violation that was the result of inadvertence, not criminal intent. The general headline for the series summed up the reporter's findings: "Justice Does Not Miscarry When the Voluntary Defender Sets Out to Help the Poor and Bewildered."[11]

Interest in the Defender's work also spread to community leaders. Cardinal Dennis Dougherty, the formidable Roman Catholic archbishop of Philadelphia, endorsed the association's fund-raising efforts, declaring in a letter to Francis Fisher Kane that the organization's mission had his "full sympathy. The cause of justice to the poor should make a strong appeal to the community at large."[12]

Despite the praise that journalists such as Morton and Lowe heaped on the Defender, the association's relationship with Philadelphia's legal community was complicated. While the Brahmins of the bar had played an essential role in creating the Defender, other lawyers were less enthusiastic about the prospect of more competition for whatever meager fees were available for defending poor people. The Depression was in full swing, and experienced criminal defense lawyers were having trouble making a living by representing defendants at trial for twenty-five dollars. "Some attorneys and judges thought the Defender encroached on the territory of lawyers," recalled John B. Martin, who became a member of the association's Board of Directors in 1936 and later its president. Every case that the Defender took was one that would not go to a private lawyer, even if the amount of money paid to court-appointed lawyers was small.[13]

Hostility from private attorneys toward public defenders was not peculiar to Philadelphia. It happened in other cities where efforts were under way to create public defender offices. New York established its voluntary defender office because the local bar turned thumbs down on the idea of a defender's office that would be part of city government. In Cleveland, opposition from the private bar scuttled plans for a public defender's office in the early 1930s.[14] In Philadelphia, however, Cogan and Steinbrook "continued their work in a manner that allayed any feelings of encroachment by the defense bar," according to Martin. They were down-to-earth, hardworking lawyers, not visionary reformers, but in Martin's view, "they were instrumental in the success and acceptance of the Defender's office."[15]

Just how hard Cogan and Steinbrook worked can be seen in Cogan's report on the association's first year. Cogan, Steinbrook, and their small staff—two investigators and two stenographers—soon found themselves stretched thin, working eight to ten cases a day. In its first year, the Voluntary Defender Association handled 2,064 cases and finished 1,466 of them. Of the finished cases, 1,115 ended with the defendant being sentenced. Defender clients entered 586 guilty pleas, along with 274 pleas of nolo contendere. Out of 635 not-guilty pleas, 337 ended in acquittal; 59 of the not-guilty pleas led to a nolle prosequi declaration by the district attorney, ending the prosecution. (The number of pleas does not correspond to the number of cases because more than one plea was entered in some cases.)[16]

The Defender's resources in its first year—$18,529 raised from private contributions—were not enough to hire a needed second assistant defender or another even more urgently needed third investigator.[17] However, the Defender lived up to its name as a voluntary organization when several attorneys stepped in to help during the organization's first year. Curtis Bok, one of the original directors and later a common pleas judge and Pennsylvania Supreme Court justice, agreed to substitute for the chief defender during vacations. (An article in the *Philadelphia Inquirer* noted that while Cogan received an annual salary of seventy-five hundred dollars, the terms of his employment did not include vacation time.)[18] Two younger lawyers, Walter Stein and Gilliat G. Schroeder, volunteered as assistant defenders, devoting full-time to the work. Two or three students came aboard as unpaid assistants to the two investigators.[19]

A small executive committee of the board supervised the Defender's work, although the real boss was Kane, who served as the organization's secretary once it was incorporated. "Make no mistake about it, the Voluntary Defender Association was Frank Kane," recalled Morris

Duane, one of the association's original directors. "The rest of us did what he asked. We helped raise money. We talked it up among members of the Bar and among friends who might support it financially. We attended meetings and helped select and persuade lawyers to participate in it."[20] The father of the Voluntary Defender Association was a hands-on parent. "Francis Fisher Kane . . . was everywhere," Schroeder recalled. "For a small man, he could be remarkably full-throated when in apprehension of injustice." He also kept a close eye on the lawyers doing the association's work. "Kane was occasionally in court, maybe more often than I knew, to monitor the professional acuteness of the defenders," Schroeder added. "He encouraged us to meet daily and critique our performance."[21]

Martin provides a glimpse of what the Defender's day was like in the organization's early years. Cogan and Steinbrook would meet at the Harrison Building in the morning to obtain the day's files. By 10:00 A.M., they were in court, usually with several cases to try. Trials went quickly. The district attorney would call police witnesses; then the court would hear the defendant's story. "The charge was brief," Martin recalled. "The foreman then polled the jury while the jury was in the box and if all were in agreement, the verdict was reported. If the jury disagreed, they were sent to a jury room."[22] By 1:00 P.M., court was adjourned. Cogan and Steinbrook grabbed lunch, then hopped a trolley to Moyamensing Prison to interview defendants in jail awaiting trial. Then it was back to the crowded office in the Harrison Building to wrap up the day. "The Defenders, under the system, won their share of cases," Martin recalled.[23]

The Defender Association got a major financial boost in 1937 when it became a member agency of the Philadelphia Community Chest, a forerunner of the United Way. In 1940, the Community Chest provided about $14,200 of the Defender's total budget of $20,800 and would continue—as the United Fund—to supply the bulk of the Defender's funding for nearly thirty more years.[24]

At the same time, the public defender movement was catching on across the United States. Courts—both federal and state—were enunciating a fundamental right to counsel for indigents. In 1932, the U.S. Supreme Court ruled in *Powell v. Alabama*, reversing the conviction of nine African American teenagers in the notorious Scottsboro case for allegedly raping two white women, that an attorney must be provided defendants in all capital cases. (Eight of the defendants had been sentenced to death, and the ninth, to life in prison. One of the women later retracted the story.) The justices' decision was a narrow one, leaving open the question of whether counsel had to be provided for indigents in noncapital cases.[25]

In 1933, before the Philadelphia Defender Association had even been chartered, the Pennsylvania Superior Court ruled in *Commonwealth v. Richards*, a case of inciting to riot, that "the right to be represented by counsel is a fundamental right, going to the very basis of the administration of the criminal law, and places on the trial judge the onus to inform the defendant of his rights and to assist him in obtaining the benefits of those rights." The court reaffirmed its position in 1940 in *Commonwealth ex rel. Schultz v. Smith*, leading to the release of several defendants who were serving long terms in prison, "the Commonwealth not being able to show that they had waived their right [to counsel] at the time of trial."[26] In 1938, the U.S. Supreme Court ruled in *Johnson v. Zerbst*, a counterfeiting case, that a defendant in federal court had to be represented by counsel unless the defendant had chosen to waive that right after being fully informed of the risks.[27] By 1940, the Defender noted in its annual report that it had become settled law in Pennsylvania that every defendant was entitled to legal representation.[28]

The court decisions did not mandate free defense for indigents, but the Defender interpreted the rulings as a sign that it needed to do more. "It has necessarily increased the work of the Defender's office, requiring the presence of the Defender or his Assistants in the prison courts all the time they are in session," according to the Voluntary Defender Association's annual report for 1940. "It has intensified problems pressing for solution, particularly the need of expanding the Defender's staff, and it has forced attention to the charitable nature of the Defender's work as opposed to the work of a Public Defender, properly equipped to make good the guarantee contained in the Constitution."[29] Being a charity assured the Defender's independence but not its solvency. Without the resources to do more, the Defender's caseload did not expand as much as it might have. The Defender handled 1,896 cases in the period from April 1, 1939, to April 1, 1940, down from the nearly 2,100 cases it took on in its first year, April 1, 1934, to April 1, 1935. The annual report's underlying message was clear: Give us more lawyers, more staff, and more resources, and we can do more.[30]

Unable to add staff, the association invoked its mission as "the Poor Man's Advocate" to be strictly selective about the cases it took. "So far, the Philadelphia [Chief] Defender has been obliged to restrict his service to men and women in prison awaiting trial, and he has deemed it right to reject cases of what may be termed 'organized crime,'" according to the 1940 report. "Not only does [the Defender] turn down applicants who can afford to pay, but he also rejects cases where it is plain that the defendant intends to 'beat the rap' and, though guilty, propose by perjury to escape punishment. Doubtful cases are thoroughly investigated. Under the law, defense attorneys are furnished at the expense of the county only in murder cases, and the Defender takes no murder cases."[31]

The 1940 report identified three ways the Defender served clients: "The most dramatic and of course appealing case is where the defendant is mistakenly charged with crime. The man with an affirmative defense is in a sorry plight if he has no means of having his story checked and witnesses notified to come to court. . . . Not guilty cases are numerous in the Defender's files, and in almost three out of every ten finished cases there were pleas and verdicts of 'not guilty.'"[32]

Most of the Defender's clients, then as now, ended up being sentenced. "In almost five out of every ten finished cases in the Defender's files, a plea of guilty was entered on arraignment," the annual report stated. In those cases, "the Defender's work is socially useful to client, court, and community. The entry of a guilty plea in a proper case results in a saving of effort and time, as a jury trial is obviated. It is not the function of the Defender to get his man 'off,' but to present the case fairly and honestly."[33]

The third way the Defender served clients was by acting as a friend: "The Defender deals with persons in trouble. Every case is of moment to the defendant and his family. . . . There is the possible rehabilitation of a guilty client to be considered, and in the various, complex social relationships of the man the Defender takes a part. By sending a report of the facts to the prison where he will serve his sentence, the authorities are assisted in individualizing the man and working out a suitable program for him." The Defender was also able to help a few convicted clients get parole. One inmate serving a long sentence wrote to tell Cogan: "It's those sparks of interest that come from outsiders like yourself that tend to make our lot a little easier."[34]

By 1943, the Defender was considering the possibility of adding a social worker to the staff, "with a view to taking care of cases calling for social services as they arise in the Defender's work." The Defender's job was to provide legal counsel, not do social work, but the lawyers could not help noticing that many of their clients faced domestic issues that fell outside a lawyer's purview. As the Defender's annual report put it, "Cases do arise from time to time calling for social-service work."[35]

In one relatively simple case, Cogan defended a teenager who had run away from home after his mother deserted him and left him with his stepfather. The teen broke into a lunch stand on Cherry Street, where a police officer arrested him for stealing sandwiches and cigarettes. Cogan found that the boy had a grandmother in South Jersey, and she offered to take him in. The *Philadelphia Inquirer*'s Herman Lowe reported in his 1936 series on the Defender that Cogan got the teen placed on probation and released to the custody of his grandmother. There, he was "happier than he has ever been before in his life, . . . working hard at a job which was obtained for him in a dyeing plant."[36]

In another case, a Defender client, identified as George B., could have used a social worker's help. His "sickly, . . . moody" wife "sometimes strolled along the edge of the Delaware River, thinking to end her pain in death"—which she eventually did, two days after Cogan got George off with a thirty-day suspended sentence instead of jail time for drunk driving.[37] A staff social worker could have been immensely helpful in both cases, but the thin budget made hiring one impossible. The Defender would not be able to add a social worker to the staff until the mid-1960s. In the 1940s, the staff would have to make do with a borrowed social worker. The 1943 annual report noted that the Family Society, a private social service agency, "has generously offered us the services of a trained worker who will look into cases referred to her from time to time by the Defender. In this way, we believe much good will be accomplished."[38]

When World War II began, the Defender's directors adopted the patriotic rhetoric of the war years for their 1942–1943 annual report. By providing defense to the indigent, the report declared, "the Defender has helped to carry the lighted torch on the home front for he has, by his activities, implemented the democratic process in the administration of criminal justice." The Defender inevitably ended up representing "a number of soldiers and sailors who needed his professional services, and has given friendly advice and assistance to others."[39] Representation of active-duty military and discharged veterans boosted the Defender's caseload. During the twelve-month period ending May 31, 1946, the Defender represented 1,661 people: "This number was appreciably higher than in the year ending May 31, 1945, when the number was 1,259 and in the year ending May 31, 1944, when the number was 1,031," the association reported. "It was expected that there would be an increase in the case load with the War's end and an even greater increase must be anticipated before the period of postwar adjustment is over."[40]

Defending veterans who were returning from war presented special challenges. "In not a few of these cases it was evident that the defendant had committed an offense under severe emotional stress, due to his war experiences and sudden release from the restraints of military life," according to the 1945–1946 annual report. In those cases, the Defender supplied the court with medical histories. As a result, several defendants were committed to mental institutions instead of being imprisoned.[41]

The end of the war also saw the association expand its work beyond its core mission of representing indigent defendants in the criminal courts of Philadelphia County. The Defender's work often included providing "help and advice in penal affairs" to indigent citizens. That could mean helping the mother of a teenage son arrested by police find out her son's whereabouts or aiding a father in learning the mental condition and legal status of a son being released from a hospital where a criminal court had committed him. "The Defender is in a unique position to render such persons friendly assistance, and we think he should do so," the report declared.[42]

By mid-1946, the association was also about to expand its representation into federal court after the Community Chest agreed to provide additional funding to hire another assistant defender. The Defender became an advocate for criminal justice reform in October 1945 (a function it would continue to perform into the twenty-first century) by calling attention to release procedures for people sent to jail because they failed to pay fines or costs. A defendant who had been fined or ordered to pay costs but was not sentenced to jail could still end up in jail for a month or more for failure to pay. "The inequities in the situation seem apparent and the Defender's clients sometimes bear the full burden. . . . We hope that the whole subject of imprisonment for fine and costs will receive careful study and that remedial legislation will result."[43]

The end of the war also saw the end of an era for the Defender when Thomas Cogan stepped down in 1946 as chief defender because of health problems. Cogan had been "taken gravely ill" in March 1943 and been replaced temporarily by Assistant Defender Herman I. Pollock, who joined the Defender that year.[44] This time, Pollock replaced him permanently.[45] Cogan stayed on with the association in the position of "counsel" until he died in 1951.

2

THE ROAD TO *GIDEON*

BY THE TIME HERMAN I. POLLOCK took over as chief defender in 1945, the courts of Philadelphia—not to mention individuals charged with crime—were coming to depend on the Voluntary Defender Association as an important part of the judicial system. But as the courts began to make more and more use of public defenders, the Defender needed to grow to take on more cases without sacrificing the quality that its charter required, which would necessitate reliable pipelines of talented volunteers and leadership to develop them.

Decisions by the U.S. Supreme Court and the Pennsylvania Superior Court holding that criminal defendants had a fundamental right to legal counsel in certain limited circumstances—*Powell v. Alabama,*[1] *Commonwealth v. Richards,*[2] and *Johnson v. Zerbst*[3]—made the Defender necessary to a justice system that only a few years earlier had been content to let the accused go undefended. The Defender's work consistently won praise from the courts. Judges began marking the anniversary of the Defender's founding each year by expressing their admiration for the organization's efforts, as Judge Louis E. Levinthal did in 1941, when he declared, "The Defenders are the Poor Man's Advocate, a friend of the court and a servant of the community. . . . There is no other agency in this city more deserving of recognition than the Voluntary Defenders." It did not hurt the Defender's standing that the organization had represented fourteen thousand defendants in its first seven years.[4]

Pollock, who had become an assistant defender in 1942, was the right choice to advance Thomas Cogan's effort to make the association credible. Born in 1903, Pollock graduated from the University of Pennsylvania Law School in 1927. He had been in private practice for twelve years before joining the Defender in 1942, after volunteering there for one summer. "I guess I must have enjoyed the work; I've been here ever since," he told the *Camden Courier-Post* in 1964.[5] Widely respected for his integrity and legal acumen, Pollock kept the association true to Francis Fisher Kane's belief that every Defender client should have representation equal to anything available from a private attorney. He won the trust of prosecutors, judges, his own Board of Directors, the press, and, toward the end of his career, city government. And he did it all with unfailing courtesy, although he was remembered as a lawyer who "could turn into a tiger when faced with a miscarriage of justice, or some threat to the association."[6]

In fiscal year 1945–1946, the year Pollock became chief defender, he and his two assistants took on a total of 1,661 cases and finished 1,326 of them.[7] The workload increased in 1947 when the association agreed to extend its representation, whenever requested, to the federal court. The idea of having the Defender take on federal cases came from several judges of the U.S. District Court for the Eastern District of Pennsylvania.[8] The Community Chest, which funded the Defender, agreed to allocate money for a new assistant defender to help with the anticipated increase in cases. The Defender's caseload did grow because of the new service, but not overwhelmingly. In 1951, three years after the Defender's federal court debut, the association served as counsel in 182 cases, out of the total Defender caseload of 2,820.[9] In 1957, the Defender appeared in 163 federal cases and 3,157 state cases.[10]

Hiring another full-time assistant defender was not the only way the Defender's legal staff grew. In 1948, a group of the city's big firms came to the rescue, responding to a suggestion from University of Pennsylvania law professor Edwin R. Keedy that they lend young lawyers to the Defender, at the firm's expense, one at a time for one-month periods, tapping the enlarged sense of professional responsibility that had long existed in the Philadelphia bar.[11] The volunteer program was an instant hit, one welcomed by the hard-pressed Defender. The association's directors praised the program in their annual report for 1946–1947: "It is felt that the arrangement will not only benefit the association but will offer to the participants a valuable experience in actual trial work. It should also offer them an enriching experience in bringing them close to community problems outside their usual professional activities."[12] For the most part the volunteers came from major law firms with strong ties to the original incorporators and directors of the Defender in 1934. Seasoned lawyers frequently volunteered to take a month out of their own practice to help the Defender.

The city's two law schools, Penn and Temple, also helped out by allowing their students to volunteer with the Defender. In 1949, Penn decided that its students could earn academic credits by working one hundred hours for the association, either part-time during their third year of law school or full-time during the summer between their second and third years. In 1953, Temple University started a similar program. Throughout the 1950s, two or three law students were working for the association at any given time, doing everything but trying cases. By the late 1950s, they were handling many of the Defender's interviews with clients and other sources. The students listened to defendants' stories, checked their mental and employment status, and tried to determine if they were poor enough to qualify for the Defender's services.[13]

Scores of volunteer lawyers had experiences that many would never have again, while the Defender got much-needed help. In addition to relieving the full-time Defender staff of some of its burden, the program gave the Defender a cohort of lawyer alumni with fond memories of their time as volunteers and an attachment to the cause of indigent defense. After they finished their month of service, volunteers were placed on a list of lawyers the Defender could call on in the event of an emergency, as happened in 1958 when the Philadelphia courts added five courtrooms in an effort to reduce the number of defendants waiting in jail for the disposition of their cases. The Defender was able to mobilize twenty-one lawyers from the reserve list to help out, working full-time for at least a week. Some welcomed the opportunity to support the Defender through service on the board. On the association's fiftieth anniversary in 1984, at least ten of the association's directors (including five of the six officers) had served as volunteers.[14]

The volunteers' accomplishments after their service with the Defender reinforced the association's standing in the legal community. Most prominent among the volunteer alumni was Arlen Specter, who went on to become district attorney of Philadelphia and a U.S. senator. Specter, who was loaned to the Defender in March 1958 by the firm of

Barnes, Dechert, Price, Myers and Rhoads, recalled that the experience whetted his appetite for public service. Other alumni achieved distinction in the Philadelphia bar or took leadership roles in civic organizations. Frederic L. Ballard Jr., who volunteered in the late 1960s, would become an authority in public finance law and help lead the transformation of a small local law firm, Ballard Spahr, into a major national firm with more than five hundred lawyers. Benjamin H. Quigg, who volunteered in the late 1940s, would become a partner in the firm of Morgan, Lewis and Bockius and president of the Big Brothers Association of Philadelphia, a board member of the United Way of Southeastern Pennsylvania, and a trustee and chairman of the board of Presbyterian Medical Center. William White Jr., who also volunteered in the 1940s, went on to specialize in trusts and estates and served in the 1960s as chairman of the United Fund Torch Drive. One volunteer, Arthur R. G. Solmssen, who went on to specialize in securities cases for Saul, Ewing, Remick and Saul, even wrote a well-reviewed novel, *Rittenhouse Square*, whose protagonist was a young securities lawyer on loan to the Defender.

The loaned lawyers generally began their service by conducting interviews with clients awaiting trial behind bars at the dreary old Moyamensing Prison at Tenth and Reed Streets in South Philadelphia. They progressed from prison interviews to courtroom appearances several days a week, working their way through a pile of eight to ten files the night before as they tried to figure out which cases to try and which to recommend the client plead. "Our lack of legal talent was offset only by our interest and sincerity," recalled one volunteer.[15] Talented and hardworking though they were, the volunteers—as well as the full-time assistant defenders—were relative newcomers to the legal profession. A major part of Pollock's job was to sand off their rough edges and train them to be trial lawyers—in just a few weeks. Pollock's classroom was his office in the frayed elegance of the ornate Harrison Building at Fifteenth and Market Streets. Those meetings would become part of Defender lore.

Pollock's understanding of the clients he served and the lawyers he led revealed itself little by little in the daily meetings. Pollock was a soft-spoken perfectionist, a stickler with a gentle manner. Assistant Defender Edmund E. DePaul described Pollock's technique as "show and tell": "'Show me what you did and I'll tell you what you did wrong.' None of us were ever spared. Yet with his understanding gentleness, we constantly improved our legal arsenal."[16]

Pollock's efforts paid off. The authors of a 1958 *University of Pennsylvania Law Review* article on legal representation of indigents in Philadelphia and New Jersey found high respect in the Philadelphia legal community for the competence of the Defender's lawyers. The consensus among members of the bar and bench that they interviewed was that Defender attorneys "provided much better representation than does the average attorney in Philadelphia private practice," though not as good as that of the private bar's best criminal lawyers. District Attorney Victor H. Blanc told the authors that the lawyers of the Defender Association were "more formidable opponents" than most that his staff faced. In 1957, the district attorney's office lost 18.8 percent of the cases it tried overall and 21.9 percent of its cases against Defender clients.[17]

While the afternoon sessions in his office usually focused on active cases, Pollock sometimes steered the conversation to the need for reforms affecting all aspects of life for the Defender's client base: law, prisons, sentencing, discharge, rehabilitation, and even family life. These made an impression that would shape how many in the Philadelphia bar would view the challenges and necessity of indigent defense. As one assistant defender recalled years later, those group meetings with Pollock created "the basis for a lifelong memory of a competent individual whose major concern was to improve the lot of the less fortunate."[18]

Some assistants and volunteers also got a chance to learn by watching Pollock in action. This included the chief defender's cross-examination of a four-year-old child to determine if she was qualified to be sworn in as a witness:

> Pollock: *Where do good little girls go?*
> Child: *Heaven.*
> Pollock: *Where do bad little girls go.*
> Child: *To the Navy Yard.*

The judge qualified her.[19]

Many of Pollock's observers say his open-mindedness was ahead of his time and won him the trust of his clients. When one young volunteer wondered aloud why homosexuality was so frequent in prisons, Pollock wryly observed, "What other kind of sex can a prison inmate get?" The same volunteer asked Pollock what to do about a client with impeccable manners who had been arrested for soliciting in drag and wanted to wear female clothing to court. Pollock advised letting him do it, waiving a jury trial and leaving the matter in the hands of the judge. Sure enough, the very next day the judge set the elegant cross-dresser free, with an order to get out of town on the first bus.[20]

Despite the heavy caseload, Pollock's assistants had what one remembered as "a rollicking good time." Exciting, too. Defender lawyers raced from City Hall courtrooms to prison interviews with clients and back to the office to prepare the next day's cases. In whatever time was left over in a hectic day, the defenders did research, paperwork, investigations, social services, and even some housekeeping around the association's offices. At least one made a habit of filching legal pads from unwary assistant district attorneys to help keep costs down. "Every paper clip counted, and so did every legal pad," former assistant defender DePaul remembered, long after the association had grown into the equivalent of a big law firm. "It was a different time, it was a different practice, it was a different Law. Mom and Pop left a sound corner grocery, and the heirs turned it into a successful million-dollar corporation. But we had more fun."[21]

Helpful though it was to the Defender, the volunteer program also had its risks. The reason that the Defender took only one volunteer a month was fear that too large a concentration of unseasoned lawyers would create opportunities for error. While the volunteers learned fast and accomplished much, their inexperience could create an opening for a client to appeal a guilty verdict on grounds of incompetent counsel, as Specter found out in 1967. Specter had been a volunteer defender in 1958. In 1967, he had been elected district attorney and was running for mayor when a former client from his Defender days claimed in an appeal that Specter had botched his defense in an armed-robbery case, resulting in a long prison sentence. Specter's client, James McCaskill, was accused of robbing four cab drivers at knifepoint in separate incidents. The case perplexed the young Specter, who agonized over whether to advise his client to plead guilty, seek a jury trial, or ask to be tried by the judge. "After dutifully advising the defendant of the situation, I was really as befuddled as he as to which would be the least undesirable course," Specter recalled years later. "In a joint decision, we proceeded with a waiver on one of the charges."[22]

During the trial, one of the cabbies who had been robbed told common pleas judge Ethan Allen Doty that the defendant had held a knife to his throat and demanded money. The judge, "not surprisingly" in Specter's recollection, convicted the defendant. That left three charges still to be faced, and Specter realized he would confront three more cab drivers ready to tell a similar story. So Specter and the defendant jointly decided the best course would be to plead guilty to all the charges. Specter's client got twelve and a half to twenty-five years in prison.[23]

In the spring of 1967, McCaskill filed a petition for a new trial, claiming that Specter had given him incompetent counsel. The case was listed for a hearing before Doty just days before the mayoral election in which Specter, a Republican, was facing incumbent mayor James H. J. Tate, a Democrat. The district attorney's office, claiming that it only found out by accident at the last minute that the petition had been listed for a hearing, requested a postponement, which Doty granted until after the election. Doty said it was a mystery to him how the case had been listed. McCaskill was represented by G. Fred DiBona, a high-profile lawyer with Democratic connections, who argued that Specter in 1958 "knew practically nothing about criminal law" and that Specter had "erred in submitting the case on waiver. He placed the defendant in a very precarious position."[24] McCaskill's appeal failed, and Specter felt vindicated. "Although my competency to be Mayor was severely questioned that year, my competency as trial counsel almost a decade before was upheld," Specter recalled with satisfaction. Still, the incident demonstrated the problems inexperience could bring the Defender.[25]

The volunteers, who came mainly from corporate law firms, knew little of criminal procedure and sometimes surprisingly little about both the U.S. and Pennsylvania Constitutions. They were quick to discover the gaps in their knowledge and to find that criminal defense was a profession within a profession, as Ballard did when an assistant defender asked him to prepare a memorandum on a point of constitutional law. The assistant defender "took strong and justified exception" to Ballard's work, Ballard recalled nearly two decades later. "This job was probably the one type of chore a volunteer should have done well—library research, right up our alley. But I didn't."[26]

By the end of the 1960s, the volunteer program was in decline, but not simply out of concern over possible mistakes by inexperienced lawyers. In 1963, the U.S. Supreme Court ruled in *Gideon v. Wainwright* that indigent criminal defendants had a constitutional right to free counsel, leading to an instant need for more public defenders across the country. In Philadelphia, the Defender began building up its full-time legal staff. With more lawyers on staff, there was less need for volunteers. As a result, the volunteers were getting fewer opportunities for courtroom experience, which made the firms reluctant to send more volunteers. The volunteer experience was simply not the same as it had been a decade earlier, when there had been only three or four assistant defenders. The annual report for fiscal year 1970–1971 noted, "This year the Association has had difficulty in obtaining a volunteer for each month. [There had been no volunteers for the months of January through May in 1971.] . . . The Association is in the process of evaluating this program."[27] The program fell into disuse after that, although there was an abortive attempt to revive it in 1972 to help ease a backlog of criminal cases clogging the court system.[28]

Because of *Gideon*, the Defender grew dramatically during Pollock's tenure, expanding services and staff in response not just to *Gideon* but to an array of substantial changes in criminal law and procedure in the 1950s and 1960s. When Pollock joined the Defender in 1942, the three attorneys who made up the legal staff represented seventeen hundred clients. By the time he stepped down in 1968, the office had forty-eight lawyers and represented twenty-three thousand clients.[29] The increased caseload intensified the perennial problem of pay for the full-time staff. Defender lawyers made less than their peers in the district attorney's office and the private bar. In the late 1950s, the association established a ceiling of seventy-five hundred dollars a year for the assistants, but none of the four assistants earned that much. In contrast, eleven of the twenty-six assistant district attorneys made more than eight thousand dollars in 1957. Not surprisingly, given the low salaries, turnover was frequent among the assistants, compounding the experience problem.[30]

Since 1937, the Defender's funding had come almost exclusively from the Community Chest and its successor agency, the United Fund, but by 1959, it was becoming clear that the United Fund could not keep up with the Defender's needs. Anticipating a seismic shift in the funding landscape, the Defender dropped the word "Voluntary" from its name in January 1958 to become the Defender Association of Philadelphia. The purpose of the name change, according to the directors' annual report for 1958–1959, was to counter "the misleading impression that the services performed by the Association are casual, part-time and not compensated. When, in fact, the opposite is true."[31]

Evidence that the Defender would need more than United Fund dollars came in 1959, when the organization fell ten thousand dollars short of the amount it needed for the year and sought assistance from the city government. In response, the city granted ten thousand dollars to the

Quarter Sessions General Fund to help the association carry on its work. However, that sum was less than one-eighth of the Defender's budget.[32]

The idea of accepting money from government went against the long-standing aversion with which charity defender organizations like the Defender Association of Philadelphia met anything that would undermine their independence of government. "The Defender Association has always been devoted to the principle of obtaining financial support solely from private sources," Pollock wrote in 1961. Nevertheless, the Defender could not rely on private funding to meet its basic requirements, "let alone the expanded program needed to make the defender system a first-class operation." In Pollock's view, looking to government for finance was a risk the Defender had no choice but to take. Justifying the necessity, Pollock pointed out that "having a private defender program maintained by tax funds is not altogether new." Private defender associations in New York and Ohio were already receiving government support. The city funneled the money through the Quarter Sessions Court "to insulate the Association from political influence," according to Pollock. He thought that the Defender could preserve its independence "by maintaining a fixed and balanced ratio between private and tax support."[33] When common pleas judge Raymond Pace Alexander suggested in 1960 that lawyers be taxed or fees added to civil and criminal cases to support the Defender, Pollock did not think the bar alone should have to carry the load. "It is a community problem for citizens and government," he said. Pollock, who was seeking $23,000 from City Council in 1960, urged "a mixed system of support" that would make the Defender "a public-private agency." (The Defender's total budget in 1960 was $82,000, of which $63,331 came from the United Fund.)[34]

As it turned out, Pollock was right about the necessity of private and public cooperation to produce a dynamic indigent defense operation but wrong about keeping a fixed balance between private and public support. Private support just could not keep up with the Defender's needs as a series of U.S. Supreme Court decisions created more demand for public defenders. Over the course of the 1960s, the Defender would come to rely more and more on funds from the city, until by fiscal year 1967–1968, the city was providing almost half of the Defender's income. The association's days as a charitable enterprise were numbered.

3

AFTER *GIDEON*

I N 1963, THE U.S. SUPREME COURT handed down a decision that would shake the U.S. legal system and trigger explosive growth in the Defender Association's caseload, straining the organization's resources so severely that it almost did not survive. Until 1963, across the country, free legal representation for indigent defendants had been restricted to cases in federal court, as established in *Johnson v. Zerbst* in 1938,[1] and to capital cases in state courts, as the justices decided in *Powell v. Alabama* in 1932.[2] However, the United States' steadily developing concern for the rights of indigent criminal defendants hit a snag in *Betts v. Brady* in 1942,[3] when the Supreme Court ruled that the Fourteenth Amendment's guarantee of due process did not extend to state courts and that indigent criminal defendants had no constitutional right to free counsel except in capital cases. Justice Owen J. Roberts, one of the incorporators of the Voluntary Defender Association of Philadelphia, wrote the majority opinion.

Roberts was a strong supporter of the Defender and had spoken eloquently of the plight of criminal defendants who had to face the courts alone. "Shall the difficulty and despair of thousands who come before the courts without representation and with little knowledge of their rights be no longer relieved?" he asked in 1934. "The principle under which the public defender [operates] . . . is, thrillingly, 'Equal Justice

Under Law.'"[4] The following year, Roberts supported a campaign to raise fifty thousand dollars for the Defender.

In 1942, though, Roberts's opinion in *Betts* contained no such ringing endorsement of indigent defense. Instead, he wrote that providing counsel for impoverished defendants was "in the great majority of the States . . . not a fundamental right, essential to a fair trial." It was up to the legislature of each state to decide how it would handle the representation of indigent defendants. There was no constitutional obligation on the states "to furnish counsel in every such case," Roberts concluded. "Every court has power, if it deems proper, to appoint counsel where that course seems to be required in the interest of fairness."[5]

However, *Betts* was "vague" and proved to be only a bump in the road to the court's eventual recognition of legal representation as a constitutional right.[6] The ruling allowed for reversal of the conviction of a defendant who had been tried without a lawyer if the lack of counsel had rendered the trial unfair. The Supreme Court, throughout the late 1940s and 1950s, after Roberts had left the bench, found exceptions to *Betts* in a series of cases that effectively undermined the ruling. By the early 1960s, momentum had built for overturning *Betts*.[7]

In 1962, the U.S. Supreme Court agreed to consider an appeal from Clarence Earl Gideon, a penniless drifter and habitual thief who had been convicted in 1961 of burglarizing a pool hall in Panama City, Florida. Pleading poverty, Gideon asked the judge to appoint a lawyer for him. The judge refused, saying that only defendants accused of capital crimes could get free counsel in Florida. Gideon then represented himself at trial, lost, and was given a five-year prison sentence. In 1962, he penciled a handwritten appeal to the U.S. Supreme Court, claiming he was entitled to counsel under the due process clause of the Fourteenth Amendment—the same position that the court had rejected in *Betts*. This time, the justices—seven of them newcomers to the court since *Betts* and two who had dissented—agreed that penniless defendants facing felony charges should come under the protection of the Fourteenth Amendment. In *Gideon v. Wainwright* they voted unanimously to overturn *Betts*.[8] The State of Florida retried Gideon after his successful appeal, but this time he was represented by counsel and was acquitted.

Three other Supreme Court decisions in the 1960s would amplify the rights of defendants and profoundly affect the Defender's role in the criminal justice system: *Mapp v. Ohio* (1961),[9] *Escobedo v. Illinois* (1964),[10] and *Miranda v. Arizona* (1966).[11] *Mapp* forbade the use of illegally obtained evidence in state court prosecutions. It gave lawyers a tool, the exclusionary rule, for enforcing the constitutional prohibition of unlawful search and seizure. (The bride of a young Defender Association volunteer came to court in 1961, post-*Mapp*, curious to watch her new husband at work. She was impressed to see him get one case dismissed on grounds that the evidence was illegally obtained. She was even more impressed when she heard the defendant exclaim, as he got into a City Hall elevator on his way to unexpected freedom: "I don't know what happened in there because I was guilty as hell.")[12] *Escobedo* defined the right of suspects to have counsel present during interrogation but was quickly eclipsed two years later by *Miranda*, which required that criminal suspects be informed at the time of arrest of their right to remain silent and have counsel, including free, court-appointed counsel if they were indigent. Both of these encouraged defendants to avail themselves of their right to a lawyer and forced law enforcement personnel to play their roles by the book if they wanted a conviction.

Even while the justice system was trying to come to grips with these expanded rights for defendants and with the defense representation guaranteed by *Gideon*, the court expanded the scope of indigent defense significantly in *Argesinger v. Hamlin* (1972),[13] ruling that any impoverished defendant facing the possibility of jail time, whether for a felony or misdemeanor, must be provided counsel. "*Gideon* started the explosion, and then came *Argesinger*, which expanded *Gideon*'s requirements to misdemeanor cases, where a sentence of imprisonment was a possible outcome," said Benjamin Lerner, who would serve as chief defender from 1975 to 1990. "The number of those cases was so great that that was like a second explosion that was, in some ways, larger than the first one."[14]

Not only did indigent defendants have to be provided counsel after *Gideon*, but the counsel had to be competent, the U.S. Supreme Court decided in *Strickland v. Washington* (1984).[15] That meant public defenders were going to have to be well trained and the offices behind them were going to have to be professional and efficient, causing more financial pressure for organizations such as the Defender. The criminal justice system, in Philadelphia and across the nation, had entered an era of mass defense and needed to develop strategies and structures to deal with it.

States scrambled to cope with the new reality. *Gideon* was not a surprise but a step in the Supreme Court's efforts to put the "justice" in the criminal justice system. "Many legal and constitutional treatises have been written on the constitutional right of an accused to counsel and the various methods adopted to assure that right," Chief Defender Herman I. Pollock wrote in 1961.[16] He noted that the court, through an "unbroken series of cases"—*Betts* to one side—had expanded its interpretation of a defendant's right to counsel so far that any defendant denied legal representation in a serious case was also being denied the protection of the Fourteenth Amendment's due process clause. By the time *Gideon* was decided, thirty-five of the fifty states already required their courts to appoint counsel for impoverished defendants in serious, noncapital cases. *Gideon* meant that all the states would have to do the same, and the scope of their responsibility would only grow as the court piled decision on decision buttressing the rights of indigent people in the criminal justice system.

In the months after *Gideon* was announced, there was concern in the Philadelphia legal community over its impact on a court system already clogged with a backlog of sixteen thousand criminal cases. Pollock said the courts were uncertain how to deal with all the cases likely to arise under the new mandate. "It was recommended some months ago that our office handle them," Pollock told a newspaper reporter.[17] However, he added, the Board of Judges that determined the procedures of Philadelphia's court system had put the matter aside, believing that it was up to the state to solve the procedural problems arising out of *Gideon*. If the judges really were expecting the state to make the difficult decisions necessary for the smooth running of the court system, they were in for an unpleasant surprise.

While *Gideon* told the states what they had to do, it did not tell them how to do it or how to pay for it. The Pennsylvania legislature responded by eventually passing a Public Defender Act late in 1968—nearly six years after *Gideon*. Pennsylvania, instead of coming up with a statewide system of indigent defense as other states did, turned over implementation of *Gideon* to the counties. "In each county except the County of Philadelphia, there shall be a public defender, appointed as herein provided," the act ordered.[18] Philadelphia, as the legislators well knew, had the Defender Association, which at the time was trying to get more funding from the city. The General Assembly of the Commonwealth of Pennsylvania gave no sign of wanting to be involved in the administrative challenge it had just posed to its most populous county.

The passage of time has brought no change in Pennsylvania's approach. The state legislature showed as little enthusiasm for funding indigent defense in the second decade of the twenty-first century as it had in the years immediately after the *Gideon* decision. By 2020, Pennsylvania was the only state that laid the burden of funding indigent defense exclusively on the counties.[19] The state also exercised no oversight of public defenders; it simply required every county to have one. The result was that many defender offices across the state found themselves without sufficient means to do their work.

Even so, Pennsylvania is not unique in its reluctance to pay for public defenders. Several states provide only minimal funding for indigent defense.[20] Louisiana took the unique approach of funding its public defender offices mostly with the proceeds from traffic fines. When revenues fell short and the state made cutbacks to public defender services in 2017, lawyers filed a class-action lawsuit on behalf of fifty thousand indigent defendants in the state.[21] While the situation may not have been as dire in other states, public defenders across the country decry their inadequate funding and impossible caseloads even more than fifty years after *Gideon*.

While *Gideon* and other Supreme Court cases were defining the rights of the accused and the obligations of a competent and effective defense, other forces were at work in American society that reflected the public's growing unease with rising crime rates. "Law and order" became a popular catchphrase beginning in the late 1960s. Violent crime more than tripled nationally between 1960, when there were 288,000 violent crimes nationwide, and 1975, when there were more than one million. In Pennsylvania, the number of violent crimes more than tripled from 11,203 in 1960 to 38,933 in 1975, while the population of the state increased by only 4 percent. Over the same period, crimes against property also tripled from 107,586 to 357,206.[22]

Politicians of both major parties quickly responded to the public's concern over crime. In 1964, conservative Republican candidate Barry Goldwater made "law and order" an issue in his campaign.[23] Goldwater lost, but concern over crime lived on, forcing Democrats to respond as well. In 1965, President Lyndon B. Johnson, who had defeated Goldwater, created a presidential commission to recommend changes in the justice system. The same year, Johnson signed the Law Enforcement Assistance Act, which for the first time gave the federal government a role in helping fund local law enforcement, courts, and prisons. The Johnson administration described the legislation as part of its "war on crime."[24]

But fear of crime did not fade as the years went by. In the 1980s, even though crime rates had been falling across the United States, the country was now worried about illegal drugs.[25] The Reagan administration focused heavily on drugs and crime, and the war on crime became, in large measure, a war on drugs. Appearing tough on crime had not lost its luster for politicians. In 1994, President Bill Clinton signed the Violent Crime Control and Law Enforcement Act, a federal law passed with bipartisan support in Congress. In Pennsylvania, the state legislature embraced anticrime policies enthusiastically. Being tough on crime was good politics.

In Philadelphia, fear of crime fueled the political rise of Frank L. Rizzo, who billed himself as America's toughest cop. Democrat James H. J. Tate won the mayoral race in 1967 in part because his Republican opponent, Arlen Specter, would not promise to retain Rizzo as police commissioner.[26] Four years later, Rizzo himself, running as a Democrat, was elected mayor. The issue of crime remained potent in Philadelphia, just as it did in the rest of the country. Pennsylvania's system of electing district attorneys and judges helped keep crime alive as a political issue, as it did in other states where judges were elected. For example, California chief justice Rose Bird lost a retention election in 1986 after Republican governor George Deukmejian opposed her because she had never voted to uphold a death penalty.[27] A study of Pennsylvania judges published in 2004 found that the closer a judge was to facing voters in a retention election, which happens every ten years, the more likely the judge was to hand out stiffer punishment to defendants.[28] However, the tactic of criticizing judges as soft on crime did not always work. Just before the 1973 election, Rizzo issued a list of four Philadelphia common pleas judges up for reelection whom he excoriated as the softest on crime in the city. All four judges were reelected by comfortable margins.[29]

The war on crime raised the stakes for the Defender's newly expanded clientele. Getting tough on crime meant putting more people in jail. As the war on crime progressed, incarceration rates went up in Philadelphia and in the country at large. The incarceration rate for Philadelphia was 241 per 100,000 city residents in 1970 and 242 in 1980, but it soared after that as the war on drugs intensified, reaching 470 in 1990 and 893, its all-time high, in 2009.[30]

Squeezed by two diametrically opposed forces, the expansion of defendants' rights and the war on crime, the Defender's caseload mushroomed after *Gideon*, forcing it to become a big operation. When *Gideon* was decided in 1963, the Defender had a staff of six lawyers, handled about 6,000 cases, and had a budget of $94,000. By the end of

1966, the staff numbered thirty-three lawyers. Between June 1, 1965, and May 31, 1966, those lawyers worked on 15,000 cases. In 1968, the organization handled 28,307 cases, an all-time high at that time. In 1969, the number went down to 22,993, but only after the Defender curtailed services sharply in the second half of 1968 because of financial difficulties. Before the financial problems took their toll, the Defender legal staff had grown to forty-nine lawyers and the budget to $681,000.[31]

In addition to taking on more cases in *Gideon*'s wake, the Defender expanded its services dramatically. With financial help from the city and a three-year grant in 1964 from the National Defender Project of the National Legal Aid and Defender Association (NLADA), the Defender Association of Philadelphia extended its range to include representation of juveniles accused of criminal acts as well as impoverished clients who had problems stemming from failure to pay child support, who faced hearings before a U.S. commissioner, who were accused of violating probation, or who were the subject of a legal effort to have them committed for inpatient mental health treatment against their will. The Office of Economic Opportunity (OEO), a federal agency, also chipped in with money for supervision of the criminal courts branch of Community Legal Services.[32]

The NLADA grant made it feasible for the Defender to file more appeals. In its early days, the association appealed only one or two cases a year, which was similar to the number of appeals a private law firm might file in nonmurder cases. The number increased modestly to four or five a year through the mid-1960s. At least one director of the Defender Association in the late 1950s thought that the Defender should file more appeals as a way of helping not just individual defendants but also a whole class of defendants. The problem was cost. The Defender estimated that each appeal would cost the association between two hundred and three hundred dollars. In Pollock's view, the contributions that supported the Defender were meant to provide counsel to individual defendants, an effort that should take priority over appeals.[33] That approach changed with the arrival of the NLADA money. Between June 1964 and June 1965, the Defender filed twenty appeals, and the number would grow over the years.[34]

The expansion of the Defender's appellate practice would have a significant impact on Pennsylvania law. An early example occurred in 1968, when the Defender filed an appeal on behalf of two Philadelphia women convicted of burglary that ended with the Pennsylvania Supreme

Court invalidating the Muncy Act, a law passed in 1913 that mandated more stringent sentences for women than for men convicted of serious crimes. The state high court ruled that the Muncy Act was "arbitrary, discriminatory and invalid under the Fourteenth Amendment of the U.S. Constitution." Thanks to the Defender's work in the case, thirty-two female prisoners and another fifty parolees would sign petitions to have their sentences reconsidered.[35]

Even with aid from NLADA, OEO, and the city, the strain on the Defender's resources was severe. In 1964, a little more than half of the Defender budget was still coming from the United Fund and a little less than half from the city. By 1969, the Defender was getting nearly two-thirds of its budget from the city, with the United Fund contributing only 7 percent. The last United Fund support came in 1973, when the fund contributed $33,000 to the Defender's total budget of $2.5 million.[36]

"After *Gideon*, which turned what was aspirational into what was constitutionally required, it became obvious that the organization had to grow faster and charitable contributions or annual appropriation from the United Way just weren't going to be sufficient," Lerner said.[37] Like indigent defense groups in other cities such as New York, the Defender turned primarily to local government for assistance. When the NLADA grant ran out in 1967 and the OEO decided unexpectedly in 1968 to stop funding criminal courts programs, the result was a financial crisis that "came close to destroying the Association altogether."[38]

The Defender began warning in May 1968 that it was running out of money and enlisted the support of Vincent A. Carroll, the administrative judge of the Court of Common Pleas, to help the association secure more from the city. Carroll wrote to Mayor Tate on May 27, backing the Defender's request for more city funding and telling Tate that the association provided its services "at a relatively nominal cost per case." The alternative, Carroll warned, was to appoint private counsel to defend indigents, which would cost the city about $2.5 million per year.[39]

During the summer of 1968, the Defender Association suspended its activities in appeals, postconviction issues, trial advocacy for clients free on bail, and magistrates' courts. Lawyers and other staff members began leaving or being laid off.[40] As if that were not trouble enough, health problems forced Pollock, who had suffered at least one heart attack, to step aside. Martin J. Vinikoor became acting chief defender on June 24.[41]

At the beginning of November 1968, Vinikoor announced that the Defender would stop taking new cases and would go out of business in six weeks without funds from the city.[42] On November 19, he petitioned the Court of Common Pleas to allow the Defender to withdraw from all criminal cases, beginning on November 29. "We used to be just a charitable group," Vinikoor told the *Philadelphia Inquirer*, "but the Supreme Court said our work was the duty of the State. Now, we handle 65 to 70 percent of the courts' caseloads."[43] Before *Gideon*, the association had represented almost exclusively defendants who were being held in jail awaiting trial because they could not make bail. The scope of the association's services expanded dramatically after *Gideon*. District Attorney Arlen Specter warned that the Defender's demise would cause chaos in the court system. "The defenders are an indispensable part of the justice system," Specter said.[44]

The Defender asked the city for five times more funding than it had ever sought before. The city agreed on November 22 to advance the Defender seventy-six thousand dollars, but this allocation was only a stopgap. "When you're dying, you'll take anything you can get," Vinikoor said. He added that the money would allow the Defender to continue operations for another five weeks.[45] The Defender needed a steady, reliable source of revenue, and since the United Fund could no longer supply it and the state would not, the Defender's directors sought a deal with the city. They were aiming to change an independent private charity into an arm of the criminal justice system without sacrificing its independence, an ambitious task to be sure.

The association's leadership, while trying to work out an agreement with the city, also had to fend off proposals, one in the state Senate and another in City Council, to create a public defender's office as a government agency for Philadelphia County. The state threat soon vanished when the Senate bill's sponsors, lobbied by friends of the Defender from both political parties, dropped Philadelphia from the legislation. Vinikoor and Joseph N. DuBarry IV, president of the Defender's Board of Directors, mounted a media-savvy campaign against the measure, sending out letters to newspapers, television stations, politicians, leaders of community groups such as the United Fund, and state legislators. On November 19, State Representative Richard Tilghman, a Republican from Montgomery County who had just been elected to the state Senate, wrote a letter to DuBarry informing him that amendments had been made to the Public Defender Act and that Philadelphia would not be included.[46] Vinikoor wrote letters to Mercer D. Tate (no relation to the mayor), a liberal Democrat influential in Harrisburg and longtime member of the Defender's board, and State Representative Louis Sherman, a Democrat from Philadelphia, thanking them for helping exempt Philadelphia from the Public Defender Act and thereby maintain the association's office as an independent entity.[47]

That left the proposed City Council measure, which Mayor Tate had suggested and the association vigorously opposed. The Defender's advocates argued that having a city agency responsible for providing counsel to the indigent could create a conflict of interest; the city would be responsible for overseeing the robust defense of the same people it charged with crimes. "Defense counsel must, in performing his duties, stand between the client and the government prosecuting him," the association's 1968–1969 annual report declared. "If counsel is, or even appears to be, under government control, the client cannot be sure that that counsel will act in the client's best interests."[48] Friends of the association argued, as they had in opposing the state Public Defender Act, that it made no sense to create a new public defender office when Philadelphia already had one that was "nationally recognized for its standard of excellence."[49] Theodore Voorhees, former chancellor of the Philadelphia Bar Association and one of the founders of NLADA, sent a letter to the Board of Judges asking that they go on record opposing the establishment of a new city public defender office and supporting "the existing Defender organization."[50]

On December 5, 1968, Councilman George X. Schwartz introduced a bill in the council calling for creation of an Office of Public Defender, whose chief would be appointed by the mayor. A hearing on the proposal was scheduled for December 16.[51] Primed by Vinikoor's efforts to muster opposition to the bill, the *Bulletin* ran a pro-Defender editorial on December 1 and the *Philadelphia Daily News* tore into the mayor in its editorial on December 9: "Is Jim Tate kidding? At a time when the city is clubbing everyone in town for new taxes to make ends meet, the Mayor proposes to establish a new department. Tate wants to appoint a Public Defender at $20,000 annually and who knows how many deputies at an unspecified cost to the city." To many people, the *Daily News* observed, the proposal looked like "a patronage grab." The paper suggested that the mayor just increase funding for the existing Defender, which was doing "an admirable job."[52] On December 10, the *Daily News* reported that the Board of Judges had sent the mayor a resolution opposing creation of a new public defender. The judges based their opposition in part on conflict of interest and in part on the practical consideration that representation by a city-run office would cost much more than representation by the Defender.[53] Facing opposition from the Defender Association, the district attorney, the Board of Judges, and the Philadelphia Bar Association, the Tate administration quickly dropped the proposal.[54]

With any idea of a new defender organization off the table, the city government and the Defender Association were ready to talk about rescuing the old one. City solicitor Edward G. Bauer Jr. was the point person for the city; Vinikoor and DuBarry represented the Defender. Along with money, a key issue was how much representation the city should have on the Defender's Board of Directors. In December 1968, the city had only two representatives on the Defender's fifty-two-member board: council members Schwartz and W. Thacher Longstreth. If the city was going to greatly increase its support of the Defender, then the city should have something to say about how the money was used, Bauer said.[55] The talks had a sense of urgency because the Defender was in grave danger and the court system was choking on a backlog of cases.

It was to the advantage of both sides to reach an agreement quickly. Some judges were particularly interested in having the Defender begin providing representation in Juvenile Court in response to the 1967 U.S. Supreme Court decision *In re Gault*, which held that juveniles accused of crime in Juvenile Court had the same right to counsel and the same procedural protection as adults. First, though, Mayor Tate wanted something. The mayor insisted that Vinikoor, the acting chief defender, must resign. Vinikoor, who had political ambitions and had once been a Democrat, had angered Tate, a Democrat, by running for City Council as a Republican; Tate insisted that if the Defender Association wanted to remain outside politics, it could not have a chief defender who was politically active.[56]

Tate's demand did not sit well with some members of the Defender's board; Vinikoor was a capable and popular lawyer who had worked for the Defender in several positions, and some on the board thought he should stay.[57] However, Vinikoor, recognizing that Tate's position put the Defender in peril, agreed to step down, but not without leveling a blast at Tate. "I resigned when it became obvious that my retention would have meant that the Tate Administration would deny the Association the necessary funds to continue providing legal service," he told a news conference. "Rather than see the accused poor in Philadelphia denied this very important service, I resigned."[58] At Specter's invitation, Vinikoor became the assistant district attorney in charge of Family

Court and then a professor at Temple University Law School. The Criminal Justice Section of the Philadelphia Bar Association honored him posthumously in 1977 for accomplishments in the administration of criminal justice, and the Philadelphia Bar Association recognized him after his death in 1976 as one of its Legends of the Bar. First Assistant Defender Vincent Ziccardi replaced Vinikoor as acting chief defender, Tate was mollified, and the negotiations went forward.[59]

The talks produced an agreement that the city would fund the Defender Association. In return, the association would amend its articles of incorporation to allow city representation on the Board of Directors. The board now would have thirty members, in three classes, instead of the previous fifty. The city would choose ten directors, the association would select another ten, and the combined group of twenty would name the final ten.[60] "There was at the time a great fear that the city would somehow interfere with the work of the Defender," recalled Louis Natali, a Temple University Law professor and current member of the Defender Association Board of Directors who was an assistant defender at the time. "The idea was to try to insulate the Defender from the city by having this board."[61]

Under the agreement, the board would name the chief defender and the first assistant defender. The chief defender, in turn, would appoint the professional and nonprofessional staff. All employees were to be full-time, unless two-thirds of the directors agreed to an exemption. The agreement was to be automatically renewable, subject to cancellation by either party, on June 30 of any year, with ninety days' notice. In addition, the Defender could cancel the agreement with thirty days' notice if the directors deemed the funding from the city insufficient. All employees of the association were forbidden to run for office or engage in political campaigning.[62]

The directors narrowly approved the agreement by a vote of nineteen to sixteen in January 1969. It came just in time to save the Defender. By then, the Defender's financial woes had shrunk the legal staff to eighteen attorneys, down from more than thirty at the beginning of the fiscal year. For about six weeks, it looked as if the Defender might have to close its doors for good, but the infusion of city money enabled the association to restore the services it had cut during the summer and begin hiring new staff to replace those who had left. By the end of fiscal year 1968–1969, the Defender had restored nearly all services.[63] However, the Defender's new funding arrangement, which had squeaked through its Board of Directors, had to survive a legal challenge. Any change in the association's charter required the approval of the Philadelphia Court of Common Pleas, which it received in 1969. While the Defender Association had successfully fought off the threat of a state-appointed or city-run public defender office on the grounds that the office's independence was paramount, even the compromise regarding the association's Board of Directors represented to some too steep a price for that same independence.

Opponents of the agreement, led by Penn criminal law professor Louis B. Schwartz, argued that the deal would give the mayor undue influence over the Defender. Schwartz had already resigned from the Defender's board and from its Executive Committee to protest the agreement. In his letter of resignation, Schwartz declared that he could not accept "the surrender of the independence of the poor people's lawyer and the 'deal' with City Hall which has been approved. Dominance of the defense by political forces linked to the prosecution presents an intolerable conflict of interest: no one who could afford his own lawyer would tolerate such a relationship. Even worse is the Association's concurrence in this conflict situation without consulting its clients, the poor, speaking through available organizations of the poor."[64] Ironically, the objectors raised the same concerns about government interference that the Defender had raised in opposing establishment of a public defender office as part of the state government.

Those who favored going along with the city's demand for representation on the board reasoned that the association could not very well ask the city for millions of dollars a year and then tell city officials they had no right to a voice. They also thought that the Defender Association's structure as a nonprofit corporation would enable it to remain independent of government.

The association took the position in hearings before common pleas judge John McDevitt that the amendments provided an appropriate balance between legitimate government interest in how tax dollars were spent and the independence essential to the operation of a sound defender service. The association buttressed its position with testimony from John J. Cleary, deputy director of the National Defender Project of NLADA. Cleary was responsible for assisting communities across the country in developing defender systems where none had existed and improving the operation of those already in existence. He told the court that the defender system in Philadelphia, as it would exist under the amendments, would be in compliance with standards promulgated by NLADA and adopted by the American Bar Association (ABA). In fact,

Cleary declared, the agreement offered "a model, if not exemplary, method" of balancing public interest with independence.[65]

McDevitt ruled in favor of the association, declaring that any scenario that envisioned city interference with the Defender was "pure speculation on the part of the objectors." While he sympathized with the objectors' concerns, McDevitt could not accept their argument that the amended charter would "create a corporate monster." Schwartz and prominent Philadelphia attorney Bernard L. Segal, a former assistant defender, appealed McDevitt's decision, first in 1971 to Superior Court, where they lost, and then to the Pennsylvania Supreme Court, where they lost again in 1973. Schwartz and Segal argued that although the city would have only ten members on the thirty-member board, it would have the power to nominate five of the ten community members, potentially giving it control over half the directors. The state high court found the scenario outlined by Segal and Schwartz to be highly improbable and upheld the deal, but it sent a clear message to the city to keep its hands off the Defender: "Evidence of improper influence or pressure, whether overt or covert, will trigger an appropriate judicial response."[66]

That still was not enough for Schwartz and Segal, who appealed to the U.S. Supreme Court. The high court denied their petition for a writ of certiorari in December 1973. At that time, Schwartz—who had actually done the Defender a favor by eliciting the state Supreme Court's blessing for its agreement with the city—comforted himself with the thought that his appeal might have had some good impact: "Maybe the red flag run up by our litigation helps maintain the tradition of non-political independence of the Defender Association."[67]

For whatever reason, the city respected the Defender's independence. It did not become a den of patronage, and no administration tried to influence its policies. Even Rizzo, as tough on crime as he was, did not interfere with the Defender. The city, in fact, increased its contribution to the Defender during Rizzo's two terms as mayor, the start of steady growth in city contributions to the Defender.[68]

4

LAWYERS NEEDED

WITH THE AGREEMENT between the Defender Association and the city of Philadelphia in place, the association was free to work at the enormous task of dealing with the mass defense that *Gideon* required. So great was the demand from indigent defendants that from July 1969 to June 1970, just after the contract took effect, the association reported serving more than forty-three thousand people "in all stages of the defense process (except homicide cases), ranging from representation during interrogations or line-ups through developing parole plans." That number was up by more than fifteen thousand from the number served in the year before the financial crisis of 1968, which had been a Defender record.[1] By 1972, the Defender Association of Philadelphia grew to become the second-largest nongovernmental public defender organization in the United States, with 91 lawyers. The growth was not surprising, given the requirements of *Gideon* and the city's demographics. By July 1, 1973, the legal staff had grown to 111, plus First Assistant Defender Vincent J. Ziccardi, First Assistant William Stewart, and Deputy Defender Dennis Kelly. There was plenty to keep them busy.[2] Crime was on the rise in Philadelphia—up 24.9 percent in the first quarter of 1970 over the rate for the first quarter of 1969, according to Federal Bureau of Investigation (FBI) statistics.[3] More than 15 percent of Philadelphia's 1.9 million residents lived in poverty.[4]

Everything about the association had to grow to cope with the huge expansion of its client base: legal staff, support staff, and office space. And it would all have to happen with new leadership. Herman I. Pollock resigned because of health problems in June 1968, and Martin J. Vinikoor, the acting chief defender, resigned at the end of 1968 at the insistence of Mayor James H. Tate. Leadership of the organization then fell to Ziccardi. After his retirement, Pollock stayed with the Defender as counsel. He was also a zealous recruiter who until his death in 1972 visited law schools in an effort to attract talented young lawyers to indigent defense.

Pollock was a tough act to follow. He had been the chief defender since 1946 and was a revered figure among public defenders across the nation, thanks to his active participation in NLADA, the nationwide umbrella organization of public defender offices. In 1963, NLADA honored Pollock with its annual Reginald Heber Smith Award, recognizing exceptional achievement by an attorney representing indigent clients in civil or criminal court. Pollock's accomplishment, according to NLADA, was to make the Defender Association an outstanding advocate for impoverished criminal defendants. Pollock spent so much time interviewing inmates at Moyamensing Prison in South Philadelphia that he observed in 1957, after fourteen years with the Defender Association, that he had spent nearly three years behind bars, a story that was picked up by newspapers across the country. To many in Philadelphia's legal community, Pollock was the personification of the Defender, and their support for the organization may well have grown out of their respect for him. When Pollock died, Robert M. Landis, chancellor of the Philadelphia Bar Association, eulogized him as the "moving and guiding light" of the Defender Association and lauded him for building "a strong cadre of lawyers whose often thankless responsibility was the defense of the indigent, service to the disadvantaged and the forgotten." Landis singled out Pollock's "inspiring preceptorship of the scores of lawyers here and around the country who learned their craft from him." The Defender's directors adopted a memorial resolution declaring that Pollock had adhered to the principles laid out by Francis Fisher Kane and Thomas Cogan that each client "must be defended by the Association as well if not better than he would be by private counsel."[5]

The Defender would miss Pollock's efforts to turn young lawyers into effective advocates. Ziccardi had a less systematic approach to recruiting and training. The two men also had very different styles. Pollock exuded a gravity that suited his role as preceptor, while Ziccardi was a colorful character, with a touch of Damon Runyon about him. Fortunately for the association's continuity, Ziccardi was a Pollock acolyte, just as devoted as his mentor to providing high-quality legal counsel for indigent defendants. A graduate of Temple University Law School, Ziccardi had been a clerk for the Third U.S. Circuit Court of Appeals and an assistant district attorney before joining the Defender Association in 1964. He brought to his work a thorough knowledge of Philadelphia's criminal justice system and a relentless determination to fight for his clients. By 1968, he had risen to the rank of first assistant defender. After Vinikoor's resignation, the Defender board named him acting chief defender and in September 1970 made him chief defender.[6]

Ziccardi quickly proved himself a worthy successor to Pollock and Vinikoor. In its 1970–1971 annual report, the Board of Directors praised Ziccardi's accomplishments during his first nine months in office: "He has successfully developed an efficient, well-staffed organization designed to provide effective representation in all areas and has skillfully encouraged new ideas to improve and expand services and to generate new programs."[7] In February 1971, a survey of the Defender's operations by NLADA (which had already conducted similar evaluations of other large public defender offices, including those in Detroit, San Francisco, Las Vegas, and Seattle) concluded that the Defender Association was "one of the finest [defender offices] in the country" and praised Ziccardi as "an outstanding Chief Defender."[8]

While he shared Pollock's devotion to indigent defense, Ziccardi brought a much different personality to the post of chief defender. Where Pollock was understated and wry, Ziccardi was boisterous, street smart, and down to earth, a charming South Philly corner guy who often seemed to operate on instinct, especially in regard to hiring assistant defenders. A master of the pithy comment, Ziccardi once told a member of the association's Board of Directors that the Defender's mission was "to get our client out of the criminal justice system with as little leather on him as possible."[9] This proved a marked change of tone from the early days, when the Defender's 1940 annual report had assured a skeptical city, "It is not the function of the Defender to get his man 'off,' but to present the case fairly and honestly."[10] Pointing out in a 1972 interview that only one in thirty of the Defender's clients ended up in jail, Ziccardi declared, "[That] is what it is all about. Not whether our client is guilty or innocent, but whether he goes to jail or goes home."[11]

Ziccardi's interaction with his lawyers was much different than Pollock's. While Pollock had met with his assistants in the afternoon to review how their cases had gone that day, Ziccardi wanted to hear funny courtroom stories, and he got his wish. There was a story about a bank robbery defendant who expressed amazement at his preliminary hearing that the police were waiting for him when he came home the day of the robbery. He did not realize that he had handed the teller a demand note written on the back of a letter addressed to him. And one burglary defendant could not hold his tongue. His defender, Frank DeSimone, was cross-examining the arresting officer and doing an effective job of casting doubt on the reliability of the officer's testimony—until the officer said he was sure the defendant was the man he saw emerge from a house on Lehigh Avenue and run west. That was too much for the defendant, who yelled to the judge, "Your honor, when I came off the porch, I ran east on Lehigh Avenue. The cop is lying." The judge asked DeSimone if he had any further questions, and DeSimone replied, "Judge, I think my client has corrected the officer." DeSimone made a note in the client's file: "This is a guilty plea." Stories such as these amused Ziccardi, but they also bred camaraderie among the assistant defenders.[12]

As chief defender, Ziccardi had to become the public face of the association, but it was not a role that came easily to him, despite his personal charm. "Vince was the kind of guy that would not play well in the larger community," said Benjamin Lerner, who succeeded Ziccardi as chief defender in 1975 and had been an assistant defender in the 1960s. "He did not have any interest in public relations and speaking to wider audiences."[13]

When he did speak to a wider audience, as he did in the *Inquirer* article, Ziccardi had a knack for saying the kinds of things that invited angry letters to the editor. He told the *Inquirer* that he gave job applicants a hypothetical case: "You have a client who has raped a girl and admits it to you. But the prosecution's witness is a little shaky. There is a good chance of winning the case if you plead the defendant not guilty. As his attorney, what do you do? If the applicant starts talking about pleading him guilty for the good of society, he flunks the interview. Good of society? He is supposed to be defending the defendant *against* society. It's Joe Schmuck against the Commonwealth."[14]

One letter writer fumed after reading Ziccardi's remarks that "these bright young lawyers put acquittals and soft sentences ahead of the safety of law-abiding citizens." Another wrote, "If that kind of justice is his goal, then the people of Philadelphia should do without him. And to think that taxpayer money is paying him and his assistants."[15] Fortunately for the Defender, if city officials shared the letter writers' indignation, they also knew the city had no choice but to fund public defense. The city actually increased the Defender's budget to $2.3 million for 1973–1974, up from $2.1 million the previous fiscal year. "During the fiscal period of 1972–73, we found that when necessary we were able to obtain adequate funding to perform all the necessary services," the Board of Directors' annual report for 1972–1973 noted.[16]

Ziccardi enthusiastically embraced the adversarial nature of the criminal justice system, describing criminal law as an exercise in "gamesmanship." In his experience, the lawyers who approached their jobs this way had a more enduring mind-set and proved better advocates for the many clients they served than the idealists who might quickly become disillusioned.[17] "Justice is not the function of the Defender's office; our job is to represent the client to the very best of our abilities," he told the *Inquirer*. "Our job isn't to prove that the client is innocent; it's to make it as difficult as possible for the prosecution to prove that he's guilty."[18]

Representing the client to the best of the Defender's ability meant shopping for sympathetic judges or using the court system's backlog of cases for leverage by threatening to take cases to trial if an advantageous plea bargain was not offered. (Ziccardi blamed the district attorney's office and the police for creating a situation where the tactic could work. The police created what Ziccardi blasted as "junk" cases, where either the evidence was inadequate or the offense was "relatively harmless.") "We hide behind junk cases and the backlog they create," Ziccardi said, adding that 70 percent of the cases the authorities brought should never have made it to court.[19]

As the "junk cases" reference made clear, Ziccardi was not shy about criticizing the district attorney in the press. In May 1972, Ziccardi claimed that District Attorney Arlen Specter had violated ABA disciplinary standards by holding a news conference to talk about a trial pending in the Court of Common Pleas. Ziccardi asked the court to impose sanctions on Specter. A judge did criticize Specter's action as "a disservice to the court and a disservice to the administration of justice to the defendant." However, he declined to sanction Specter.[20] In December 1972, Ziccardi told the city council that Specter's reluctance to engage in plea bargaining was actually leading to acquittals for Defender clients. Ziccardi claimed that two out of three people arrested in Philadelphia were acquitted; Specter shot back that Ziccardi's claim was preposterous, unless he was counting "some 40,000 drunks arrested each year who are not prosecuted." Specter said that his office won 73 percent of all cases brought to trial each year.[21]

To his credit, Ziccardi extended his esteem for scrappy adversarial defense over diplomacy or idealism beyond his public statements to the Defender's hiring practices and workplace culture. One of Ziccardi's most important challenges during his tenure was to rebuild the association's legal staff, which had shrunk to eighteen during the financial crisis. Despite the havoc the financial storm had wrought, Ziccardi still had a nucleus of very good young lawyers to build on, including a group of top-flight law graduates who had come to the Defender in a fellowship program founded by civil rights expert Anthony Amsterdam, then a law professor at the University of Pennsylvania. In addition to being talented, the lawyers from the Amsterdam program had the added advantage of not costing the Defender anything. Their salaries were funded by a grant from the Ford Foundation.[22] To the lawyers he inherited from Pollock and Vinikoor, Ziccardi added his own hires, favoring street-smart lawyers with Philadelphia roots who would stand up in court and do whatever it took to get a client off.

Having Philadelphia roots was an important point in Ziccardi's hiring checklist. "He preferred guys—although there were some women—from the Philadelphia streets, from neighborhoods that he understood, who had gone through the local school system, who were street smart," Lerner said. "A lot of those people turned into really good trial lawyers because they were perfectly comfortable with standing up and opening their mouth and making arguments even if they didn't have much to work with. A lot of those people—not all of them but a lot of them—were really outstanding trial lawyers."[23]

One of the Ziccardi hires who turned into an outstanding trial lawyer was DeSimone, an assistant defender from 1970 to 1973. DeSimone's account of his hiring mirrors perfectly Lerner's description of Ziccardi's approach. DeSimone, a graduate of Villanova University School of Law, had just passed the bar in early November 1970 when he applied to both the district attorney's office and the Defender Association. He interviewed for an assistant district attorney job on a Monday. He was told that the office would be hiring in the first week of December and would get back to him. The next day, DeSimone interviewed for a job with the Defender. When he arrived for the interview, the receptionist told him Mr. Ziccardi would see him. This surprised DeSimone because he had interviewed at the district attorney's office without talking to the district attorney, Arlen Specter. "I was in kind of shock because I expected to be interviewed by somebody else, like the D.A.'s Office had just done," DeSimone recalled. When he went into Ziccardi's office, he found the chief defender standing behind his desk. "He had my résumé in his hand, and he looked at my résumé, and he looked up at me, and he said, 'Where are you from, Frank?' To my ears, as a Philadelphian, he didn't ask me where I lived; he asked me where I was from. That kicked into being what corner I was from, growing up. I said, 'Eighteenth and Ritner, Mr. Ziccardi.' He looked up with a big smile. He said, 'Kid, you gave the right answer. You're from a corner. I like kids from corners. Guys from corners make good trial lawyers. You're hired.' I said, 'Excuse me, Mr. Ziccardi. Wait a minute. I'm going to hear from the D.A.'s office in about five weeks.' He said, 'Forget about them. You hear me? You start here Monday. Next Monday, you start here, ninety-five hundred dollars a year, and you're going to have a lot of fun, kid. You're going to learn a lot.' It was the best move I ever made in my life." (It was also the beginning of a long friendship between DeSimone and Ziccardi. "I loved Vince," DeSimone said. "He was a Renaissance man. He just was a different kind of person. He was a wonderful guy. He was a good judge of people.")[24]

Although Ziccardi's Philly corner-guy persona made for charming stories such as DeSimone's, his hiring was not strictly parochial. During his tenure, the Defender made recruiting forays into major law schools outside the Philadelphia area, including Harvard and Duke, as well as local schools. Defender recruiters interviewed about 250 students each year on those campus visits and selected 125 from that group for further interviews.

One of Ziccardi's most unusual hires was Joseph M. Snee. Not only was Snee far older than most new assistant defenders—he was well into his fifties when he joined the Defender in 1971—but he had been a law school professor for years, teaching constitutional and criminal law at Georgetown University. And perhaps most unusual of all, he was a Catholic priest, a member of the Jesuits, the order that operates Georgetown. Snee joined the Defender at the recommendation of Samuel Dash, another Georgetown faculty member and a former assistant district attorney in Philadelphia who would go on to serve as special counsel to the Senate Watergate Committee. Snee quickly advanced to the Major Trials Unit and stayed with the Defender for nine years. He saw his work at the Defender as an act of service to the poor. He quipped that the saints had other priests to attend to them, so he thought it should be his job to serve the sinners. He wore standard lawyerly attire—coat and tie—rather than clerical garb and took care not to flaunt his religious identity, but apparently at least one of his clients found out and said he did not want a priest to represent him because a priest would not lie on his behalf.[25]

"[Ziccardi] was good at picking people," said Paul Conway, who was hired by Ziccardi and went on to become head of the Defender's Special Defense Unit and then the Homicide Unit for years. "He picked some of the best trial lawyers. He would pick these street fighters for trial lawyers and all these smart Ivy League guys for the appeals section."[26] Not all of Ziccardi's hiring hunches worked out. Dennis Kelly, who was for years the deputy defender and made up the legal staff schedule, recalled one new lawyer who botched a cross-examination badly. "The guy was out at a preliminary hearing case," Kelly said. "A delivery man was held up, and the accused allegedly stepped into the delivery truck, pointed a gun at him, and took the money. So the direct examination is done, and they get to the cross-examination, and this guy says, 'Are you from New York?' The assistant district attorney objected, and the defender told the judge: 'Your Honor, give me a chance to get an answer to the question, and you'll see its relevance.' The judge allowed the question. 'Are you from New York?' the assistant defender asked. 'No, I'm not,' the driver replied. 'No further questions,' the defender said. He did join the ranks of the departed here," Kelly said.[27]

The mixture of elite and street could also cause some friction. Philadelphia civil rights lawyer and Temple University Law School professor David Kairys, an assistant defender during the late 1960s who studied law at Cornell and earned a master's degree in law at Penn, recalled that one assistant defender took him to task for seeming to downplay the importance of interviewing clients: "'Don't let anyone hear you say you got nothing to do but interview. That's a vital function around here. We all do it, even the Ivy Leaguers.' The Ivy League comment reflected a tension in the office that I would become familiar with."[28]

Many of the young lawyers joining the Defender came with minimal preparation beyond their law degrees and licenses. Courtroom experience was one part of the appeal of working as a Defender. Law schools offered their students very little in the way of courtroom training. The Defender did have an orientation program, which, according to the annual report for fiscal year 1972–1973, was designed to acquaint new attorneys with "the daily procedures of an Assistant Defender, the nature of the Association, and with the Philadelphia court system."[29]

Mostly, though, it was learn by doing and had been before Ziccardi became chief defender.

In the hurly-burly of expansion after *Gideon*, there was little time for training. "Here was my training when I started," recalled Lerner, who first worked for the Defender in 1966, while Pollock was still the chief defender. "We had preliminary hearings at the different police districts in those days. I started on a Wednesday, and my first assignment was on the following Monday; I was going to represent clients at preliminary hearings in West Philly. When I mentioned to the guy who was running the office that I didn't even know what a preliminary hearing was at the time, since I spent my first year out of law school out in San Francisco clerking for a federal trial court judge, he said, 'That's okay; you'll go with one of our experienced lawyers over the weekend to South Philly to watch him do preliminary hearings.'"[30]

The "experienced" lawyer was John Packel, who would later lead the Defender Association's Appeals Unit for many years but had graduated from the University of Pennsylvania Law School just a year before Lerner. "I went out with him on Saturday—they had hearings seven days a week in those days—and before we were through the morning session, he got himself kicked out of court for arguing with the judge about representing somebody." Packel objected that the judge could not throw him out of court because there would then be nobody from the Defender Association to represent indigent defendants. The judge spotted Lerner and said, "What about him?" "That's how I started," Lerner said. "I was a relatively warm body on the wrong side of the courtroom."[31]

Later, as chief defender, Lerner would replace the seat-of-the-pants introduction to indigent defense with a training program that brought the Defender national accolades. However, the do-it-yourself approach was still in effect in the Ziccardi era, and some liked it. DeSimone, like Lerner, had no courtroom experience at all when he started work for the Defender. As a Villanova law student, he had been self-conscious about his South Philadelphia accent and shy about speaking in class, but all that changed when he started work for the Defender. "When I got into the Defender's office, I never was shy a moment," he recalled. "I don't know what happened. I started at those hearings, and like I said, they throw you in the swimming pool, you swim. And I swam and I swam and I swam and I swam."[32]

Ziccardi had a definite route he wanted his young lawyers to swim. "First, he would send you to the prisons, and you'd have a couple of weeks in the prisons," DeSimone recalled. "You'd learn a little bit; you'd talk to the guys. You didn't know a lot, but you got a little bit of the ability to talk to the clients. Then, while that's going on, he'd have you down to the Roundhouse [the Police Administration Building, so called because of its shape] during the preliminary arraignments."[33]

After about a month of arraignments, the new defenders would move on to represent clients at preliminary hearings in the police districts. Then they moved on to Municipal Court, where they could watch some of city's best private-practice criminal lawyers, such as Cecil B. Moore and A. Charles Peruto Sr., at work. "They didn't put any witnesses on at the preliminary hearing," DeSimone recalled. "All they would do is cross-examine. They'd cross-examine the police, cross-examine the rape victim, cross-examine a robbery victim. It was wonderful to watch it unfold, to watch these experienced lawyers ply their trade. And I'm getting paid to watch them for two hours." From Municipal Court, it was on to the Court of Common Pleas and then to the Major Trials Unit. After a year and a half, Ziccardi assigned DeSimone to the Major Trials Unit.[34]

DeSimone, who went on to try murder cases for the district attorney before entering private practice, credits the Defender with helping him become a successful advocate. "Because of the Defender's office, because of the abilities I was able to hone, because of what happened in the office, because of listening to people and being able to judge people and size them up, and people like Vince who had street skills, I was able to become a lawyer, a trial lawyer," he said. "A lot of my success in the D.A.'s office came about because of my Defender's office experience. I was a D.A. with a defender's mind." DeSimone knew where all the traps for the prosecution were and how the defense attorney might sow doubt about the defendant's guilt.[35]

Surprisingly, a good number of lawyers have worked for both the Defender and the district attorney or U.S. attorney; two former defenders have been elected Philadelphia district attorney—Specter, who had been a volunteer defender, and Larry Krasner, who was a full-time assistant. Another former assistant defender, Stephen J. McEwen Jr., was elected district attorney of Delaware County. Both Ziccardi and Vinikoor had worked in the district attorney's office, and Vinikoor went back to work there after leaving the Defender. Several lawyers, such as DeSimone, joined the Defender after interviewing with the district attorney's office. "Good lawyers can do both prosecution and defense," said Paul Conway, the longtime chief of the Defender's Special Defense Unit and the first head of the Homicide Unit. "The worst lawyers are the zealots on either side," said Conway, who had interviewed with the district attorney's office but went with the Defender, as DeSimone did, because Ziccardi unexpectedly offered him a job during an interview.[36]

The willingness of some lawyers to work as both prosecutor and defense counsel raises the question of what kind of person becomes a public defender. Young lawyers looking for trial experience? Advocates concerned that every defendant have a fair trial? Competitors who thrive on the battlefield of the courtroom? Idealists? Activists? Or some combination? The answer appears to be all of those, and often in the same person. Abbe Smith, a former assistant defender in Philadelphia who went on to become a law professor at Georgetown University, explains: "There are as many motivations as there are defenders." Smith has written that she tells her students she became a defender because as a child she read the novel *To Kill a Mockingbird* and saw the movie many times. She wanted to be a trial lawyer so she could be like the book's protagonist, Atticus Finch, an attorney in a small southern town who defends an African American man falsely accused of raping a white woman.[37]

Temple University law professor Louis M. Natali Jr., who was an assistant defender in the late 1960s as part of Penn's Amsterdam program and later led the Defender's training programs as first assistant, believes you can find three kinds of people in a public defender office: mavericks, who like to "stick a stick in the grinding wheels of justice"; true believers, who aspire to make an unfair system fair; and people worn out by the work who are just putting in the time and drawing a salary. "If you can combine the maverick and the true believer, I think you have a really solid person," Natali said.[38]

The culture of a public defender office is extremely important to attracting and nurturing good defenders, said Jonathan Rapping, cofounder of Gideon's Promise, a training center for public defenders in Atlanta. The best offices—including Philadelphia's—have "a culture of spirited, client-centered, zealous advocacy," according to Rapping. The lawyers who work in those offices are "a different breed of public defender. . . . They don't do this work because it's a stepping-stone to becoming a judge or a district attorney or a high-paid private lawyer. They don't do this work because they want trial experience on the backs of poor people. They do this work because it's a mission, it's a calling."[39]

Natali's view of the importance of office culture is similar to Rapping's and counteracts what Natali described as a "tremendous" burnout danger. "It's so great to work at the Defender because the people you work with give you approval and give you satisfaction," he said. "That's why people stay." The defenders support one another and learn from one another. "Generally, people watch what's going on," he explained. They watch what their peers are doing in court and offer advice and encouragement. "A lot of what happens in the office, the best thing that happens in the office, is not ever going to be the formal training," Natali said. "It's the informal training that you get from your office mate, from your floormate, or you go in and you say, 'Hey, I just came from court, and this judge said I couldn't do this.' And somebody said, 'Well, wait a minute,' and they gave you three cases why the judge was wrong, or they gave you an argument [to use in court]."[40] As an example of the Defender's camaraderie, Kelly recalled waiting around until 1:00 A.M. for a verdict from a jury that had gone out at noon. "My fellow defenders hung around, waiting for the verdict with me, and that's the kind of dedication [one finds at the Defender]," Kelly said.[41]

Hiring lawyers was one thing; keeping them was another. Pay for public defenders, not just in Philadelphia but everywhere in the country, has traditionally been low. "A lawyer [working for the Defender] who started in 2008, at the point of the financial meltdown, started around forty-eight thousand five hundred dollars," said David Rudovsky, who was president of the Defender's board during that period. "Eight years later, if that lawyer is still at the Defender, if they're making sixty thousand dollars now, they're doing well."[42] Beyond the low salary, the work is not easy. Caseloads are huge. Most of the clients are found guilty or plead guilty. There are petty indignities, at the hands of judges, prosecutors, even clients. ("I don't have a lawyer; I have a public defender" is not an uncommon sentiment among clients.) And zealotry, for those who are most motivated by it, can be draining.

Abbe Smith, considering the problem of defender burnout, concluded that the key to having a satisfying, long-lasting career as a public defender was an ability to blend idealism and cynicism. The disappointments that go along with being a defender can lead to disillusion and cynicism, according to Smith. "Yet, a certain measure of idealism remains even in the most seasoned, seen-it-all defender," she writes. "Idealism—believing in something—is a powerful thing. Believing that the fight itself makes a difference, whether or not one prevails in the end, is both powerful and essential for defenders. There is fuel there."[43]

The trick is to strike a balance between cynicism and idealism. Some defenders cannot do it; they yield to the cynicism and leave indigent defense. Others embrace the paradox. "Every defender I know who has lasted in the business—frankly, every poor people's lawyer—is both reverential and irreverent, hopeful and doubtful, in short, a cynical idealist," Smith believes. "Idealism keeps you going; cynicism keeps you grounded."[44]

5

REORGANIZED AND RELEVANT

I F THE DEFENDER'S LEGAL STAFF had to grow to cope with the demands of *Gideon*, so did its support staff and infrastructure. Revitalized by the contract with the city, the Defender was now able to expand its services beyond anything that Francis Fisher Kane could have imagined or Herman Pollock could have hoped for. And in a pioneering effort on behalf of prison reform, the Defender would soon show that it could have a significant impact on Philadelphia's justice system.

Early in 1968, the Board of Directors asked the Defender's leadership for a projection of the organization's needs and growth over the ensuing five years. The subsequent report, "Defender Services—Trends and Directions, 1973," recommended that the association find new quarters of at least 16,500 square feet to accommodate a staff of lawyers expected to grow to seventy by 1973 and hire an office manager. Other goals included a strong recruitment program, pay parity with the district attorney's office, a more formal training regimen, more sophisticated information retrieval, more individualized representation, and expansion of social services. The Defender would have varying levels of success in meeting those goals, but the hiring of an office manager and the move to new quarters were accomplished quickly. First came the manager, then the move.[1]

In June 1969, the Defender hired Dorothy Lynch, who had been an office administrator for ten years with the firm of Wolf, Block, Schorr and Solis-Cohen, as the association's first business manager. Lynch would run the Defender Association's affairs for twelve years, but when she showed up for her first day on the job in the summer of 1969, she must have wondered what she had gotten herself into. With a noir flair, she described her first impressions of the Defender offices in a memoir for the Defender's fiftieth anniversary in 1984. "I crossed the cooled but sleazy lobby of One North 13th Street [then the home of the Defender] and took the elevator to the eighth floor to begin my new job," she recalled. "When I stepped out of the elevator, I realized that the narrow public corridor outside the office was the clients' 'waiting room'—a crowded space with chairs in various stages of disrepair lined against the wall. Although not yet 9 A.M., the space was hot and so crowded with people that some had to stand or sit on the floor. I soon learned that their wait would be long, because few lawyers were available for interviewing. I remember the closely huddled desks and typewriters, all of various sizes, shapes and colors and generally in poor condition, a hand-operated ditto machine, a file room more like a walk-in closet. Grit, seeping in through ill-fitting windows, was everywhere."[2]

Fortunately for the Defender's operational efficiency over the next twelve years, Lynch's welcome from the association's staff far outweighed the dreary setting. "Almost everyone I met in those first few days made me glad I had chosen this new job," she recalled. Lynch described Herman Pollock, who had resigned as chief defender by that time but had stayed on as counsel, as "a revered father figure to the young lawyers." Vincent Ziccardi, who was then the acting chief defender, was "warm and knowing in the way things worked."[3]

Lynch's description of the Defender's cramped and shabby digs underscored the importance of finding a new home. The search for new quarters actually had its roots in fiscal year 1966–1967, toward the end of Pollock's tenure as chief defender, when the association commissioned Price Waterhouse and Company to evaluate its office practices. Price Waterhouse recommended changes in "attorney assignments, case document flow and control, accounting systems and procedures, and presentation and accumulation of statistical data."[4]

The Defender's struggle to survive in the financial crisis of 1968 shoved relocation and improved operations momentarily aside, but soon after the contract with the city was signed and Ziccardi became the acting chief defender, the association again commissioned Price Water-house to do a second study of the Defender's office operations. The report, completed in October 1969, focused on the flow and control of case documents and on office space. Price Waterhouse concluded that insufficient office space—only about eighty-five hundred square feet—and poor layout were hampering the Defender's efficiency. The inefficient office arrangements led to inadequate file-preparation procedures, which handicapped the Defender's courtroom activities and added an additional burden to the defense the association was able to provide for its clients. The study recommended that the Defender begin planning immediately to move into new office space.[5]

Finding that space was not easy. Some building owners were reluctant to rent to the Defender for fear that their tenants would not want to rub shoulders with the Defender's clientele. However, the association was able to find more than sixteen thousand square feet, formerly occupied by stockbrokers, in a building at 1526 Chestnut Street, above the Stouffer's restaurant. The association moved into the new space on June 30, 1970, before work on the site was even complete. When Pollock toured the new offices, he took Lynch's hand in his and said tearfully that his dreams had come true; the Defender Association was firmly established at last.[6]

Even with the move and improved layout, however, the Defender offices did not present the same face to the world that a private law firm of similar size would have shown. The 1971 NLADA report noted that it was hard for visitors to find the office: Directions to the elevator and the stairwell were "neither prominent nor clear," the stairwell looked like it led to a parking lot rather than a law office, and the "sparsely furnished" reception area appeared "more appropriate to a welfare than an attorney's office." However, the office was close to the courts and, once a visitor got inside, was "furnished . . . in a manner appropriate to the dignity of the legal profession, with a library of sufficient size and equipment for efficient operations."[7] Spartan though the Defender's reception area may have been, the NLADA team gave the office a thumbs-up for functionality: "In terms of administrative and clerical staff, record keeping, and availability and use of machines (e.g., dictating machines, automatic typewriters) . . . [the Defender is] vastly superior to any other [public defender office] observed."[8]

Expanding the staff and moving into new offices were far from the only changes for the Defender in the Ziccardi years. In March 1969, the association began providing representation in the Juvenile Division of

Family Court. The Defender had represented juveniles throughout its history, but not often. In 1940, for example, the association represented 13,695 clients, 15 of them under the age of sixteen and another 215 between the ages of sixteen and eighteen.[9] In the early 1960s, Pollock expressed interest in expanding its juvenile representation, but aside from a brief involvement with the Family Court program of Community Legal Services (CLS), nothing happened.[10]

Then in May 1967, the U.S. Supreme Court ruled in the case of *In re Gault* that juveniles charged with delinquency had a right to counsel, just as adults charged with crime did under *Gideon*.[11] *Gault* was a game changer for juvenile law. In practical terms for Philadelphia, it meant that the city would have to provide lawyers for juvenile defendants. CLS, funded by the federal government, had been providing that representation, but Congress in 1967 banned CLS from criminal or juvenile delinquency cases after September 1, 1968. The city needed to find a substitute in a hurry, and the Defender was the obvious choice, at least as far as one key judge, Frank J. Montemuro Jr., was concerned. Montemuro, the administrative judge of Family Court, warned in June 1968 that chaos would result unless the city could contract with the Defender Association to supply the necessary juvenile representation. The alternative would be to appoint private counsel, which could cost the city $22 million, even if enough lawyers were available. Montemuro thought the Defender could do the job for $350,000 per year.[12] The judge repeated his warning of impending chaos early in September: "We're in real serious trouble in juvenile court, and we'll be in trouble until the city fathers come up with the money to purchase legal services from the Defender Association to represent these juveniles."[13]

The city's need for juvenile representation to replace CLS, coming in the midst of the Defender's financial troubles, was a bit of serendipity for all concerned—or as the 1970–1971 annual report of the Defender's Board of Directors succinctly put it, "a factor in the resolution of these difficulties."[14] Family Court needed public defenders, and no other agency was available to provide them, the directors noted: "Therefore, the contract entered into between the City and the Association in January 1969 provided for legal representation in the Family Court as well as representation in the Criminal Courts."[15]

The Defender began its juvenile representation on March 10, 1969, with four attorneys working out of borrowed office space with borrowed furniture in the Family Court building. By the end of June, the legal staff had increased to six lawyers and one law clerk, representing every child who appeared at a detention hearing, even if the child would later have private counsel.[16] The following year, the number of assistant defenders working in Family Court increased to twelve. They helped the court establish procedures for hearing pretrial motions and writs and for determining whether there was probable cause for keeping a juvenile locked up pending an adjudicatory hearing. The Family Court defenders also conducted regular reviews of juveniles detained while awaiting hearings and worked on expediting trials, cutting the wait time from arrest to adjudicatory hearing from five weeks to four.[17]

The Juvenile Unit's small social-service unit worked out rehabilitation plans to keep the youngsters from being committed to a residential facility. If a minor had been charged with "incorrigibility"—meaning ungovernable by parent or guardian, a classification peculiar to juvenile law—the social-service investigation might find another relative that the youngster "could live more happily with," the directors' 1968–1969 report explained.[18] The social-service unit also recommended plans for minors who were committed, evaluated community resources available to help them, and kept the lawyers informed of ways to make use of available community services for the young clients.[19]

The Defender also created an Adult Social Service Unit in 1968. The department's mission was to help Defender clients with their nonlegal problems, including drug use, unemployment, housing, and homelessness. The emphasis was on "the rehabilitation of the client toward maximum social utility," according to the Board of Directors' 1969–1970 annual report.[20] The NLADA report described the department as "one of the unique and far-sighted features" of the Defender Association.[21]

While the social-service department came into being at the end of Pollock's tenure, the Defender's financial crisis of 1968 disrupted its operation, and it would fall to Ziccardi to move the department forward. Ziccardi believed that a strong social-service program would be a great help in getting Defender clients sent home rather than to jail, anticipating by more than two decades the holistic approach to indigent defense of the 1990s. "Before this was fashionable anyplace else, let alone indispensable, Vince put in place a growing social-services division to provide programmatic recommendations about treatment/rehabilitation for clients that could be presented to judges by way of sentencing alternatives," Lerner said. The Defender listed fifteen social workers on its staff for fiscal year 1971–1972.[22]

An *Inquirer* feature story on the Defender in 1972 noted that "Philadelphia's is one of only two or three defender systems in the nation which have a social service agency within their framework. Social services, which can provide the client with jobs, medical care, schooling and counseling, is still a novel concept." Richard Boroch, who was the Defender's director of social services in 1972, explained the Defender's approach: "We try to give the courts a realistic alternative to prison, one that the courts can respond to."[23] In 1972, the Defender even hired its own psychiatrist, Dr. Perry Berman, to help determine the competency of defendants. Court-appointed psychiatrists had been doing only about forty evaluations a year. With a psychiatrist on staff, working twenty hours a week, the association could now get psychiatric examinations for about 250 of its clients each year, Ziccardi reckoned.[24]

At the same time the Defender was expanding programs to help keep its clients out of jail, it began to focus on helping those of its clients who were in jail, either awaiting trial or serving a sentence. That effort played a major role in beginning a drive for jailhouse reform in 1970 that would carry into the second decade of the twenty-first century. On July 4, 1970, inmates at Holmesburg Prison rebelled over conditions at the jail. The incident left more than one hundred inmates and guards injured.[25] After the conflict, Defender Association staff lawyers began hearing from their clients locked up in Holmesburg that some inmates were being physically abused by prison staff and sexually abused by other inmates.[26] Even before these incidents, Defender attorneys had known that overcrowding, a lack of programs, and an insufficient number of guards made being locked up at Holmesburg dangerous. The long waiting time between arrest and trial, combined with lack of anything to do but wait, created an explosive situation.[27]

On July 13, Assistant Defender David Rudovsky, who would become one of Philadelphia's premier constitutional lawyers and president of the Defender's Board of Directors from 2006 to 2018, applied for a writ of habeas corpus on behalf of a Holmesburg inmate, Cephus Bryant. On July 16, Rudovsky filed a second petition on behalf of another inmate, James Goldstein. Both prisoners claimed that pretrial detention in Holmesburg amounted to cruel and unusual punishment because the association's clients were subject to possible physical or sexual abuse and because conditions at the jail were primitive.[28] "It was kind of unusual that we would get involved in a case that was usually litigated as a civil rights matter," Rudovsky said. However, the Defender was able to represent Bryant and Goldstein in the habeas corpus petition because they were Defender clients and the Defender was concerned about their well-being at Holmesburg. "We thought we had a duty not only to represent clients at trial, but if they were incarcerated, either pretrial or after a sentence, we had a continuing obligation to make sure that they were being treated fairly," Rudovsky explained.[29]

President Judge Vincent A. Carroll of the Court of Common Pleas assigned three judges—Edmund B. Spaeth Jr., Robert N. C. Nix Jr., and Theodore B. Smith Jr.—to take evidence and hear arguments in the case. Among those testifying were former and current Holmesburg inmates, a chaplain, the superintendent of prisons, and other officials. Their testimony painted a shocking picture of substandard conditions in almost every aspect of Holmesburg's institutional life: Inmates were injecting heroin and carrying knives, rats and roaches were everywhere, cells were unfit for habitation, the mess hall was filthy and stank, and the kitchen was "a pigpen."[30]

On August 11, the court granted the writs and the two inmate plaintiffs were transferred to other jails. In a sixty-six-page opinion, the three judges described Holmesburg as a "cruel, degrading disgusting place, likely to bring out the worst in a man." They concluded that "to continue to imprison petitioners, who are untried and are in Holmesburg Prison, Philadelphia, rather than out on bail only because they are poor, is to impose upon them cruel and unusual punishment in violation of the Eighth and Fourteenth Amendments of the United States Constitution," and they ordered the city to fix the situation.[31] District Attorney Arlen Specter immediately appealed, but the Pennsylvania State Supreme Court rejected his appeal and ruled that inmates could file habeas corpus petitions "to secure relief from conditions constituting cruel and unusual punishment." Chief Defender Ziccardi announced that the Defender would seek the release of six hundred other Holmesburg inmates on writs of habeas corpus if conditions did not improve at the jail within a month.[32]

Conditions did appear at first to be improving. Efforts to get prisoners released on bail had been going well, reducing the prison population by nearly three hundred, and Ziccardi announced he was temporarily dropping his plans for filing the six hundred habeas corpus petitions.[33] However, the Defender's satisfaction with the city's efforts was short-lived. "We were monitoring the conditions and decided that, in our view, they were still unconstitutional," Rudovsky said.[34] So in February 1971, Rudovsky was back in court, this time filing a class-action lawsuit in the Court of Common Pleas, *Jackson v. Hendrick*, on behalf of five Holmesburg inmates.[35] By this time, Rudovsky had left the Defender to begin his own law firm with Defender colleague David Kairys, so the case was not a Defender Association case. As a civil case, *Jackson* was outside the Defender's sphere of activity. However, *Jackson* would remain in litigation for three decades, and Defender lawyers kept Rudovsky informed about conditions their clients were confronting behind bars. Rudovksy also continued working on the case when he returned to the Defender to work as first assistant in the mid-1980s. "When I went back in as first assistant defender, I litigated it there as a defender," he said. Much of *Jackson* "came out of the original Defender interest in jail conditions: In a lot of ways, [*Jackson*] was a Defender project."[36]

The *Jackson* case was assigned to the same three-judge panel—Spaeth, Nix, and Smith—that had heard the habeas claims the previous year. The trial lasted a full month. In April 1972, the judges ruled in a 260-page decision written by Spaeth that prison conditions in Philadelphia were so bad that they violated the constitutional rights of the inmates. The judges pronounced the city's jail systems to be "in almost every aspect of its operations a failure" and ordered the city to undertake a six-month program to reform the system. The ruling applied not just to Holmesburg but to the City House of Corrections and the City Detention Center. The judges also ordered the appointment of a master to monitor conditions in the jails and ordered specific changes related to health care, environmental conditions, and overcrowding. Once again, as with the habeas petitions, the city appealed and the State Supreme Court affirmed the three-judge panel's ruling.[37]

The *Jackson* Supreme Court decision led to decades of monitoring "in which we continued to litigate the case," Rudovsky said. "The [common pleas] court ordered reforms over the years, the city did or didn't do the reforms, they were held in contempt on several occasions for not [complying], [and] they were fined significant amounts."[38] Then in 1982, as the prison population in Philadelphia began to rise again significantly, some inmates complained that the state courts had failed to alleviate conditions in the prisons and filed a separate action in federal court, *Harris v. Pernsley*, making the same claims *Jackson* had been making in state court.[39] "Since the issues were pretty much the same in *Jackson* and *Harris*, and the city was the defendant in both cases, [the lead counsel in the cases] agreed the federal suit would mainly focus on overcrowding issues," Rudovsky said. "The *Jackson* case, which I was still litigating, would deal with the conditions of confinement—medical care, food, recreation, visits, use of force, and environmental issues."[40] In 1986, with Philadelphia's jail population at 4,300, the city entered into a consent decree providing that whenever the inmate population reached 3,750, no untried defendants would be admitted unless charged with crimes of violence or major drug offenses. Convicted defendants could still be incarcerated in the city's jails, regardless of the population.[41] Although the consent decree did act as a brake on the growth of the jail population, it did not bring the number down to the level that decree envisioned. The jail population remained around 5,000, and both cases continued on, running along parallel tracks.[42]

In the early 2000s, both cases were ended under an agreement in which the city pledged to control the jail population and the conditions. "That didn't happen," Rudovsky said. By 2006, the inmate population had spiked so high that the prison commissioner determined that there was no more room in the jails and decided to keep defendants in the police districts where they were taken after arrest. However, the police stations were not prepared to provide food, medical treatment, or even a place to sleep, Rudovsky said. "Hundreds of our clients were there for days, and we were getting reports of serious problems and abuses."[43]

In response, Rudovsky and David Richman, the lead attorney in *Harris*, filed a new federal lawsuit, *Bowers v. Philadelphia*.[44] (Both Rudovsky and Richman were private attorneys, but each had a Defender connection: Rudovsky was named president of the Defender board in 2006, and Richman was a board member.) The court found for the plaintiffs and ordered an end to the practice of holding prisoners in the police districts. When the jail population continued to rise, Rudovsky filed yet another lawsuit in federal court, *Williams v. Philadelphia*,[45] which led to a settlement agreement with the city in 2016. Under the settlement, the city agreed to reduce its jail population, cut the number of lockdowns, and limit the use of triple celling for mentally ill inmates. By this time, too, all the agencies involved in the justice system—courts, the district attorney's office, the Defender, the police, and city agencies—had cooperated on a plan that made further lawsuits unnecessary.[46]

The legal battles that began with the Defender's habeas corpus petitions in 1970 had an impact not just in Philadelphia but across the country. "If you go back to 1970, when we filed the habeas petition, nobody was looking at [prison conditions]; no court was looking at it," Rudovsky said. The common approach of judges to the operation of jails and prisons was "hands off." "There were a couple of cases in the South, in Arkansas, where lawyers had challenged some of the conditions, but around the country, there was hardly any case law," Rudovsky said. "It wasn't clear what powers the courts had to deal with conditions in prisons and jails, so the *Jackson v. Hendrick* opinion by Judge Spaeth was kind of a leading opinion very early on, a kind of a road map for lawyers around the country to do prisoners' rights litigation. This was kind of a big change in civil rights litigation."[47]

6

TONY'S FELLOWS TAKE CHARGE

I N NOVEMBER 1974, Vincent Ziccardi submitted his resignation, effective January 15, 1975, to enter private practice and pursue a business venture related to the city's upcoming celebration of the nation's bicentennial.[1] He had led the Defender in its rebound from the near disaster of 1968, building up the legal staff from eighteen lawyers to more than one hundred by 1974, representing thirty-six thousand clients annually.[2] The job Ziccardi left was quite different from the one he had inherited, to his credit. His successors would need to pilot this substantial office through a difficult period of politics locally and nationally, with the lives of thousands of accused and the functioning of a city's justice system resting on their leadership. Fortunately, the opportunistic Defender had established a unique stream of leadership to tap into in this moment.

Ziccardi told the *Philadelphia Daily News* that he "was getting a little bored with the job." He had also been dealing with a unionizing effort by some of the Defender's lawyers, dissatisfied with the low pay and with the Defender practice of having a different lawyer represent defendants at each step in the judicial process except in major cases. The pro-union campaign fizzled, but not before taking a tense turn in November 1974 when Ziccardi fired one of the organizers, leading to a strike threat until Ziccardi hired him back at the urging of D. Donald Jamieson, president judge of the Court of Common Pleas. Ziccardi denied that his decision to retire had anything to do with the labor situation and told the *Daily News* that he had been planning the move "for four or five months."[3]

Whatever Ziccardi's reason, the Defender Association needed a new leader, and it found one quickly in Benjamin Lerner, who had served as an assistant defender from 1966 to 1968. Lerner got the job despite his age: He was only thirty-four when he took over an office that represented more than 70 percent of Philadelphia's criminal defendants on charges ranging from shoplifting to rape to manslaughter (but not homicide, which was still reserved for representation by private attorneys). Lerner was confident he knew the criminal justice system and understood the Defender's role in it, but he had never managed anything as big as the Defender, which was then the second-largest nongovernment public defender office in the nation.[4]

Young though he was, Lerner was well prepared by training and by experience for his new responsibility. A 1965 graduate of the University of Pennsylvania Law School, Lerner had clerked for a federal judge in San Francisco before returning to Philadelphia to join the Defender in 1966 as part of an innovative fellowship program created by Anthony Amsterdam, then a law professor at Penn. The program, funded by the Ford Foundation, hired young lawyers to work as assistant defenders three weeks out of every four and spend the fourth week brainstorming ways to improve the justice system. After the term of his fellowship was up, Lerner had worked first for a large Philadelphia law firm and then for the Pennsylvania attorney general's office, where he ran the criminal law division, but it may have been the Amsterdam program that did the most to prepare him to become the chief defender.[5]

Law students and young lawyers just starting out did not get much clinical training in the 1960s, which Amsterdam thought was a mistake. Inspired by the E. Barrett Prettyman Program, a fellowship program in criminal law run by Georgetown University for young lawyers, Amsterdam came up with a clinical project of his own. "The aim was to combine the resources of a law school with those of a small, overworked, full-time public defender's office," Lerner said.[6] Amsterdam applied to the Ford Foundation and got a five-year grant that would support the work of three or four fellows per year, each for a two-year period on the legal staff of the Defender Association. Because they would be working as assistant defenders, they would have to be law school graduates who had passed the bar and were licensed to practice. The program would also bring in third-year Penn Law students, whom the fellows would supervise, to help with representation at low levels.[7] The program was not limited to Penn Law alumni, and since clinical training programs for young lawyers were so rare in those days, Amsterdam found himself with a wealth of bright applicants from all over the country. "Tony had his pick of people" for his fellowship program, recalled Lerner, who was one of the first three fellows in 1966, along with law graduates of Yale and Georgetown.[8] About half of the fellows had held prestigious clerkships with federal judges. Word of the new program drew Philadelphia native Louis M. Natali Jr., a Georgetown Law graduate, back home from Richmond, where he had been clerking for a judge on the U.S. Fourth Circuit Court of Appeals. "I didn't necessarily want to come back here, but this was so interesting and exciting," he said. "It would be like if you were a baseball player and you got a chance to work with Joe DiMaggio or Robin Roberts."[9]

Lerner and the other fellows were united in an almost reverential respect for Amsterdam. "I'm a pretty cynical person, but I do have one hero in this life, and it's Tony Amsterdam," said Natali, who became first assistant defender under Lerner and later a Defender Association board member and law professor at Temple University.[10]

It is easy to understand why Amsterdam made such a profound impression. A 1960 graduate of Penn Law, Amsterdam—"Tony" to his colleagues and students—had clerked for U.S. Supreme Court Justice Felix Frankfurter before serving briefly as an assistant U.S. attorney for the District of Columbia. He joined the Penn faculty in 1962 and built a stellar reputation for scholarship and advocacy, leading law students on summertime voter registration forays into the South and devising a strategy for avoiding racist southern state court judges in voting rights cases. By the mid-1960s, he was already on his way to becoming a towering figure in constitutional law.[11] In 1972, the U.S. Supreme Court would agree with his argument in *Furman v. Georgia* that capital punishment was unconstitutional because it was applied inconsistently.[12] The court reversed itself four years later, but all the legal maneuvering around the death penalty issue halted executions from 1967 to 1977. Amsterdam's reputation as one of the great civil rights lawyers of his era and one of the death penalty's mightiest opponents was firmly established.

For Lerner, Natali, David Rudovsky, and the others in the program, Tony Amsterdam was the model of what a defense attorney should be. He told his fellows, "You will have varying amounts of time to prepare for a case, and if you're a public defender with a huge caseload, with files that you don't get sometimes until the morning of the case, you might only have a couple of hours or a matter of minutes, but whatever time you have, you commit yourself. You forget everything else for that time period, and you commit yourself one hundred percent mentally and physically to that case, that assignment, for whatever amount of time you have."[13]

The Amsterdam fellowships had a significant impact not just on the fellows but on the Defender as an institution. In the short term, it brought to the Defender a group of very talented young lawyers—whose salaries came from the Ford Foundation, not the Defender—at a time when the association needed them desperately, especially during the 1968 financial crunch. In 1967, seven Amsterdam fellows were working at the Defender, Rudovsky recalled. They made up about one-fifth of the Defender Association's legal staff at the time, a percentage that went up as the regular staff dwindled in 1968. "To the extent it drew qualified and motivated lawyers who wanted to do criminal defense work, pretty high-quality lawyers from that program, I think it gave a boost to the office," Rudovsky said. "It was lawyers the Defender didn't have to pay for, so you had those extra resources there."[14] In the long term, the Amsterdam alumni provided leadership for the association well into the twenty-first century. Lerner, Natali, and Rudovsky would all assume significant leadership roles in the Defender over the next four decades. "It was a pretty talented group, both in terms of trial skills and, maybe even more important, kind of a larger vision of defense responsibility—appellate skills, legal skills, that kind of work," Rudovsky said. "I think it kind of raised the bar in terms of what the office would then be looking for in future applicants."[15]

The program also proved beneficial for some lawyers already on the Defender staff, drawing them into the creative legal thinking that the fellowship project spawned. John Packel, who had joined the Defender after graduating from Penn before the Amsterdam program began, experienced just this effect.[16] Packel would become Lerner's first mentor with the Defender and go on to put his legal creativity to use for thirty years as head of the association's Appeals Unit. "He was like the non-Amsterdam fellow, practically, because we became—all of us—very, very close social friends," Lerner said.[17]

Although they revered Amsterdam, the fellows took their orders at the Defender from Herman Pollock and his assistants. Ziccardi, then the first assistant, scheduled them, just as he did the other assistant defenders. "We were not grouped together but spread out so that each of us had as an office mate a regular defender," Lerner recalled. "From the first day that we started, we were treated like additions, much-needed additions, to the staff, and that was the thing that Tony had promised Herman would happen, and it did happen."[18]

The project exposed the fellows to two highly regarded mentors from different eras: Amsterdam and Pollock. "I knew Herman well," recalled Amsterdam, who was still teaching law at New York University in 2018. "He and I collaborated in the general design of the fellowship program, which could not, of course, have been instituted without his support."[19]

In addition to the work the Amsterdam fellows provided the Defender, the program demanded that fellows use their new perspective to develop ideas on how the criminal justice system might be reformed to work more effectively to minimize the inequalities experienced by the people living through it. These were not merely academic. The brainstorming sessions, held at Penn under Amsterdam's watchful eye, were academic only in the sense that they took place on campus. The ideas they produced had a real-world application. "The time spent at the law school is usually devoted to developing an approach to a problem uncovered through work in the [Defender] office," the association's directors wrote in their 1967–1968 annual report. "Ideas developed in this manner have made our staff more cognizant of the inequalities of the law and how they may be corrected."[20]

One of those inequalities, in the view of many in the public defender community, was cash bail, which critics complained punished poor defendants, who had to remain in jail awaiting trial because they could not afford even minimal bail. "We undertook the project of attacking the oppressive nature of the money bail system then in place in Philly," Amsterdam recalled. "Our strategy was to prepare form habeas petitions, which we would file by the hundreds every Monday morning on behalf of all weekend arrestees represented by the association, in order to flood the courts with a tide of litigation that they could not ignore in the business-as-usual way in which they handled small handfuls of bail motions. The fellows and I drafted the petitions and the timetables for filing them."[21] David Kairys, who would later partner with Rudovsky in a distinguished constitutional practice, took the lead among the fellows.[22]

Magistrates were responsible for setting bail, but a defendant could petition a common pleas judge to review the magistrate's decision if the bail seemed too high. The purpose of filing the habeas corpus petitions was to create a system that would force a review of excessive bails. It was one of the first systemic challenges to the cash bail system, Rudovsky said.[23]

The Defender attack on cash bail did not short-circuit the practice, which continued to be a problem in Philadelphia and across the country well into the twenty-first century, contributing to the problem of prison overcrowding. It did, however, put a dent in cash bail, obtaining relief for hundreds, perhaps thousands of Defender clients over the years and, in the long run, providing other opponents of cash bail with a template for getting at least some defendants released.

Amsterdam left Penn for Stanford Law School in 1969, before the fellowship program ended. He would move to New York University in 1982. Another distinguished Penn Law professor, Howard Lesnick, took over supervision of the program "just for a year or two," Rudovsky said. "I think the program would have ended anyway. It was a five-year commitment by Ford."[24] But it lasted long enough to set the Defender's course for decades.

7

BIGGER, THEN BETTER

BENJAMIN LERNER needed to take stock. As the newly appointed chief defender early in 1975, he found himself confronting a law enforcement scene in Philadelphia that was challenging for criminal defense lawyers. The mayor was Frank L. Rizzo, who as police commissioner from 1967 to 1971 had established a national tough-on-crime reputation that played well in white communities and badly in black neighborhoods, from which the majority of the Defender's clients came. The war on crime, in Philadelphia and across the country, was driving the prison population upward, beginning an era of mass incarceration. To counter the lock-'em-up rhetoric, Lerner decided to make it his mission to become an advocate not only for the Defender Association but also for criminal defense in general. He would speak out forcefully on behalf of the constitutional rights of criminal defendants and let the public know that it was actually to their advantage that those rights be respected.

First, though, he needed to craft a plan of action for the organization he had been chosen to lead. The Defender was well regarded, as the NLADA report of 1971 made clear, calling it "one of the finest in the country."[1] Nevertheless, the Defender in early 1975 needed to improve its pay scale, supervision, recruiting, training, minority hiring, and juvenile representation. Lerner would have to confront all these issues while dealing with rapid expansion.

Growth had become inevitable in the wake of *Gideon*. In little more than a decade, the Defender had changed from a small operation of half a dozen lawyers, supported primarily by charitable donations, to a large, publicly funded law firm, with a staff of one hundred lawyers working in eleven units: Municipal Court, Federal Court, Motions, Major Trials, Felony Waiver (for nonjury trials), Probation and Parole, Juvenile, Appeals, Mental Health, Law Reform, and Child Advocacy.

The organization's caseload soared after *Gideon* and grew even more because of two subsequent U.S. Supreme Court decisions. *Argersinger v. Hamlin* (1972) extended the right of free counsel for indigents to every case, including misdemeanors, in which the defendant faced possible imprisonment.[2] The impact on the Defender was immediate. In the first twelve months after *Argesinger* was decided in June 1972, the Defender served a total of 82,125 people, an increase of 8 percent over the previous twelve months.[3] The other, *In re Gault* (1967), held that juveniles accused of crime have the same right to counsel as adult defendants.[4] The Defender had agreed to take over representation of indigent minors charged with crime as part of its contract with the city in 1969,[5] and consequently it handled more than six thousand juvenile cases in 1970.[6]

While the Defender had grown to the size of a major law firm, it was not acting like one. It was getting bigger, Lerner recalled, but not better. The Defender's lawyers varied widely in competence and enthusiasm. The overarching goal of the new regime would be to reorganize the Defender and have it operate in a more systematic way, as the big firms did. "Professionalization" would become the Defender's watchword in the 1970s.

As any new leader would, Lerner wanted to put his own team in place. That meant bringing his closest friend from the Amsterdam fellowship days, Louis M. Natali Jr., on board as first assistant defender, which he did in 1976. Gruff and colorful, Natali was a superb trial lawyer who, since his Amsterdam fellowship, had developed an intense interest—and expertise—in training lawyers for the courtroom. Many in the legal community thought that trial advocacy could not be taught; one either had the gift or did not. Natali thought otherwise. He believed that the right kind of training could help turn a bright young lawyer into an effective trial advocate. He taught an approach to practicing criminal law that was both tough and cerebral: "to fight every case, think about winning every case, think about the ways of winning every case."[7] Successful defense lawyering required meticulous preparation, a discipline that training through classroom work and mock trials could develop. Natali constructed a training program for the Defender grounded on those tenets, and it succeeded brilliantly. In 1987, after the program had been in place for more than a decade, NLADA recognized the association in 1987 as the best public defender office in the United States on the strength of its training program.

However, it was not just Natali's courtroom and training skills or his friendship with Lerner that made him the ideal first assistant. Just as important, Natali had leadership ability; he could "supervise the supervisors."[8] Previous Defender administrations—like other public defender offices across the country—simply assumed that the best trial lawyers should run the office, whether they had any management skills or not. Natali had both courtroom and management skills.

Lerner thought that supervision in the Defender had been too passive. Vincent Ziccardi, toward the end of his time as chief defender, had been a distant figure, often absent from the office. Lerner was determined to be an active, hands-on leader, which he hoped would help make the Defender more effective and boost morale. He made the rounds of the office every afternoon, talking to the lawyers about what had happened that day and letting them know they had his support. He wanted Defender supervisors to take the same approach, and he knew Natali would help set the tone for that. If a Defender lawyer ran afoul of a judge, Natali backed up the lawyer. On one occasion when a judge had a young attorney locked in a holding cell for arguing with him, Natali called the judge and in a profanity-laced diatribe demanded that the judge free the lawyer. The judge did.[9]

The new emphasis on professionalization also meant adopting a more organized approach to recruiting. It was not that the Defender had neglected recruiting under Ziccardi. After stepping down as chief defender in 1968, Herman Pollock continued as counsel to the Defender, and his activities included recruitment visits to about a dozen law schools, including elite institutions such as Harvard.[10] The Defender's recruiting program continued after Pollock died in September 1972, but Ziccardi's approach to hiring was notably casual, usually based on a quick interview, a snap judgment, and a command by Ziccardi to report for work the following week.

Ziccardi hired some lawyers that way who became good defenders (along with some who did not), but it was not Lerner's way. Lerner thought that the Defender was not casting its net wide enough. He wanted an aggressive, systematic recruiting effort that would scout the best talent nationwide. That effort would require sending Defender lawyers to law school recruitment days and conferences and contacting students recommended by law school professors in an effort to reach those who really wanted to be criminal lawyers.

The recruiters held preliminary interviews with potential applicants, but the path to a job with the Defender ran through Lerner's office. Lerner decided which law schools Defender recruiters would visit, with an eye to increasing racial and gender diversity. He reviewed all the applications and then selected a group he thought worth bringing in for an interview. Those who made the cut would meet with a panel of three lawyers who would give them a hypothetical case and ask them how they would handle the client interview, conduct the investigation, cross-examine witnesses, and argue the case. Then came an interview with Lerner, who made the decision to hire or not. The young lawyers were expected, although not required, to stay for three years, and most did. Some made a career at the Defender, while others went into private practice (usually partnering with other ex-defenders rather than joining a large law firm), and still others went onto the bench or took jobs in government or academia.[11]

The number of applicants for assistant defender positions was not overwhelming in the early years of Lerner's tenure, but by the 1980s, word was getting around among the law schools that the Defender Association of Philadelphia was a good place for young criminal attorneys to get courtroom experience. The Defender even began receiving applications from experienced lawyers, including some already working for other public defenders or government agencies. There were more than enough candidates to make the application process competitive.

One big draw was the Defender's reputation as an office that took more cases to trial than most public defenders did across the country. That was not entirely because the Defender wanted to try every case; Arlen Specter, Philadelphia's district attorney from 1966 to 1974, thought that plea bargains allowed criminals to get off easy (although a *Philadelphia Inquirer* investigation in 1973 found that defendants who pled guilty were likely to be sentenced to more time behind bars than those found guilty in a trial by jury or by judge alone, a bench trial). The *Inquirer* reporters found that the district attorney tried 12,456 cases in the Court of Common Pleas in 1971, about twice the number tried in Chicago and Brooklyn and well over twice the number in Manhattan.[12] That meant a lot of courtroom work for public defenders in Philadelphia, although very few trials—1 to 6 percent of all cases in most years and only 2 percent in 1971, the year examined by the *Inquirer* series—were jury trials; 50 to 60 percent were bench trials, before a judge alone, a unique feature of Philadelphia's court system.[13] The rest were guilty pleas, which increased after Specter left office.[14]

The lure of doing trials, whether before judge or jury, attracted lawyers such as Bradley S. Bridge, who joined the Defender in 1983. Bridge had wanted to be a criminal defense attorney ever since eighth grade, when an assistant principal at his middle school in Seattle lied to him to get him to confess that he had made an obscene gesture at a school bus driver. Bridge, who previously intended to be a physicist, determined then and there that he would become a lawyer "to protect people who needed to be protected."[15]

After graduating from Harvard Law School in 1979, Bridge went to work for the state appellate defender's office in Chicago, representing indigent defendants in appeals to the Illinois Appellate and Supreme Courts and to federal court. What he really wanted to do, however, was try cases as a public defender, so he looked around the country to find the offices that did the most trial work. His eye fell on Portland, Oregon, and on Philadelphia. Portland had the advantage of being closer to his hometown of Seattle, but Portland did not have any openings and Philadelphia did. After Bridge interviewed with a three-member committee of staff lawyers, Lerner offered him a job within hours. Bridge asked for time to think it over, hoping something might open up in Portland. It did not, and after some hesitation, resolved by consulting with his father, Bridge signed on with the Defender.[16] He would become one of the organization's most respected lawyers and a vigilant watchdog over police misconduct, and he would remain on the staff well into the twenty-first century.

Philadelphia's reputation for tough policing was a draw for some applicants. Abbe Smith, who applied to the Defender when she graduated from law school at New York University in 1982, was attracted by the prospect of practicing criminal law in a city that had twice elected Frank Rizzo as its mayor in the 1970s. She was convinced she was coming to a place where she could make a difference. Like Bridge, she admired the Defender's reputation for taking cases to trial. "There's no question I'd rather be in trial than negotiating with a prosecutor or urging a client to take a plea," Smith said (although, as Smith notes, she, "like most criminal lawyers," has spent much of her time "counseling clients about guilty pleas").[17]

Smith, who would later leave the Defender to teach in law school, also found herself drawn to the people she met in the Defender's office, striking a note that Defender alumni and alumnae frequently sound. She was impressed that Lerner, an avid baseball fan, knew she was a serious softball player. When she sent in her résumé and application letter, she got a form reply acknowledging receipt, but with a note from Lerner at the bottom: "Glad you applied. We could use a good infielder." As far as Smith was concerned, that sealed the deal: "It was really good chemistry."[18]

As the recruiting effort picked up steam, the number of new lawyers hired at one time began to grow, fueled by the Defender's success at getting funding from the city—even under the law-and-order Rizzo administration. In 1983, Defender recruiting reached a turning point when the association was able to hire a group of twenty-three new lawyers—a "class," in Defender parlance—much larger than the classes of six or seven that the Defender had been hiring through the 1970s.[19] Like other classes, it was rich in talent, a fact validated by the number of Defender recruits—not just from the class of 1983—who would go on to become state or federal judges, law school professors, and successful private practitioners. Larry Krasner, from the class of 1987, would even be elected district attorney of Philadelphia in 2017.

Training all that talent became a Defender hallmark in the 1970s and 1980s, setting the Defender Association apart from other public defender offices across the country, as the NLADA award of 1987 showed. It was not just a matter of making the Defender more efficient. It was a necessary response to *Gideon*. The Pennsylvania Supreme Court made clear in its 1973 decision affirming the Defender's funding deal with the city of Philadelphia that *Gideon* demanded that indigent defendants have access to capable lawyers. "There is no dispute that any plan to provide counsel to persons who need representation in criminal proceedings should be designed to provide counsel who is both competent and independent," Justice Thomas W. Pomeroy Jr. wrote for the court in a decision that struck down the legal challenge by Penn law professor and former Defender board member Louis Schwartz to the Defender's contract with the city.[20]

Commitment to providing competent, independent representation had been the Defender's lodestar since 1934. The organization's goal had always been to provide the poor a defense as good as—or better than—any they could get if they were paying for it, but it was grounded in the practical as well as the ideal; a high level of competence was necessary just to keep public defenders from being crushed by a caseload that was exploding not only because of *Gideon* but because of the tough-on-crime attitude that politicians were pushing nationally and locally. The pressure of providing competent and effective representation for all those new clients was too great to allow budding defenders time for educating themselves in the courtroom, as had been the practice under Ziccardi.

Even without all the pressures weighing on public defenders, Lerner already believed strongly, as an alumnus of the Amsterdam program, that neophyte criminal lawyers needed professional guidance and careful supervision. That is where Natali came in. Since leaving the Defender after two years as an Amsterdam fellow, Natali had been teaching at Rutgers–Camden Law School and had been running training programs in Boulder, Colorado, beginning in 1973, for the newly formed National Institute for Trial Advocacy (NITA). In 1975, Natali invited Lerner to Boulder to see NITA's program for himself. The course consisted of four weeks of simulated trials, and Lerner was impressed. He wanted Natali to organize and supervise a similar program for the Defender, making the Defender one of the first large public defender offices in the nation to create such a program and give it the resources it needed to succeed. Later in life, Natali would consider training his greatest contribution to the Defender.[21]

All new hires were required to take the training program, which ran for three weeks, usually in September. Trainees identified themselves by their Defender class year, just as they might for their law school or college. The training included two weeks of classroom work and one week of moot court, taught by Defender supervisors, who critiqued the performance of the trainees. The classroom sessions, buttressed by training manuals and booklets, covered all aspects of public defender practice: the Philadelphia judicial system, Pennsylvania criminal law and procedure, and advocacy techniques.[22]

The training was necessary because while law school graduates in the 1970s had learned the law, they had not necessarily learned how to practice it. Clinical training for law students and young lawyers, rare in the mid-1960s when the Amsterdam fellowship was started, was still a work in progress in the mid-1970s. The bulk of legal education still focused on casebooks and on studying appellate decisions. The Defender training program taught the rookies how to apply what they had learned in the classroom in a Philadelphia courtroom. It also introduced them to a new wrinkle in criminal law: sentencing advocacy, negotiating the best possible outcome for a defendant who had pleaded guilty or been convicted, another way the Defender was expanding the range of its concern for clients. Since most public defender clients across the country are found guilty—75 percent by one estimate[23]—good representation required preparation and presentation of evidence at the sentencing hearing intended to persuade the judge to impose a more lenient sentence, appropriate to the offense and the offender. This involved further investigation of the client's background. The Defender under Ziccardi had been an early advocate of the use of social work to track down evidence for sentencing advocacy, a practice that continued and deepened under his successors as chief defender.

Even when the newcomers had completed the three-week course and headed off for their first assignments, the training was not really over. It persisted in the form of their rotations—a closely supervised journey for each new lawyer through the Defender's various practice units. First, the young lawyers would do preliminary hearings, and then they would move on to juvenile court hearings, municipal court hearings and trials, felony nonjury trials, and, finally, jury trials in the Court of Common Pleas. The whole process could take anywhere from two to three years. Unlike in the Ziccardi years, supervision throughout the rotation was very tight, virtually one-on-one in the early years. Lawyers would discuss their cases with a supervisor before and after court appearances and then take care of the follow-up paperwork. Because of the Defender's system of horizontal representation, with a new lawyer at every step of the way except in the most serious cases, the lawyers had to be trained in how to write for the file so the next lawyer on the case would know what had been done and what still remained to be done. The new lawyers could expect to see their contributions to the client's file dissected by their supervisors.[24]

A further aim of the training program was to convey to the newcomers the culture and ideals of the Defender Association. This was accomplished by inviting respected senior attorneys to talk to the trainees. One of the most effective communicators of the Defender spirit was Stuart Schuman, a revered figure at the Defender who headed the Municipal Court Unit for years until his death in 2018. Schuman was known as a tireless reader of files, acutely aware that each one, no matter how routine, represented a flesh-and-blood Defender client to whom the association owed its best effort. Marc Bookman, a member of the class of 1983 who made a name at the Defender trying murder cases, found inspiration in Schuman, even though Schuman spent his career in the less exciting world of Municipal Court, where the Defender Association did the majority of its work. "Stu talked to our class about what it meant to be a public defender, case by case, list by list, day by day," Bookman recalled. "That's the kind of phrasing he would use. His dedication to what it meant to be a public defender was impactful. If there's one person that reflected the Defender Association to me, over my lifetime, it would be Stu Schuman."[25]

To achieve the level of supervision that the rotation needed, Lerner created in the mid-1980s a cadre of interim supervisors, experienced lawyers temporarily detached from their usual duties to assist the regular supervisors. The rotating supervisor positions, which Lerner also used to provide more advancement opportunities for minority defenders, created a set of mentors who were not part of the management structure. After training, young lawyers could still turn to them for advice or just to serve as a sounding board without worrying about whether they were making a bad impression on management.[26]

The rotation that the newcomers followed was more than simply a framework for turning neophytes into competent counselors; it was a cycle they would repeat throughout their Defender careers. While a few lawyers like Bookman might be assigned long term to one of the practice units, such as Major Trials, Juvenile, or Homicide (each of which required additional specialized training), once most defenders had gone through their initial training, culminating with a stint in Major Trials, they would rotate back to where they had started and go through it all over again. Since most lawyers stayed at the Defender for about five years, they would go through the rotation twice. The purpose was to give everyone a shot eventually at Major Trials while still covering the other, less dramatic but nevertheless important areas of the Defender's practice.

Although some lawyers groused about the rotation, others simply accepted it as a necessity.[27] Besides, there were some collateral advantages: The rotation offered the lawyers a respite from the stress inherent in trial work. The experience they had gained in Major Trials made them more confident and successful as they worked their way back through less serious cases in the lower courts, where they had an advantage over the inexperienced prosecutors they were facing. It also sent an important message to the Defender's newest lawyers: There will be a spot for you when you are ready to move up because someone will be rotating out.[28]

To buttress its basic training regimen, the Defender also established a continuing education program. Staff seminars focused on substantive and procedural issues, trial tactics, and advocacy techniques. "These programs, combined with an annual evaluation system for all staff members, have improved the quality of our representation," according to the Defender's fiftieth anniversary report in 1984.[29]

In 1983, Natali resigned as first assistant to become a professor at Loyola Law School in Los Angeles. (He was elected to the Defender's Board of Directors in 1992 and remained on the board well into the twenty-first century.) When Natali announced his decision to leave, Phyllis Subin, one of the Defender's top trial lawyers, approached Lerner and suggested that he create a director of training post and appoint her to fill it.[30] Subin, a graduate of Villanova University School of Law, was a senior trial lawyer at the Defender but had also been working as a trainer with Natali and seemed naturally suited for the task. New lawyers, especially women, had been turning to her for advice for several years. Natali nurtured Subin's training talent, and the Defender sent her off to a NITA teacher training program at Harvard Law School.[31] Up to that time, running the training program had been one of the first assistant's responsibilities. Lerner agreed to separate the two jobs: Subin would be director of training, and David Rudovsky, another alumnus of the Amsterdam program, would take a leave of absence from his civil rights law firm and become the first assistant.

The Defender's continuing programs, begun under Natali, occupied much of Subin's attention as training director. When the Pennsylvania Supreme Court made continuing legal education (CLE) mandatory for lawyers in 1993, the Defender, because of its long involvement in continuing education, became one of the first organizations in Pennsylvania, and probably the first nonprofit, to be accredited as a CLE provider, before the Philadelphia Bar Association or the Pennsylvania Bar Institute.[32]

A major challenge for continuing education was the rapid introduction of new technologies. When Subin took over as training director, DNA had not yet altered the practice of criminal law. Cell phones and social media had not yet appeared. "What do you do when your client has a cell phone and your client is tweeting and Facebooking and sending out things that are damaging?" Subin asked. "One of the roles of training is to stay up to date on all of the cases and all of the changes so that your staff is fully engaged and fully involved in terms of what they need to do."[33]

Subin left the Defender in 1995 to become the public defender for the state of New Mexico and was succeeded by her assistant, Mary DeFusco, but like any dedicated teacher, Subin took pride in the accomplishments of her students. "I track my classes," she said in 2018. And she was convinced that the Defender's emphasis on training was "an absolute essential element of the process of building a strong indigent defense program for Philadelphia and as a way of communicating the high cultural standards that this office wanted to set for its lawyers and the nature of our practice."[34]

8

RACIAL DIVERSITY AT THE DEFENDER

ONE OF THE PRINCIPAL GOALS of the Defender's ramped-up approach to recruiting under Benjamin Lerner was to diversify the Defender staff. The Defender's client base had been heavily minority since the association opened for business in 1934 (1,080 of the 2,064 clients the Defender represented in its first year were African American),[1] but the Defender legal staff remained white and male until the 1960s. By the time Lerner took over as chief defender in 1975, African Americans were moving into positions of leadership in city government, but not in the Defender. Of eighty-nine lawyers on staff, only six were members of a racial minority group.[2] There were no African Americans in supervisory positions on the legal staff, although there were African American supervisors on the investigative staff.

In Lerner's view, diversifying the Defender staff was important because it was simply the right thing to do. Beyond that, he recognized that it was important to the Defender's clients to have lawyers who looked like them and for the community that the Defender served to see lawyers who looked like them. And from a practical standpoint, it made getting funds for the Defender easier in a jurisdiction where African Americans were heavily involved in government.[3]

In the first half of the 1970s, minority lawyers were more likely to find the Defender than the other way around. In 1974, Reggie Walton, a native of Donora, Pennsylvania, who had been a star football player at West Virginia State University before graduating from the American University Washington College of Law in Washington, D.C., became one of Vincent Ziccardi's team of defenders.[4]

Walton would have rather been a prosecutor, although he was willing to be a public defender, but most district attorney offices wanted job applicants to have one or two years of experience. The only job opportunity Walton found that would allow him to try cases as soon as he passed the bar came at the Defender Association, so Walton accepted its offer. Ironically, he ended up not trying many cases because John Packel, head of the Defender's Appeals Unit, asked him if he would like to work in appeals. This was not the task Walton had in mind, but the pay was better. It turned out to be a good move, not just because of the money. "I learned tremendously from [Packel], and he was very influential in enhancing my writing skills and research skills, so it was the best thing for me to have done," Walton recalled years later. After working in appeals for a year, Walton went back to the courtroom but found the experience disappointing. Some of the judges in Municipal Court at that time still did not have legal training but were filling out terms to which they had been elected before the 1968 revision of the Pennsylvania Constitution required that judges be lawyers. Walton received what he described as "very negative treatment from some of them on several occasions." He applied for a job with the U.S. attorney in Washington, D.C., was hired, and left Philadelphia in February 1976.[5]

Before he left, Walton did the Defender a great favor. In 1975, he persuaded his best friend, C. Darnell Jones II, another African American graduate of American University's law school, to join the Defender. Jones, like Walton, was looking for work as a prosecutor, not as a public defender. A native of Oklahoma, Jones had come east to attend law school because he wanted work for the U.S. State Department, but his father, a *Perry Mason* fan, urged him to become a trial lawyer. Before he had finished law school, Jones decided his father was right. He would be a trial lawyer.[6]

During his third year at American University, Jones applied for a job with the Philadelphia district attorney's office and was hired. When he arrived in Philadelphia after graduation, he paid a call on his friend Walton at the Defender office. "A number of defenders heard us talking, and Reggie introduced me," Jones recalled. "The guys there were razzing me about being a D.A.: 'No, you don't want to go over there; we wear the white hats, blah, blah, blah.'" The razzing was quickly followed by an invitation to interview. Jones responded that he already had a job: "They said, 'Come anyway.' So I went the next morning for an interview. I think they probably hired me on the spot, but in any event, I jumped ship. I never went to work as an assistant district attorney."[7]

A year after Jones signed on, another talented young African American lawyer, Gregory Sleet, joined the Defender staff after graduating from Rutgers–Camden Law School. The son of a Pulitzer Prize–winning photojournalist for *Ebony* magazine, Sleet had decided he wanted to become a lawyer after reading a biography of the legendary defense attorney Clarence Darrow in high school. He interned for the Defender while he was in law school and, once he had become a staff attorney, quickly advanced to the Defender's Major Trials Unit and became known for his commitment to his clients as individuals, not just as cases to be won or lost.[8]

Walton, Jones, and Sleet would all go on to distinguished careers on the bench. President Ronald Reagan named Walton to the Superior Court of the District of Columbia, and President George W. Bush appointed him a U.S. District Court judge in 2001. He would later become head of the FISA (Foreign Intelligence Surveillance Act) Court, which rules on requests for surveillance of foreign agents by U.S. intelligence services and law enforcement agencies. Jones stayed with the Defender for ten years and became chief of the Juvenile Unit, the first African American supervisor on the Defender's legal staff. In 1987, Governor Robert Casey nominated him for a vacancy on the Philadelphia Court of Common Pleas, making him the first person ever to go directly from the Defender Association to the bench. In 2008, President Bush named Jones a U.S. district judge for the Eastern District of Pennsylvania. Sleet left the Defender in 1983, worn down by the stress of trial work, to start a private practice with another Defender alumnus. He would later serve as a deputy attorney general for the state of Delaware and as U.S. attorney for Delaware before President Bill Clinton named him a U.S. district judge in 1998, the first African American ever to be appointed a federal judge in Delaware.[9]

The small number of African Americans on the Defender's legal staff in the 1970s reflected the small number of African Americans in the legal profession generally. In 1970, there were 111 African Americans practicing law in Philadelphia—about 2 percent of the total number of lawyers in the city.[10] Nationwide, African American attorneys made up only 1.3 percent of the total number of lawyers.[11] African Americans also were underrepresented among prosecutors. In 1974, the

Philadelphia district attorney's office had only 6 African American attorneys on a staff of 125.[12]

Even if there had been more young African American lawyers in the early 1970s, the Defender might still have had trouble increasing the number on its staff. Several prominent African American lawyers in Philadelphia conceded that their young colleagues were not especially interested in working for public law agencies like the Defender for the simple reason that the pay was too low. Moreover, African American lawyers in the private bar saw public defenders as unwelcome competitors for their potential client base. In a commentary for the *Villanova Law Review* in 1970, Charles L. Mitchell, an African American attorney, spelled it out: "Whereas in the past, criminal defendants often obtained from their family and friends the funds to pay the fees necessary to retain a private attorney, the availability of public servants to indigent individuals makes this occurrence less likely."[13]

Yet the number of African American staff attorneys at the Defender rose slowly but steadily in the years after Jones signed on in 1975. In some years, the Defender would add as many as three new African American lawyers to the staff out of a class of about half a dozen, while in other years, there would be none; then the number would go back up. Jones attributed the increase to an uptick in the number of African Americans attending law school, which he characterized as "more, but not that many, in general."[14]

Over the course of Lerner's fifteen years as chief defender, the number of minority lawyers jumped from 6 among a staff of 89 (7 percent) in 1975 to 28 among a staff of 127 (22 percent) in 1989, a year before he stepped down.[15] The Defender did slightly better than the district attorney in maintaining racial diversity on staff. In 1997, the Defender had 186 lawyers: 20 percent were African American, 5 percent were Latino, and 2 percent were Asian American; thus, 27 percent of the legal staff was minority. The same year, 17 percent of the district attorney's 261 attorneys were African American, 2 percent were Latino, and 2 percent were Asian American. At that time, only 7 percent of the Philadelphia bar was African American.[16]

In the early 1980s, Darnell Jones became the first minority supervisor on the Defender's legal staff, serving as assistant chief and then chief of the Juvenile Unit. In 1987, Lerner created two full-time supervisory positions meant for minorities. He also intended to use the rotating supervisory positions created to help with training as slots for minority lawyers. However, some African American defenders thought the association was moving too slowly in promoting black lawyers to supervisory positions.[17] On May 24, 1989, a group of lawyers, social workers, and office staff, calling themselves the Concerned Minority Defenders, filed a complaint with the Equal Employment Opportunity Commission (EEOC) alleging racial discrimination at the Defender. Four African American assistant defenders also sent a letter to Lerner explaining their position: "Many minority employees feel that you are not truly interested in having a workplace that is free from discrimination. The sad truth is that despite numerous competent minority attorneys who have passed through the Defender over the years, you have never promoted a minority defender to the position of chief of any of the adult divisions, the heart of the organization." The letter pointed out that only 25 of the Defender's 125 lawyers at that time—20 percent—were African American and only one was Hispanic, while 80 percent of the Defender's clients were African American or Hispanic.[18]

Lerner's method of choosing people for promotion did little to soothe the ire of the Concerned Minority Defenders. Charles Cunningham, an African American assistant defender who was not a party to the EEOC complaint, said that Lerner's practice was to send out a memo announcing that a position was open, telling anyone who was interested in applying for the post to get in touch with him. When the applications were in, Lerner would make a choice. "No one got an interview," Cunningham recalled. "Ben just said, 'OK, I'm picking this person,' and that was the end of the story." Unsuccessful applicants believed that they never got a chance to state their case. It caused some hard feelings.[19]

The Concerned Minority Defenders considered as evidence of discrimination the 1989 selection of a white lawyer, Maureen Rowley, to be chief of the Defender's Federal Court Division. The group contended that Rowley got the job over more qualified applicants, including an African American, Thurgood Matthews, assistant chief of the Special Defense Unit. They also objected to the selection of two white lawyers over two African American lawyers for clinical teaching assignments.[20] Lerner responded that six of the twelve new supervisory positions he had created as chief defender went to minorities. He added that the Defender also was devoting more resources to hiring minorities and had named an African American lawyer to coordinate minority recruiting. Concerning Rowley's appointment to the federal defender post, Lerner's position was that Rowley had more extensive federal court trial experience than Matthews and the other candidates. He added that the two

African American lawyers whom the Concerned Minority Defenders noted had not been named to the clinical teaching assignments had since been assigned to supervisory positions.[21]

The issues raised by the nonlawyer staffers included charges that "decisions of hiring and promotions are made on the basis of personal friendship, affinity." Lerner said he had been unaware of the problem but conceded that the complaints were legitimate. "As soon as I became aware of the nonlegal staff's concerns in this area, we started a process to address those concerns and they were resolved," Lerner said.[22] The issues with the lawyers were not so easily resolved. Finally, Matthews sued the Defender Association in U.S. District Court in 1994, alleging discrimination. Matthews had joined the Defender in 1981 after graduating from Howard University School of Law and rotated, like other Defender lawyers, through different units until he was assigned in 1985 to Special Defense, which handled the Defender's most complex, high-profile cases in state court. He then spent a year with the Federal Unit, where he received positive performance evaluations. His first supervisory position was as assistant chief of Special Defense, one of the posts that Lerner had created to provide supervisory opportunities for minorities.[23]

Matthews's lawsuit went to a nonjury trial in 1997 before U.S. District Court judge Lowell A. Reed Jr. According to testimony at the trial, all the applicants for the federal Defender job received interviews, conducted by a four-member panel that included Lerner and Ellen Greenlee, who was then the first assistant. The panel was to make recommendations, but the decision was to be Lerner's. In testimony during the trial, Lerner and Greenlee described Matthews as "a well-experienced, excellent trial lawyer and trial strategist." Two of the panel members, Lerner and Greenlee, rated Rowley the best of the applicants. The other two panelists recommended Assistant Defender Jeffrey Staniels, who was white, and ranked Rowley second. Only Lerner had Matthews ranked as high as the third choice among the four applicants. The other three panelists ranked him fourth. Lerner chose Rowley for the job.[24]

Reed ruled in favor of the Defender Association, finding that Lerner made his decision based on "legitimate factors and without regard to the minority race of plaintiff." When he was interviewed for the position, Matthews "showed no real interest in the integral administrative issues confronted by the chief of the federal division." He also favored a "more adversarial and confrontational position within the federal criminal justice system" that Lerner and Greenlee, cognizant of the style of litigation rewarded in that court, thought would be "antithetical to the best interest of the federal division."[25] Despite losing the lawsuit, Matthews remained with the Defender Association. He would later be named assistant chief of the Homicide Unit, supervising some of the Defender's best trial lawyers and trying several of the unit's highest-profile cases himself.

By the time Matthews's suit made it to court, Lerner had retired to private practice in 1990 and would later become a common pleas judge. However, the ruckus raised by the federal Defender appointment convinced some that it was time to have an African American in the top echelon of Defender leadership. Jules Epstein, then a highly respected senior trial and appellate attorney for the Defender and later a professor at Temple University Law School, told the *Legal Intelligencer* that it was "extremely important . . . that the Defender Association have a black person in a top administrative position."[26]

That vision would be realized after the Defender board, at Lerner's suggestion, named Ellen Greenlee to succeed Lerner as chief defender and the popular Charles Cunningham, a superb trial lawyer, to succeed her as first assistant. "There is no one—black or white—more qualified than Charles Cunningham," Epstein told the *Legal Intelligencer*.[27] Cunningham and Greenlee would lead the Defender for a quarter of a century.

9

PIONEER WOMEN

THE *GIDEON* DECISION, which changed the American criminal justice system in so many ways, indirectly brought the Defender its first full-time female attorney, Carolyn Engel Temin. Temin graduated from the University of Pennsylvania Law School in 1958 but did not go directly into legal practice, opting to concentrate on raising a family. She did not sit for the bar exam until the early 1960s. Instead, she volunteered with the Defender at the suggestion of her father-in-law, who was also an attorney. She had not yet been admitted to the bar when she began her volunteer work at the Defender in the mid-1960s, so all she could do was interview prisoners. At first, her clients comprised only female prisoners who arrived at City Hall from the House of Corrections to appear in court. The interviews took place three Fridays a month in a holding cell at the sheriff's office. Men and women were held together in the cell, but Temin was allowed to interview only the women—until the day when there was nobody else around to interview a male prisoner. "They let me do it, and I didn't disappear or dissolve; nothing bad happened," she recalled later. "I was hoping maybe that would prove to them that women could do the same job as men, but it didn't."[1]

When *Gideon* made it necessary for the Defender to hire more lawyers, an acquaintance from law school who was connected to the association encountered Temin on the street in 1964 and recommended that she apply. He told her that the Defender was planning to hire one female attorney. "This was the token woman thing," she remembered. "It was quite acceptable to say, 'We're going to hire one woman.' So I went down and I got interviewed, and I got the job, and they let me do everything. That's how I became the first actual woman to appear in criminal court on a regular basis in Philadelphia."[2]

It did not take long for Temin to prove herself an impressive legal force. "My proudest accomplishment came very early in my career," she recalled years later. "When I became a criminal lawyer, I noticed that there had been a law on the books since 1913 that was called the Muncy Act," after the women's prison in Lycoming County, Pennsylvania.[3] Because of the Muncy Act, women often ended up serving longer terms than men for the same type of crime. Temin convinced the Pennsylvania Supreme Court in 1968 to declare the law unconstitutional. (This story and many other appeals before the state Supreme Court appear in Chapter 10.)

Despite her success in the Muncy Act appeal, Temin still found herself confronting discrimination. "People could say things then that you could be indicted for saying now." She faced the challenge of being not only a female lawyer but also a female public defender. Although the Defender had been around for more than thirty years, prejudice against public defenders persisted in the court system. A lot of people around City Hall did not think of defenders as real lawyers, according to Temin.[4]

Temin had to deal with attitudes, even within the Defender, that would evoke eye rolls in the twenty-first century. "It was quite a different era and quite a different time," she recalled. "Someone told me a few months after I was on the staff of the Defender, the person who was responsible for hiring me said, 'We knew you would be a good choice because you have a happy marriage, so we knew you'd get along well with men.'" But that was not all. It was considered a plus that she already had two children and presumably would not have more.[5]

When the chance came to practice as a defender exclusively in U.S. district court rather than the state courts, Temin jumped at it as an opportunity to practice in a more congenial environment. She promised herself that she would never set foot in City Hall again, and she kept that personal vow until she took a job with the district attorney's office in 1971.[6] She would later be elected a judge on the Court of Common

Pleas, where she served for twenty years, and in 2018 returned to the district attorney's office when District Attorney Larry Krasner, a former defender himself, named her his first assistant.

Temin was followed into the Defender by a wave of female lawyers, a group that one of them, Phyllis Subin, described as "pioneers."[7] Subin arrived at the Defender nearly a decade after Temin, in the early 1970s, but her recollections of those days are similar. "There was a time when none of the women had any children, and I think there really was a sense that women had to prove themselves, as to whether or not they could do it," Subin recalled. "I remember going into court; there were no women judges, no women D.A.s. All the cops were men, and primarily the court officers were male, so we were really trying to prove that we could be very, very good advocates and lawyers and understand how the system worked, and it wasn't always easy."[8]

After joining the Defender in the mid-1970s, Subin, like Temin, made a mark in the courtroom "at a time when many doubted that women could do criminal defense work," as Subin described the era. She became the first woman appointed to the Special Defense Unit, which tries the Defender's highest-profile cases, and later director of training.[9]

Another pioneer was Rita Levine, who concentrated on juvenile cases and later on the rights of persons who were the subject of involuntary commitment proceedings. She began working on the legal aspects of mental health issues when Pennsylvania's Mental Health Procedures Act of 1976 "was in its infancy," Benjamin Lerner said.[10] The law provided for the court appointment of counsel in involuntary commitment cases (which were civil, not criminal, proceedings), turning a process that had once been governed by the recommendation of psychiatrists into an adversarial contest in which the person being committed saw his or her rights and perspective represented.[11]

Differences over involuntary commitment led to sharp disagreements between doctors and lawyers. Psychiatrists wondered why lawyers were opposing treatment that mentally ill people needed. Lawyers believed that deferring to the judgment of mental health professionals had led to the warehousing of patients. Levine, who became known for fierce advocacy on her clients' behalf, was often sharply critical of mental health professionals, claiming that the doctors should treat mentally ill patients "with a little more dignity and respect and more professionalism than I see."[12]

"Rita really pioneered the procedural rights of mentally ill people to have a say in whether they would be committed against their will," Lerner explained. "She had a very difficult time in doing so." Her advocacy for her clients rubbed some in the mental health community the wrong way "because she dared to question, to cross-examine doctors, and to do so in an effective way," Lerner told the *Philadelphia Inquirer* at the time of Levine's death in 1989 from injuries sustained in a terrorist attack in Israel.[13]

Also part of the pioneer wave was Ellen Greenlee. Like Temin, Greenlee first worked for the Defender as a volunteer before she was hired full-time in April 1974. She worked quickly up through the ranks, trying twelve jury cases and winning six of them, representing clients accused of a variety of offenses, including rape, robbery, and aggravated assault.[14] (A juror once remarked that he had voted to acquit a Greenlee client because he didn't believe "such a classy lady" would represent a guilty person.)[15] Like other Defender lawyers, Greenlee also tried numerous bench cases, heard by a judge without a jury, in the Court of Common Pleas and Municipal Court, and she argued one appeal before the Pennsylvania Superior Court.

The appeal case in which Greenlee's client was fighting his conviction and a hundred-dollar fine for sexually harassing a female University of Pennsylvania student was notable mostly because Greenlee had to quote the explicit language her client used in an indecent proposition to the young woman. The issue was not whether he used the language; it was whether the language itself constituted harassment, since the defendant did not follow it up with any action. The appeal failed on a four-to-three vote.[16]

Like other Defender lawyers, Greenlee found defending clients exhilarating: "It's exciting, actually, to be on trial," she said. "I think primarily it was being able to represent a client and make a difference for that client, for the client to see that you were prepared and interested in their welfare, especially that you were prepared."[17] In 1980, Greenlee was named assistant head of the Defender unit that handled preliminary hearings and felony waivers, bench trials in which the defendant agreed to be tried by a judge alone rather a judge and jury. Four years later, she became supervisor of the unit and in 1986 was appointed first assistant defender, the second in command of the Defender Association. In 1990, the Defender Association named her the chief defender, replacing Lerner in the top spot.[18] Unlike Temin, Greenlee did not feel that she faced any real gender discrimination, maybe because she was thirty-six when she joined the Defender. "I already had the maturity and the respect of people. I didn't have to earn it," she told the *Inquirer* in 1986. "I came in with a distinct advantage over younger women directly out of law school." Judges who addressed female lawyers as "honey" seemed to do it more with young female lawyers, she observed.[19]

When Greenlee joined the staff, there were about a dozen female attorneys at the Defender. With each new class of hires, there were slightly more women. The lawyers that the Defender hired in the Lerner years were split about fifty-fifty between male and female.[20] In 1984, as the Defender marked its fiftieth anniversary, twenty-five of the ninety-nine assistant defenders were female. Four of the women, including Greenlee, were supervisors. By the time she became first assistant, just two years later, the number of female staff attorneys had climbed to forty. When Greenlee stepped down as chief defender in 2015, women made up more than 60 percent of the staff.[21]

The increase in the number of female attorneys at the Defender reflected a national trend. The number of women in public defender offices was rising across the country as more and more women went to law school. In 1970, there were thirteen thousand female lawyers in the United States, making up 4 percent of the total number of attorneys; by 1980, the number was up to sixty-two thousand, or 12.4 percent of the total.[22] In 2014, the ABA reported that 34 percent of its members were female, a percentage far lower than the 60-plus percent at the Defender.[23]

By the late 1980s, with Greenlee as first assistant and Subin the director of training, many women joining the Defender found the female presence near the top of the association's leadership reassuring. Claire Rauscher, who joined the Defender at that time and would later go on to practice white-collar criminal defense in North Carolina, considered Greenlee and Subin "cheerleaders" for the female attorneys. "Their confidence in my abilities empowered me to push through the large dockets and difficult moments," she recalled. "I recognized if they were able to be successful in a system almost exclusively dominated by men (at the time), I could certainly plow through a system weighted against the indigent clients and fight for just results."[24]

Rauscher recalled that Greenlee had backed her up after a judge had told the mother of a client not to listen to Rauscher because she did not know what was in the son's best interest. This came after the judge had spent an entire week belittling her. When she got back to the office, she told Greenlee what had happened. "[Greenlee] immediately picked up the phone and called the judge," Rauscher recalled. "She demanded that he apologize and fully defended me. It was a day I won't forget (the judge did make a half-ass apology the next day). She took on a powerful judge that could have taken some action against me and/or the office but she fought for me and what was right."[25]

Women bring something unique to criminal defense work, according to Abbe Smith, the New York University law grad who joined the Defender because she wanted to represent poor defendants in Frank Rizzo's Philadelphia. Smith, who later became a professor and head of a criminal law clinical program at Georgetown, observed that female lawyers seemed to be "gravitating to criminal trial work—especially on behalf of the poor."[26] Female attorneys, in Smith's view, were more open to "holistic" defense, which delves into every aspect of a defendant's life—childhood, intelligence, education, family, income, neighborhood, immigration status—to find the sort of information necessary for negotiating a plea, preparing for trial, or suggesting alternatives to incarceration, whichever may be necessary. "Women might be particularly drawn to holistic work—to representing the whole person and not just their particular legal case," Smith said. "But that doesn't mean women can't be 'trial jocks'—as much into trying cases as guys."[27]

Being a trial jock while raising a family can be daunting. Women in the major trial units of public defender offices often have been single or childless. Because the tasks involved in raising children still fall mostly to women, Smith believes that some female defenders who have children tend to move into units with more regular schedules, such as appeals or juvenile, although others said they have not noticed such clustering. Smith, who raised a son while trying cases, thinks that women seek out more stable schedules because of "the persistence of traditional gender roles in domestic life—women keep the home fires burning once there are children." Being in court, Smith recalled, forced her to miss many a parent-teacher conference "because judges wouldn't release me."[28]

Another reason that few women work on jury trials may be the strain that being constantly in court can put on a relationship when the attorney's partner is not prepared for the required commitment to the office. "Trial work is very intense, very demanding, very immersive; I love being in a trial," Smith said. But it can be very hard on a relationship unless the spouse or partner either is a criminal lawyer or really understands how demanding trial work can be—and how self-absorbed those who do the work can be.[29]

One lawyer who did manage to balance trial work and family life despite the social expectations around motherhood was Mary DeFusco, who like Smith was a member of the class of 1982 and went on to become director of training and recruitment. She was the first among the lawyers who joined the Defender in 1982 to make it to the Major Trials Unit, but she became pregnant before she could get a jury trial and had to skip her turn. However, she made it back into Major Trials despite having five children. When one court session ran into the evening, her husband brought their latest baby to the courtroom to nurse. The judge told DeFusco that she could use the robing room. DeFusco felt the allure of more stable hours. "Looking at it in hindsight now, I would have stayed with my kids [instead of staying in the Major Trials Unit]," she said. "I would have changed my schedule, gone to Appeals or Juvenile, or whatever."[30]

As the number of women in the Defender ranks grew, so did their impatience with the small number of female supervisors. When Lerner promoted Darnell Jones to be head of the Juvenile Unit, some women felt that Lerner was leapfrogging Jones, who had been doing Major Trials, over women who had made a decision to stay in Juvenile and knew the juvenile justice system well. It looked to the women like a catch-22: they were being passed over because they did not have jury trial experience, but they did not have jury trial experience because they had spent their time becoming experts in the juvenile system.[31]

Shortly after Jones was promoted, Governor Robert Casey appointed him to be a common pleas judge, opening the top spot in Juvenile again. DeFusco thought that Mingo Stroeber, who had been in Juvenile for several years and become an expert on juvenile law, should apply to replace Jones. Abbe Smith called a women's meeting and told the participants they needed to stick together. DeFusco told Stroeber she should sue if she was passed over for one of the two top jobs in Juvenile, but that turned out to be unnecessary. Stroeber was promoted to assistant chief and then got the top job four years later, which she held for several years before going into private practice.[32]

When Lerner resigned as chief defender in 1990, the Board of Directors named Greenlee to succeed him. Lerner had asked the board to make Greenlee his first assistant in 1986 because he wanted to give her the best possible chance of succeeding him. "I lobbied hard for her to be selected," he recalled. "I was very conscious of the importance of having a woman as qualified as Ellen as the first assistant in the office."[33] The Defender had come a long way since the day Carolyn Temin heard there would be an opening for one woman.

10

APPEALS

J OHN PACKEL BROUGHT A TOUCH of whimsy to the Defender, whether composing an anthem for a Defender anniversary party, illustrating legal briefs with cartoons, or riding his bike to work, decked out in psychedelic T-shirt and red socks. The whimsy, however, went with a very sharp legal mind that Packel used to distinguish himself as the chief of the Defender's Appeals Unit for many years. Packel did not take himself seriously, but he took his work very seriously. In a 2004 article for the *UC Davis Law Review*, former assistant defender Abbe Smith described the "typecast public defender" as "anti-authoritarian, feisty, non-conformist, irreverent, skeptical, slightly voyeuristic, slightly exhibitionist, and resilient."[1] She could easily have been describing John Packel.

Packel drifted into the Defender. He graduated from the University of Pennsylvania Law School in 1963 near the bottom of his class. "I was a terrible student," he recalled. He briefly worked for the law firm where his father, Israel Packel, one of Pennsylvania's most distinguished lawyers and later a justice of the state Supreme Court, was a partner, but that did not go well. "I did not fit into the place," he said. "I don't wear ties; I don't wear suits. They gently told me I should leave."[2]

Searching for something to do, Packel turned to the Defender, where he had worked one summer while he was in law school. The office was still very small, and Herman Pollock, the chief defender, did not have enough money to hire him, so Packel began working as a volunteer early in 1966. By May, grants were coming in to help the Defender cope with a caseload that was expanding rapidly because of *Gideon*, enabling Pollock to hire Packel.[3] In June 1966, in an incident that gave a hint of what his Defender career would be like, Packel clashed with an imperious magistrate named M. Philip "Doc" Freed, a ward leader perhaps best known for his battles with other city officials, including the police.[4] (The office of magistrate was abolished by the Pennsylvania Constitution in 1968.) Packel happened to be in court on another case when two defendants charged with sodomy appeared without counsel. Packel offered to represent them, but Freed thought that the two could afford a lawyer and told Packel to stay out of it. Packel persisted, and the magistrate threatened him with contempt.[5]

Matters began to heat up. Freed told Packel to go sit down, but not at the desk designated for the public defender. When Packel would not move, Freed tried to have him arrested, but the police refused. The magistrate then came down from the bench and moved the public defender's desk to the spectators' section; Packel moved it back to its original position next to the bar of the court. Freed came down and moved the desk again, while Packel laughed. Freed, perhaps worn out by the exercise and wanting to get Packel out of his hair, turned to the two defendants and told them that he was continuing their case for two weeks and that they should hire a lawyer. The story became a Defender legend. "That was an early kind of claim to fame," Packel said.[6]

Despite the thrill of jousting with magistrates, Packel found that he was drawn to appeals: "I got real interested in doing legal research. Herman [Pollock] assigned me to the Motions Division, and I quickly became the chief of the Motions Division. We did pretrial motions and postconviction stuff, and I shared an office with Mel Dildine. He was chief of appeals, a very talented guy." When Dildine left the Defender in 1970, Vincent Ziccardi wanted to name David Rudovsky to succeed him, but Rudovsky declined and suggested that Ziccardi give the job to Packel. "That's how I became chief of appeals," Packel said. "By default."[7]

Packel quickly put his stamp on the Appeals Unit. In its 1971 evaluation of the Defender, NLADA described the unit as "not only competent, but excellent." However, the evaluators did have a few reservations. They saw oral argument as a weak spot in the Defender's appeals efforts, and the evaluators criticized the appeals lawyers for appearing in "extremely casual and inappropriate dress" and adopting an "abrasive and sometimes disrespectful attitude" during oral argument. They mentioned no names, but the description fit Packel perfectly. The report conceded that it could be difficult arguing cases before a court that would "most likely" render an "adverse" decision; despite NLADA's sympathetic advice, Packel did not change and the Defender continued to win its share of appeals.[8]

The Defender's appeals work grew along with its overall caseload in the years after *Gideon*. Until *Gideon* was decided in 1963, the Defender filed just one or two appeals a year.[9] In fiscal year 1963–1964, Defender lawyers filed five appeals.[10] In part, the Defender was simply reflecting the practice common among Philadelphia lawyers at the time of not filing appeals in criminal cases other than murder. In 1958, five years before *Gideon*, attorneys practicing in Philadelphia courts filed appeals in fewer than 1 percent of all cases that ended in a conviction.[11] At least one of the Defender's directors believed that the organization should file more appeals because he thought it had a responsibility not just to individual clients but also to indigent defendants as a class.[12] However, appeals were a drain on an organization supported by charity. Pollock estimated the cost of an appeal at $200–$300 in 1958 ($1,750–$2,625 in 2018 dollars).[13] The pro-appeal sentiment got no traction until *Gideon* and similar cases required that indigents be provided free counsel for both trials and appeals. Then the number of appeals grew dramatically.

In fiscal year 1964–1965, the number of appeals the Defender handled rose to 25.[14] Then the figure shot up, reaching 230 in fiscal year 1967–1968 and 590 in fiscal year 1970–1971.[15] It became Defender practice to at least consider an appeal in every case that might present a legal issue. Trial attorneys who lost a case were encouraged to visit the Appeals Unit if the client either requested an appeal or the lawyer wanted to talk about issues that might provide grounds for appeal. In 1967, the Defender filed its first certiorari petition with the U.S. Supreme Court, *Fairhurst v. United States*, challenging a conviction for interstate transport of a stolen vehicle, but the court denied it in 1968.[16] That disappointment, however, was followed just a few weeks later by a stunning success, engineered not by Packel but by Carolyn Temin, the Defender's first female attorney.

Temin had been looking for a case that would allow her to attack the constitutionality of the Muncy Act, the 1913 law governing the sentencing of women found guilty of a crime that carried a sentence of at least one year in prison.[17] The theory behind the Muncy Act was that women needed a different form of rehabilitation than men and should serve only as much time as it took to accomplish that rehabilitation. The fact was that under the terms of the Muncy Act, women often ended up serving longer terms than men for the same type of crime. Sentences for men carried a minimum and a maximum, but sentences for women were indefinite, although they could not exceed the maximum set by law for the offense. A woman convicted of a crime punishable by more than three years in prison was required to serve the maximum for the offense. She also had to serve the time at Muncy State Correctional Institution rather than in a county lockup.[18]

The Muncy Act did have a provision that might have seemed, at cursory glance, an advantage for female prisoners: They could be paroled at any time, beginning on the first day of their sentence. However, that did not happen. "As a practical matter, they had a laundry list of minimum sentences that they would make people serve," Temin said years later, even though the Muncy Act prohibited setting a minimum sentence for women. Female prisoners were also subjected to more rigorous treatment than male prisoners. They could get in trouble for such things as "sassing a guard," Temin said. "If you go to a men's prison, sassing a guard is generally the way guards are addressed—this is just what's done—but the women were put in solitary confinement and were denied water. They didn't have water to flush the toilet or wash."[19]

After searching diligently, Temin came across the case of a woman, Jane Daniels, who was appealing a conviction for robbing a tavern. She had been found guilty by a judge in a nonjury trial in 1966, and he had sentenced her originally to one to four years. A month later, however, prison authorities advised the judge that the Muncy Act required him to resentence her to an indeterminate term not to exceed the maximum of ten years prescribed by law for robbery. The judge reluctantly complied, and Daniels, who had been looking at a maximum of four years, was now facing a maximum of ten, so she appealed. "[The Defender] gave me her case and said I should do the appeal because I was a woman; I think that's why they gave it to me," Temin recalled. "I asked Herman Pollock, who was then the chief defender, if it would be okay if I raised the issue of the unconstitutionality of the Muncy Act, and he gave me permission to do that."[20]

Temin argued on Daniels's behalf that the Muncy Act violated the equal protection clause of the Fourteenth Amendment to the U.S. Constitution because it treated men and women differently. Her first stop in the appeals process was at Pennsylvania Superior Court, where she lost in 1967. The court declared, by a six-to-one margin, that while Pennsylvania's sentencing laws did discriminate against women, the discrimination was not unconstitutional because it was meant to meet the peculiar needs of female offenders, "allowing the time of incarceration to be matched to the necessary treatment in order to provide more effective rehabilitation."[21]

So Temin took the case up to the state Supreme Court, and while it was pending there, she found another woman doing time at Muncy to add to the appeal. Her new client, a prostitute named Daisy Douglas, had been convicted with a male codefendant of robbing her customers. When they were arrested, he got three to ten years and Douglas got the required indeterminate sentence, with a maximum of twenty years. "At the time that I came in contact with her, she had already served seven years because of 'disciplinary problems,'" Temin said. "[Her male accomplice] had already been out after three years and had violated parole and was back in again."[22]

The Supreme Court ruled unanimously in favor of Temin's clients on July 1, 1968. The court found that "an arbitrary and invidious discrimination exists in the sentencing of men to prison and women to Muncy, with resultant injury to women."[23] In the wake of the court's ruling, the state legislature quickly passed a bill, which Governor Raymond Shafer signed into law, allowing judges to impose a specific sentence on female offenders, but maintaining the prohibition on minimum sentences. This meant that the parole board would still have the power to release a female prisoner at any time, so a difference remained between the sentencing of women and men.[24]

The discrepancy lasted until a Monroe County man, Ronald Butler, appealed his 1971 second-degree murder conviction on grounds that his sentence of ten to twenty years violated his right to equal protection under law because women could be paroled at any time while he, as a man, could not. Butler wanted the appeals court to strike down the 1911 Pennsylvania sentencing law that authorized a minimum and a maximum on sentences for men. Instead, the state Supreme Court ruled that the part of the revised Muncy Act prohibiting minimum sentences for women was unconstitutional, thus denying Butler's appeal while benefiting Pennsylvania's female inmates.[25] "When you look at cases involving women's rights, it's always a man that gets women their full rights," Temin observed wryly. "The court finally said, 'Enough of this. Everybody will be sentenced the same way.' So it took a man to vindicate women's rights, and if you look at other cases in other women's rights, it very often takes a man."[26]

The Defender won another major appeals victory in 1973, this time with Packel as the lead attorney. In November 1972, Packel argued before the Pennsylvania Supreme Court in *Commonwealth v. Hall* that evidence used in the conviction on drug charges of his client, William Hall, should have been suppressed.[27] Packel challenged the validity of the search warrant that the police used to gather the evidence. The application for the warrant relied on information from an anonymous informant. The police told the court that tips the informant provided them had previously resulted in convictions in three of five cases, with the other two pending. At trial, the Defender sought the names of those who were convicted to test the reliability of the police claim for the informant's effectiveness but not to unmask the informant.[28]

Packel was convinced the police were lying. He went through two-years'-worth of search warrants, did a statistical analysis, and submitted the warrants to the court as evidence. The police had been claiming that 80 percent of the information that tipsters provided led to conviction. Packel's analysis of the data found the conviction rate to be around 14 percent. In his brief to the court, Packel wrote that the Defender's numbers led to "the inescapable conclusion that police are committing perjury in the preparation of search warrants with alarming regularity."[29] The justices found Packel's data convincing and in March 1973 remanded the case for a new suppression hearing, although they were not ready to attribute the discrepancies to police perjury. Justice Robert N. C. Nix Jr. pointed out in a concurring opinion that "every misstatement need not be a result of perjury and could just as likely result from inadvertence or negligence."[30]

Commonwealth v. Hall expanded the right of the defense to challenge the validity of search warrants and have "meaningful cross-examination" in preliminary hearings to test the reliability of police information. Defense attorneys would now have to be given the names of defendants fingered by police informants so they could check the informants' reliability.[31] Packel was proud of the accomplishment. The court's decision "probably changed the practice of the police" and made them "a little less unforthright, double negative, in obtaining search warrants," he said.[32]

Wins like *Daniels* and *Hall* helped cement the Defender's reputation for top-notch appeals work. Packel and his team scored another major victory in 1996 when the Pennsylvania Supreme Court ruled that twelve vials of cocaine discarded by someone the police were chasing could not be admitted into evidence because the police had no probable cause to chase him. The decision in the case, *Commonwealth v. Matos*,[33] extended the right of freedom from unreasonable search in Pennsylvania beyond that required by the Fourth Amendment to the U.S Constitution. The case, argued by Assistant Defender Helen Marino, arose out of an incident in April 1991 when two police officers approached three men on a playground. The men ran away, so the police ran after them. An officer said he saw one of the men, Danny Matos, discard a plastic bag that was found to contain the vials of cocaine. Matos still had five vials of cocaine in his possession when the police caught him.[34]

At Matos's trial, the judge ruled that the drugs were inadmissible. The district attorney appealed to Superior Court, which reversed the trial judge's ruling, so the Defender took the case to the state Supreme Court, arguing that the vials of cocaine were obtained as the result of an illegal seizure because the police had no probable cause to stop Matos. If there had been no seizure, the vials he discarded would have been admissible. The Defender conceded that stopping Matos was not seizure under the Fourth Amendment but was a seizure under the Pennsylvania Constitution. Therefore, the state Supreme Court ruled, the evidence was inadmissible.[35]

District Attorney Lynne Abraham called the decision a gift to criminals, but the Defender called it a victory for the rule of law.[36] The issue was an emotional one. A federal judge in New York, Harold Baer Jr., who made a similar decision suppressing evidence in a 1996 drug trial, found himself the object of a withering attack that included two hundred members of Congress writing to President Bill Clinton, calling on him to seek the judge's resignation. Baer survived the criticism but later reversed his decision.[37]

Assistant Defender Bradley S. Bridge, acknowledged as the association's expert on police misconduct, said *Matos* required police to respect the law. "Matos says that police officers need a lawful basis to seize a citizen," Bridge told the *Philadelphia Inquirer*. "When they don't have a lawful basis, then any evidence found should not be admitted."[38]

Packel deflected praise for the Appeals Unit's accomplishments to the other lawyers in the unit, which numbered ten by the early 1990s and about fifteen when he retired in 2003. He counted himself lucky to lead them. "I was a lousy administrator, but I was a good leader," he said. "I just loved the people I worked with. In the beginning especially,

I had this group of just really terrific lawyers, and we were like best friends. Then, they started leaving. . . . It just tore me up, losing these friends."[39]

Despite his love for appeals work, Packel knew the Defender could not appeal every case it lost. Even after *Gideon*, the number of cases the Defender appealed was still only a very small percentage of its total caseload—"almost minuscule," according to Packel. "There were a lot of totally slam-dunk cases that there were obviously no-appeal issues."[40] If he saw no appealable issue, Packel wrote the defendant a letter explaining why. He cautioned clients who had received relatively short sentences—eleven and a half to twenty-three months, for example—that if they filed an appeal without any good appellate issues, they risked having a vindictive judge deny them parole.

Nevertheless, Packel also sent convicted clients a set of appeals papers, with instructions to fill them in and send them back if they wanted to file an appeal. "All you have to do is sign these and send them to court, and they'll appoint us to represent you," Packel informed the clients.[41] The problem was that a lot of defendants wanted to file appeals even when their case fell into the category of "slam-dunk, no issue to appeal." The decision on whether to appeal was up to the defendant. "If he mentions the word 'appeal,' we have to file it," Packel said.[42] And as a result of a 1987 U.S. Supreme Court decision in a Pennsylvania case, *Pennsylvania v. Finley*, appellate lawyers who concluded that a client's proposed appeal had no merit and was unlikely to succeed were obliged to prepare a brief for the court explaining their conclusion.[43] Rather than do that, essentially torpedoing the client, the Defender filed the appeals.

By 2003, what Packel had once described as "a great job" was becoming burdensome. "I was getting real frustrated by having to file a lot of totally wasteful appeals, and at the same time, the court was getting more demanding and ridiculous in creating hoops to jump through," he said. "The notion of assigning all these bad appeals with all this wasted work to my lawyers was really grating on me, and one day, my wife and I went out to dinner . . . with a guy I had gotten friendly with, and he happened to mention that he played softball in this senior league in Montgomery County twice a week. The next day, I went in and gave notice, and I've been playing softball ever since."[44] Packel's departure may have deprived the Defender of a colorful character and a sharp legal mind, but other sharp legal minds took up the slack, including his successor, Karl Baker, who had been Packel's deputy.

On Baker's watch, science handed appeals lawyers some powerful new tools. Psychological research had shown that eyewitness identification in criminal cases was not always reliable, especially if the suspect was of a different race or the perpetrator displayed a weapon.[45] Research had also shown that confessions could be false; suspects sometimes said they committed crimes that they did not commit.[46] Efforts by the Defender over the years to have the courts recognize and address these issues were unsuccessful. Then developments in DNA identification gave defense attorneys a new way to prove that in some cases a convicted defendant could not have committed the crime despite confessing or being identified by an eyewitness. However, even though DNA testing showed eyewitness identification and false confession to be two leading factors in wrongful convictions, Pennsylvania courts long refused to allow testimony from experts about the reliability of these tests.[47]

The Defender took on the eyewitness issue in an appeal to the Pennsylvania Supreme Court of a conviction in a robbery case, *Commonwealth v. Benjamin Walker*,[48] and the false confession issue in an appeal of a murder conviction, *Commonwealth v. Alicia*.[49] The justices handed down decisions in both cases on May 28, 2014. The court was divided in each case and went in opposite directions with its decisions. In *Walker*, the court held that expert testimony concerning witness unreliability was admissible, while in *Alicia*, the majority held that expert testimony concerning false confessions was not admissible.[50]

Defender client Benjamin Walker brought his appeal after he was convicted of robbing two University of Pennsylvania students in October 2005 and sentenced to seventeen and a half to thirty-five years in prison. The conviction was based on the students' eyewitness identification of Walker as the robber. At trial, Walker's lawyer wanted an expert to explain to the jury how the mind works and how its ability to recall events and people accurately can be compromised. The judge refused, citing Pennsylvania's Rules of Evidence, so Walker appealed to Superior Court, which upheld the trial judge. Walker then appealed to the state Supreme Court. This time, he got the result he wanted.[51]

The prosecution argued that allowing experts to testify that some eyewitness identification was unreliable would undercut the validity of all eyewitness evidence. The Supreme Court disagreed, highlighting the new primacy of DNA rather than eyewitness testimony as the gold standard of identification and the possibility of the two to conflict. Justice Debra Todd wrote in the majority opinion: "The recent advent of DNA has raised the prospect of erroneous eyewitness identification and the resulting overturning of convictions based in part upon such testimony has made the concern over the accuracy of eyewitness testimony manifest. Further, DNA testimony has brought to the fore the damaging impact of erroneous eyewitness identification as well." The justices remanded the case to the Court of Common Pleas for a retrial.[52]

Owen Larrabee, the assistant chief of appeals, said the decision could help prevent the innocent from being convicted in Pennsylvania courts.[53] The *Walker* ruling had a "huge impact" on criminal law reform in Pennsylvania, said Rudovsky, then the Defender board president.[54] Jose Alicea was not so fortunate. Alicea, whose name was misspelled on the Supreme Court docket, had been charged with murder arising out of a fight between two groups at a café in the Olney section of Philadelphia in 2005. Shots were fired, and a bystander was killed. Eyewitnesses identified two people as the shooters, neither of whom was Alicea, but after six hours of questioning by police, Alicea, who had an IQ of 64 and mental health issues, confessed to the killing. However, in a pretrial motion, Alicea asserted that his confession was not voluntary, although he did not claim police coercion.[55]

Alicea's counsel moved to allow the admission of an expert on wrongful confessions, arguing that there were more than 185 cases nationally in which convictions had been reversed on DNA evidence even though the defendant had originally confessed. The trial judge, former chief defender Benjamin Lerner, agreed that expert testimony was admissible to educate the jury on the possibility that a confession might be false, as long the expert witness did not address the validity of Alicea's confession.[56]

The district attorney appealed the ruling to Superior Court, which upheld the ruling in the trial court. The prosecution then took the case to the state Supreme Court. The majority of the justices decided that expert testimony in the matter of false confessions would not meet the requirement that such testimony be helpful to the jury. Rather, the court ruled, it would constitute "an impermissible invasion of the jury's role as the exclusive arbiter of credibility."[57] The high court remanded the case to Philadelphia Court of Common Pleas, where Alicea pleaded guilty to third-degree murder in 2015 and was sentenced to seventeen to thirty-five years in prison.[58]

The Supreme Court's *Alicia* decision drew prompt criticism. Lawrence S. Krasner, the lawyer who filed Alicea's motion for expert testimony (and would later become Philadelphia's district attorney), said that the ruling was "a wrong decision by a court staking out an unscientific position that will continue to convict innocent people, encourage improper interrogations by police and cost citizens a fortune in lost lives and lost taxpayer dollars."[59]

The divergence of the *Walker* and *Alicia* decisions gave rise to some head scratching. An article in the American Psychological Association's *Judicial Notebook* described them as "discrepant" and suggested that the court had applied established social science research differently in the two cases and that the effect was to leave the application of social science research to the whims of the judges.[60] Jules Epstein, a former assistant defender and at the time of *Walker* and *Alicia* a professor of law at Widener University, called the decisions "incompatible. Either the science is good or it's not. Either the jurors should know this stuff or they should not."[61]

FRANCIS FISHER KANE, the moving force behind the 1934 creation
of the Voluntary Defender Association of Philadelphia, later renamed
the Defender Association of Philadelphia.

(Defender Association of Philadelphia. Photo by Peter Tobia.)

THIRD. The place where the business of the corporation is to be transacted is the City of Philadelphia, State of Pennsylvania.

FOURTH. The corporation shall have perpetual existence and perpetual succession by its corporate name.

FIFTH. The names and residences of the subscribers to this Certificate of Incorporation are:

A. H. Wintersteen	1601 Morris Building
Chester N. Farr, Jr.	1018 Real Estate Trust Bldg.
Henry S. Drinker, Jr.	1429 Walnut Street
William W. Montgomery, Jr.	Morris Bldg. 15th fl.
Francis Shunk Brown	1005 Morris Building
Frederic L. Ballard	1035 Land Title Bldg.
Maurice Bower Saul	2301 Packard Building
Morris Wolf	1204 Packard Building
John Hampton Barnes	1601 Morris Building
A. A. Jackson	Girard Trust Company
F. B. Bracken	2107 Fidelity-Philadelphia Bldg.
Edward Hopkinson, Jr.	N. E. cor. 15th & Walnut St.
Francis Fisher Kane	1215 Guarantee Trust Bldg.
Charles Edwin Fox	1732 Bankers Trust Bldg.
Owen J. Roberts	Morris Bldg. 15th fl.
Stevens Heckscher	1617 Land Title Building
Robert Dechert	S. E. cor. 6th & Walnut St.

SIXTH. The officers of the corporation shall be a President, one or more Vice-Presidents, a Secretary, a Treasurer, and such other officers as the Board of Directors may deem necessary, and the names and residences of those who have been chosen as officers for the first year are as follows:

	Name	Address
Pres.	John Hampton Barnes	1601 Morris Building
Vice-Pres.	Chester N. Farr, Jr.	1018 Real Estate Trust Bldg.
Sec.	Francis Fisher Kane	1215 Guarantee Trust Bldg.
Treas.	Albert A. Jackson	Girard Trust Company

A page from the Charter of Incorporation for the Voluntary Defender Association of Philadelphia, with the names of the incorporators.

(Defender Association of Philadelphia. Photo by Peter Tobia.)

THOMAS E. COGAN, chief defender, 1934–1946.

(Defender Association of Philadelphia. Photo by Peter Tobia.)

HERMAN I. POLLOCK, chief defender, 1946–1968.
(*Defender Association of Philadelphia. Photo by Peter Tobia.*)

VINCENT J. ZICCARDI, chief defender, 1970–1975.
(*Defender Association of Philadelphia. Photo by Peter Tobia.*)

BENJAMIN LERNER, chief defender, 1975–1990.
(*Defender Association of Philadelphia, Photo by Peter Tobia.*)

ELLEN T. GREENLEE, chief defender, 1990–2015.
(*Defender Association of Philadelphia. Photo by Peter Tobia.*)

KEIR BRADFORD-GREY, chief defender, 2015.

(Defender Association of Philadelphia. Photo by Peter Tobia.)

ELLEN GREENLEE, chief defender, 1990–2015, and
CHARLES CUNNINGHAM, first assistant defender, 1990–2015.
(*Defender Association of Philadelphia. Photo by Peter Tobia.*)

LOUIS NATALI, first assistant defender, 1976–1983.
(Temple University Beasley School of Law.)

DAVID RUDOVSKY, first assistant defender, 1983–1986;
Board of Directors president, 2007–2018.

(University of Pennsylvania School of Law.)

11

LAW REFORM

BENJAMIN LERNER'S INTEREST in finding ways to make the justice system fairer and expand the rights of defendants dated back to his days as an Amsterdam fellow. The program encouraged fellows to think critically about the justice system and brainstorm reforms. So it was hardly a surprise when Lerner appointed Leonard Sosnov as the Defender's first chief of law reform in 1980. Sosnov was a perfect fit for the new post. He had joined the Defender in 1972 after graduating from Harvard Law School and clerking for a federal judge in Philadelphia. He spent his first eight years with the Defender doing waiver trials, jury trials, and appeals, so he knew his way around a courtroom as well as a law library.[1]

Sosnov's job would be to search the Defender's files for issues that could be appealed as test cases, with an eye to setting a precedent helpful to Defender clients as a class. He advised staff lawyers about issues that were worth bringing up in the lower courts and had them file motions (or filed them himself) to preserve issues for later appeal. He alerted the trial lawyers if he thought significant appeals issues were lurking in a new statute: "I would say, 'If we can get to the Pennsylvania Supreme Court with this issue, I think we have a really good chance of winning, so I want you to raise this issue, please, and let me know if you need help litigating it.'"[2]

Patience was an important part of the job. Sosnov might raise a constitutional issue, but it could take a long time for the courts to accept it. He lost his biggest case as chief of law reform, *McMillan v. Pennsylvania*, which he argued before the U.S. Supreme Court in 1986.[3] However, he had the satisfaction of seeing the court eventually accept his line of argument nearly thirty years later in a case from Virginia, *Alleyne v. United States*, in which he was not involved.[4]

Many of Sosnov's cases worked to challenge mandatory minimums. The Defender was suspicious of mandatory minimums because they restrict the judge's ability to impose a sentence responsive to the particularities of an individual case, often resulting in a harsher sentence. *McMillan* challenged a 1982 Pennsylvania law that established a five-year mandatory minimum sentence for committing a crime with a firearm. Under the law, it was up to the sentencing judge to decide, based on a preponderance of the evidence, if the defendant "visibly possessed a firearm." Sosnov argued that if possessing a firearm were to be a consideration in sentencing, it had to be an element of the crime itself, as decided by the jury beyond reasonable doubt, not by the judge as a "sentencing factor" on the less stringent standard of preponderance of the evidence.[5]

The court rejected Sosnov's argument five to four, but the loss did not bury his argument—far from it. In 2000, the court ruled in *Apprendi v. New Jersey* that judges could not increase a sentence based on an aggravating factor unless a jury had found beyond reasonable doubt that the aggravating factor was part of the crime.[6] Another lawyer tried to use the same argument in a 2002 case from North Carolina, *Harris v. United States*, which went before the U.S. Supreme Court and failed. The court decided on a five-to-four vote that *McMillan* was still constitutional because it applied to a mandatory minimum sentence, while *Apprendi* involved a judge imposing a sentence that went beyond the maximum prescribed for the crime, which only a jury could do.[7] Then, in 2013, the court ruled in *Alleyne*, a case from Richmond, Virginia, that it had wrongly decided both *Harris* and *McMillan*.

In 2015, long after he had left the Defender, Sosnov was part of the defense team that won a case in the state Supreme Court, *Commonwealth v. Hopkins*, in which the court ruled unconstitutional a Pennsylvania law that imposed a mandatory minimum sentence of two years for dealing drugs within one thousand feet of a school. *Hopkins* invalidated most of Pennsylvania's mandatory minimum statutes, using the same line of argument Sosnov had used in *McMillan*.[8]

Sosnov argued many other major cases in his years as chief of law reform. *Commonwealth v. Sorrell* (1982) successfully challenged the constitutionality of a statute purporting to give the state a right to demand a jury trial in a criminal case.[9] In 1998, voters approved an amendment giving the commonwealth the same right to trial by jury as the accused. *Commonwealth v. Lovette* (1982) successfully argued that transporting a suspect from one place to another without the suspect's consent constitutes an arrest and requires probable cause under the Fourth Amendment.[10] *Commonwealth v. Bernhardt* (1986) established a habeas corpus right for an accused person to be released from custody when a preliminary hearing is delayed without good cause.[11]

Sosnov left the Defender in 1990 to teach law at Widener University and was succeeded by Peter Rosalsky, who joined the Defender in 1979 and moved back and forth between the Trial Unit and the Appeals Unit before becoming chief of law reform.[12] (Sosnov returned as an assistant defender in 2016 after retiring from Widener.) Rosalsky kept up the Defender's campaign against mandatory minimums, winning victories in *Commonwealth v. McClintic* (2006),[13] which challenged a mandatory twenty-five-year sentence for a third conviction of a violent crime, and *Commonwealth v. Dickson* (2007),[14] which challenged applying to an unarmed co-conspirator the five-year mandatory minimum for showing a firearm while committing a crime.

The major function of the Law Reform Unit was preparing amicus curiae briefs for the Pennsylvania Supreme Court. The court accepts only a small number of cases for review, Rosalsky said, so when it does accept review in an important case, the Defender may want to weigh in on behalf of its defendants—especially if its analysis is likely to differ from the analysis of the litigant's lawyer.[15]

In fact, a Defender amicus brief is most effective when the Defender's view differs from the litigant's and does not simply repeat or agree with the litigant's presentation, Rosalsky added. It is up to the Defender to have the longest view in the room and anticipate the needs of those who will be accused in the future. While many of the lawyers who have cases before the Supreme Court are highly skilled appellate lawyers, others are not. Amicus briefs can make a real difference. Some Supreme Court opinions pay scant attention to them, while others rely in substantial part on an amicus brief's argument. Defender amicus briefs have played a significant role in several state Supreme Court cases.[16] In *Commonwealth v. Weigle* (2010),[17] the court included a Defender amicus brief among the materials it sent to its advisory arm, the Procedural Rules Committee, to help clarify the relationship between retail theft and robbery. The court also referred to an amicus brief that Rosalsky filed in *Commonwealth v. Hopkins*, the school-zone mandatory-minimum case in which Sosnov was part of the appellant's defense team. The court made extensive use of a Defender amicus brief in *Commonwealth v. Wolfe* (2016), in which Matthew Wolfe, an eighteen-year-old man, was convicted of having sex with a thirteen-year-old girl, an offense that carried a ten-year mandatory minimum.[18] Wolfe had been sentenced to ten to twenty years in prison, but the success of his appeal cut the sentence to six and a half to thirteen years.

Sosnov filed important amicus briefs in two cases before the state Supreme Court: *Commonwealth v. Sessoms* (1987) and *Commonwealth v. Ludwig* (1991).[19] In *Sessoms*, the court held that Pennsylvania had set forth its sentencing guidelines in violation of the constitution because the governor was not included in the process and cited the Defender brief as support for part of its decision. (The legislature later enacted the guidelines properly.) In *Ludwig*, the court held that the use of closed-circuit TV for child witness testimony violated the face-to-face provision of the state constitution. (The constitution was later amended to eliminate the face-to-face provision, and now TV testimony is allowed under limited circumstances.)

While much of the Defender's law reform effort has been aimed at mandatory minimums, the association has not limited its amicus participation in Supreme Court cases to any particular type of case or issue, from parole and probation violations to whether a judge failed to determine if a defendant could afford to pay a fine the court wanted to impose. Sosnov and Rosalsky "did outstanding work challenging some of the harshest changes in criminal law in sentencing, parole and probation," former Defender president David Rudovsky said. "And they secured a number of appellate rulings expanding the rights of defendants under the Pennsylvania Constitution."[20]

12

WATCHDOG

ONE OF THE DEFENDER'S MAJOR CONCERNS, not part of its official mission but developed over its years as the poor people's lawyer, has been to serve as a watchdog against police misconduct. Because Defender lawyers are in court every day and represent a large majority of Philadelphia's criminal defendants, they get a close view of how the police make arrests. The information that fills their files reveals patterns that few others have the vantage point to see. From their front-row seats, Defender lawyers have long exercised a key role in raising questions about police behavior, as they did twice in the 1980s.

The first instance involved the alleged framing of mugging suspects by one of the Philadelphia Police Department's elite "Grandpop Squads," a scandal that burst into view in a series of investigative articles in the *Philadelphia Inquirer* in February 1981. The Defender figured prominently among the authorities that the *Inquirer* cited in the series.[1] The undercover squads, which operated in Center City, had an officer dress as a vagrant and act as a decoy to attract would-be muggers. When someone tried to strong-arm the apparently easy target, other undercover officers swooped in to make an arrest. At least, that was how it was supposed to work. One four-man squad allegedly created suspects of their own by having the decoy yell for help as someone walked by him. The backup officers would then emerge to "rescue" the decoy and arrest the hapless passerby for supposedly attempting to mug the decoy. In some cases, the suspects were roughed up. That squad, with Officer Robert Flanagan as the decoy, recorded fifty-seven arrests in 1980, 15 percent more than any other Grandpop Squad.[2]

In 1979 and 1980, the courts appointed Defender lawyers to represent twenty-six defendants arrested by the Flanagan unit. The defenders began to see disturbing patterns in the cases. Assistant Defender Linda Backiel and Phyllis Subin, who was working the case with Backiel, put together a list of the Flanagan squad's arrests showing that thirteen of the twenty-six suspects that the Defender represented over a nine-month period in 1979 and 1980 needed hospital treatment, a number far higher than would be expected in an undercover operation.[3]

The Defender lawyers suggested in court that the Grandpop Squad officers had framed suspects to create more cases, which would lead to more court appearances and, hence, more overtime pay. The lawyers also noticed similarities in police testimony from case to case and filed a motion with the Court of Common Pleas contending that the police squad was "in the habit of describing every instance as having occurred in a particular pattern, regardless of what actually transpired."[4]

Many of the suspects that the Flanagan squad arrested seemed unlikely muggers, said Backiel: "They are typically small, non-macho men, often with physical problems." The squad also arrested "some girls and quite a few juveniles," Backiel added.[5] Backiel, who was representing two of the six defendants featured in the *Inquirer* series, pointed out that both defendants were slightly built; one was forty, and the other was thirty-six; one was epileptic and had a heart condition, and the other was a disabled veteran, also epileptic.[6]

Two other alleged muggers that Flanagan's squad arrested were teenagers, one of them a sixteen-year-old girl and the other her fourteen-year-old boyfriend.[7] A third suspect was an aide in the Camden County Sheriff's Office who was on his way to church. The district attorney dropped charges against the sheriff's aide,[8] who later sued the city and settled for thirty thousand dollars,[9] and one of the two people with epilepsy arrested by the squad.[10] The other suspect with epilepsy was convicted but was later granted a new trial and acquitted.[11] The teenagers were charged with robbery, theft, receiving stolen property, simple assault, and criminal conspiracy and agreed to spend six months under court supervision, after which charges against them were dismissed. The girl later sued the city and settled for fifteen thousand dollars.[12] On February 2, 1981, Police Commissioner Morton B. Solomon pulled

Flanagan's squad off the street and reassigned its members to the radio room at police headquarters.[13]

Louis Natali, the first assistant defender at the time, called for the U.S. attorney to investigate whether the officers might have violated the civil rights of people they arrested. He contended that Justice Department lawyers did not have a daily working relationship with the police that could compromise their independence, and a grand jury could be used to investigate the situation.[14] Perhaps in response to Natali, U.S. Attorney Peter F. Vaira asked the FBI in May 1981 to investigate the Grandpop Squad.[15] In September 1981, a federal grand jury indicted all four members of the squad on charges that they conspired to violate the civil rights of eight people they arrested by fabricating the cases against them and lying under oath. U.S. Justice Department prosecutors also charged them with assaulting four of the suspects by roughing them up or having a police dog attack them.[16] The indictment "was pretty unusual for its time," Subin said.[17]

After a legal battle that went all the way to the U.S. Supreme Court over whether the indicted officers could use the same lawyer, U.S. Attorney Edward S. G. Dennis, Vaira's successor, dropped all charges against the four officers in January 1985, citing "evidentiary problems which now make it impossible for the government to prove its case beyond a reasonable doubt." Dennis added, "The interests of justice required dismissal." He offered no further explanation.[18] Eleven suspects whom the Flanagan squad arrested between 1979 and 1981 did plead guilty or no contest to mugging charges and were placed on probation,[19] but others protested their innocence. The district attorney's office dropped charges against five of those arrested after they passed lie detector tests.[20]

Until the Grandpop Squad episode, keeping an eye on the police was something the Defender had not been equipped to do because, as Subin explained, it did not mature as an institution until the 1970s.[21] By the 1980s, the Defender had made vigilance over law enforcement an important part of its agenda. In 1988, the Defender again found evidence that police were framing people, and this time it was on a larger scale than anything alleged against the decoy operation. Paul Messing, then deputy chief of the Defender's Felony Waiver Unit and later a civil rights attorney in private practice, began noticing similarities among drug arrests in Philadelphia's Thirty-Ninth Police District, in the city's Tioga-Nicetown area. Undercover officers making drug arrests in the district were telling the same story, in virtually the same words, in case after case. They said they were working undercover, trying to buy cocaine through a hole in a door from a suspected drug dealer, when someone would recognize them as police, leaving them no choice but to break down the door and make arrests without a warrant. The only things that changed from one case to another were the date and location.[22]

During the trial in 1989 of Defender client Antonio Vasquez on charges of drug dealing, Messing asked Thirty-Ninth District officer John Baird about similarities between his testimony that day and testimony by other Thirty-Ninth District officers in a dozen different trials. The question rattled Baird and drew an objection from the assistant district attorney prosecuting the case. Common pleas judge Russell M. Nigro, who was presiding, stopped the trial, called the attorneys to his chambers, and asked the district attorney's office to investigate. However, the matter apparently never reached District Attorney Ronald Castille, later chief justice of the Pennsylvania Supreme Court. Assistant District Attorney Elois Howard, who supervised the prosecutor involved in the trial, said the matter had been brought to her attention but she concluded that it "really wasn't a big deal because the PDs were always making allegations." However, Baird did not show up to testify when the trial resumed, so Nigro dismissed the charges against Vasquez. Baird started skipping any trial where Messing would be the defense counsel, which in turn led to charges against more Defender clients being dismissed.[23] Messing later left the office to go into private practice, and since all the cases in which Baird was involved had been dismissed, they were put in a file drawer. In 1995 a federal grand jury indicted Baird and four other officers or former officers on charges of framing suspects, beating them, stealing from them, and then giving false testimony about them in court. The indictments were the result of an FBI investigation launched in 1991 after a man detained by two of the officers complained to police.[24]

The indictments caught the attention of Bradley S. Bridge, one of the Defender's top trial attorneys, who got permission from Defender leadership to reopen cases in which the officers had been involved. Bridge's work led to the overturning of more than 160 convictions.[25] The city also paid out more than four million dollars to settle false-arrest claims. Over the ensuing years, Bridge would manage to get between fifteen hundred and sixteen hundred convictions overturned because of police corruption in various cases, mostly involving guns or drugs.[26] Although the district attorney did not act when Messing first raised his concerns, that he raised them at all showed the Defender's value as a guardian against police misconduct, a role that Messing believes others in the criminal justice system were unwilling to fill. "I think a lot of people in the system see examples of misconduct, whether it is bad searches or questionable testimony, and they tend to look the other way," he said.[27]

Bridge became the Defender's leading authority on corrupt cops in the 1990s, not just because of his involvement with the Thirty-Ninth District cases. Bridge had been keeping a list of untrustworthy police since 1988. It started with two police officers who had been clearing the books at a staggering rate on crimes against property, such as burglaries, bicycle thefts, and car radio thefts. They did it by extracting false confessions from suspects. "People would admit to doing thirty or forty or fifty of these particular crimes in one statement," Bridge said. Bridge did not know how the police had gotten those admissions, but he did know they were false: "Those statements were fraudulent, demonstrably so, because on a number of those occasions, people were actually in custody—one of my clients was actually physically in custody in Virginia in a case that he admitted to stealing someone's bike. As a result, the prosecutor's office, when faced with this incontrovertible evidence of statements that were palpably false, ended up dismissing the cases. Based on that, I thought we needed to keep track of police officers."[28]

By the time the Thirty-Ninth District scandal emerged seven years later, Bridge already had nineteen names on his list. By 2018, Bridge's list had grown to more than two thousand names. Not all were then on the force, and some had died. The list included each officer's name, badge number, assignment at the time of appearing on the list, current assignment, and reason for appearing on the list. The list was not public, although its existence was known among lawyers in Philadelphia. When any of the police officers on Bridge's list was involved in a Defender case, the Defender lawyer was able to raise concerns about the officer's credibility. Only one officer, who found out through an acquaintance that his name was on the list, ever complained about being included. Bridge reviewed the entry and decided to remove the officer's name.[29]

Despite reform efforts by the city and the police department after the Thirty-Ninth District episode, the Defender did not back away from its watchdog role. "The problem, frankly, is that these same issues keep happening," Messing said in 2017. "The city just negotiated a new collective bargaining agreement with the Fraternal Order of Police that has these same very rigid arbitration provisions in it that make it almost impossible to terminate a cop."[30] Defender leadership does not see any likelihood that police misconduct will disappear. Former Defender board president David Rudovsky observed in 2014, "Basically, you can set your clock by this: that every five to seven years, we have another narcotics squad scandal."[31]

13

FUNDING AND DEFENDER PAY PARITY

ONEY WAS A PROBLEM for the Defender from the organization's beginning in 1934. The Defender's contract with the city in 1969 may have saved the organization, but it did not relieve all the association's financial difficulties. Because funding indigent defense in Pennsylvania falls directly on the counties rather than the state, the Defender had to rely for almost all of its funding on the city of Philadelphia. Perpetually strapped for money, the city government was not always enthusiastic about bankrolling an organization that represented people accused of crime.

From the very beginning of his tenure as chief defender, Benjamin Lerner knew he would have to fight constantly for more resources. When he took over, assistant defenders were making less than assistant district attorneys, and the needle on the Defender's salary scale had not moved in several years; annual pay for Defender staff lawyers in 1971 ranged from $9,500 a year for newcomers to $16,000 a year for experienced attorneys.[1] The starting salary for an assistant defender in 1974 was $10,500 a year, while an assistant district attorney started at $13,698.[2] The NLADA evaluators who reported on the state of the Defender Association in 1971 called the Defender salaries "grossly inadequate." Even the chief defender, whose salary increased from $25,000 in 1971 to $39,000 in 1975,[3] trailed the district attorney, whose salary rose from $34,000 to $42,000 as part of a wave of raises given to Philadelphia city officials late in 1973.[4]

Low pay was leading to high turnover. Without raises, it would be difficult for the Defender to keep experienced lawyers. Lerner knew the Defender could never pay its lawyers as much as they would earn in a private firm, but he did want them to be paid as much as the prosecutors they faced in court. "Parity"—as in pay parity—would become a Defender watchword.[5]

Concern about low pay for public defenders was not just a Philadelphia issue, although it may have been more pressing there. At a time when the Defender was paying lawyers less than $10,000 to start, Los Angeles paid its new public defenders $12,924 and San Francisco paid $14,698.[6] The problem of low pay for public defenders proved so persistent that in 2002 the ABA included a call for parity as part of a set of guidelines called "Ten Principles of a Public Defense Delivery System." The ABA called for parity not just in salary but in workload and "other resources (such as benefits, technology, facilities, legal research, support staff, paralegals, investigators, and access to forensic services and experts) between prosecution and public defense."[7]

Parity proved an elusive goal for the Defender Association. Lerner did manage to get enough money from the city to give the assistant defenders raises and was able to give the staff salary increases throughout his fifteen-year tenure. The raises were not always large, but they were still raises. Lerner did it by keeping the Defender staff smaller than he wanted and having staffers take on more work than he wanted. Even if they managed to achieve parity, Lerner liked to point out, Defender Association lawyers would make less than city prosecutors because the city's benefits package covered only city employees, and the defenders were not public employees.[8]

When Lerner became chief defender, Frank Rizzo was the mayor, and most Philadelphians might have bet that getting more money for criminal defense from his tough-on-crime administration would be a daunting challenge. It was not. Lerner and Louis Natali emphasized to Rizzo administration officials the enormous scope of the Defender Association's work. Rizzo did not much care for criminal defendants, but he knew that they had a constitutional right to a defense.[9] "We got more money under Rizzo than we ever got under any other administration for parity," Natali said. He and Lerner visited the city's finance director and showed him a list from the Philadelphia law journal, the *Legal*

Intelligencer, of all the courtrooms the Defender was staffing. They argued that the assistant defenders were doing the same amount of work as assistant prosecutors but were not getting paid as much. "They agreed to provide us with parity," Natali said.[10]

Parity was not instant. It took several years of raises, but by the mid-1980s, the Defender had gotten there—after Defender leaders demonstrated to Mayor William J. Green III, as they had to Rizzo, the Defender's cost effectiveness. For a while, the Defender's pay scale came very close to the district attorney's. Green's team thought at first that if they audited the Defender, they would find places to cut the organization's budget, but instead they found that the Defender was operating very efficiently. The Defender ended up with a substantial budget increase.[11]

Even the district attorney supported Lerner's effort to achieve parity in the late 1970s and early 1980s. Edward G. Rendell, who was district attorney from 1978 to 1986, accompanied Lerner to City Council appropriation hearings. "In my eight years as District Attorney, I often found myself in the position of going to bat for them financially because money for defenders seems very easy to cut at budget time," Rendell told the *Philadelphia Inquirer* in 1987. "They have no powerful constituency."[12]

Still, parity was never a sure thing. Though the Defender had demonstrated to city government that it cost the city less than having the courts assign private attorneys to indigent defendants, the city faced financial difficulties that affected not just the Defender but all municipal services. Twice during his tenure as chief defender, Lerner threatened to curtail Defender services if the city did not provide sufficient funding for its operations, a move that Lerner called "the nuclear option." Each time, the city came through with the needed funding.[13]

The Defender Association was hardly alone among public defender offices across the country in facing financial troubles. In 1983 and 2003, the ABA conducted hearings on funding for public defenders and heard frequent complaints of low pay, high-volume caseloads, and inadequate funding.[14] Some public defenders sued states for more funds, while others used their own version of the "nuclear option" by declining to take more cases. These tactics had occasional success, but indigent defense in the United States remained in bad health during the first two decades of the twenty-first century. Public defense in general was "a huge national failure," William Leahy, New York's chief public defender, told Pew Foundation researchers in 2017.[15]

In 1984, as the Defender marked its fiftieth anniversary, the association once again faced a financial crisis. "Budget Pinch Spoils Public Defenders' 50th Anniversary," a headline in the *Inquirer* proclaimed on June 22, 1984. Lerner asked for an extra $1.5 million beyond the $8.9 million appropriation the city had approved for the fiscal year beginning July 1, 1984. Without the added funds, Lerner warned, the Defender would be unable to staff all of the city's more than fifty criminal courtrooms or give raises to Defender staff and would have to cut its caseload by 20 percent. Reducing the Defender's caseload would actually cost the city money, Lerner argued, because the Defender worked more cheaply than private court-appointed counsel. The average Defender case cost the city about $250, according to Lerner, while the average cost for representation by private court-appointed counsel was $500.[16]

Lerner had support for his request from Rendell, common pleas president judge Edward J. Bradley, and Pennsylvania chief justice Robert N. C. Nix Jr.[17] Mayor W. Wilson Goode responded that the city government was in financial distress and might not even be able to come through with the $8.9 million already appropriated, let alone anything extra. "Obviously, no commitment for additional funding would be prudent at this juncture," Goode wrote to Bradley, who had adopted Lerner's position that the city would end up spending even more if it did not come up with the additional funds for the Defender.[18]

In a compromise, the city finally provided an extra $750,000 to the Defender that Lerner quickly used to hire twenty-four new lawyers, twelve for existing openings and twelve for new positions. Under the compromise, the Defender would delay salary and benefit increases until January 1, 1985. Because of the delay, an assistant district attorney would be paid more than an assistant defender for fiscal year 1984. "In effect, our existing staff will be giving up something that everybody else is getting," Lerner told the *Philadelphia Inquirer*. "It was the feeling of the staff that it was the best we could do, and that the delay would be acceptable as a one-time thing."[19]

In 1987, Lerner warned the city that the Defender would have to close down in June for the last three weeks of the fiscal year if the city rejected a Defender request for an additional $400,000 to cover the expense of staffing ten new courtrooms that had not been part of the original planning for fiscal year 1987. Without the extra money, Lerner said, the Defender could not meet its payroll.[20]

Such year-end requests were routine for the Defender as the organization dealt with unanticipated expenses. This time, things got complicated. City officials wanted the Defender to borrow the money from a bank and then repay it out of the following year's appropriation. Lerner did not like that plan and said that he was not certain he could even get a loan unless the city pledged that it would be repaid. City Councilman John Street, a powerful member of council who would later be elected mayor, angrily told Lerner in a council meeting that he did not want to hear anything about closing the Defender down. He shouted that Lerner had disrespected him by going to the city finance director for funding the previous year instead of coming to council and that this was his chance to retaliate. In the end, though, Lerner offered soothing words to Street, and the Defender got its money.[21]

Still, the days of parity were numbered, as municipal finances spiraled downward. Although the Defender got decent increases for a few years, the district attorney got greater increases that destroyed parity. By the time Lerner left the Defender in 1990, there was a 25–30 percent gap between the pay of assistant defenders and assistant prosecutors. In 1991, Rendell was elected mayor amid an economic crisis. The city was running a deficit of $250 million and teetered on the edge of bankruptcy. As part of his effort to turn the city finances around, Rendell held the line on spending for all agencies. This was not a good situation for the Defender, which got almost all of its money from the city. The district attorney's office had other funding sources because it was eligible for law enforcement grants and the Defender was not. As a result, the district attorney's office could scale back its funding requests during the crisis, while the Defender could not. City officials did not forget the forbearance of the district attorney's office. When the financial crisis ended, the city was more generous with the district attorney's office than with the Defender.[22] The problem of parity would persist into the twenty-first century.

14

TAKING STOCK AT A MILESTONE

THE DEFENDER CELEBRATED its fiftieth birthday in 1984 in a modest way, fitting given its financial challenges. Despite its money woes, the organization had a lot of reasons to be satisfied. It had grown from 2 lawyers in 1934 to 133 lawyers and 135 support personnel in 1984, making it the fourth-largest public defender operation in the United States. The annual budget had increased from $18,528 to more than $9 million over that span, an astounding change for anyone who had been around long enough to remember the Defender's pre-*Gideon* days as a small, voluntary association.[1]

Over its first fifty years, the Defender had established a nationwide reputation for independence and successful representation of the poor. The Defender's approach to training had become the gold standard for public defender training in the United States. It was recognized as such in 1987, when the NLADA and the ABA presented the Philadelphia Defender with the Clara Shortridge Foltz Award as the outstanding public defender office in the country, largely because of its training program.[2] An advisory commission in San Diego County, California, recommended that the county, which was about to establish a public defender's office, model the agency on the Defender Association of Philadelphia. One San Diego lawyer tried unsuccessfully to convince Benjamin Lerner to apply for the job of running the new office.[3]

The Defender—so long looked at askance by others in the criminal justice system, from bench to bar—also garnered accolades at home. Edward J. Blake, administrative judge of the Philadelphia Court of Common Pleas, praised the quality of the Defender's work. "The defenders do an excellent job," he told the *Inquirer* in 1987. He added that in the ten years he had been assigned to conduct postconviction hearings for defendants claiming ineffective counsel at trial, he had granted a new trial in fewer than 1 percent of Defender cases.[4] Ed Rendell, who had gone up against the Defender for two terms as district attorney, also praised the association as necessary to the system. "If we had 200 judges and 400 prosecutors, so we could open 200 courtrooms, we still couldn't go to trial without defenders," Rendell said. "The accused must have adequate representation. Philadelphia is very fortunate to have excellent defenders. Thanks to Ben Lerner and a lot of others in the organization, defenders are staying longer, and they're recruiting a lot of good young lawyers."[5]

The Defender celebrated its fiftieth anniversary in part with a little bit of stress-relieving silliness. John Packel, the Defender's resident free spirit, proposed a midnight party in which Defender staff would gather round and sing the Defender anthem. The only problem was that the Defender did not have an anthem, which to Packel's mind was no problem at all. Defender staffers would be encouraged to write anthems, which they would unveil at a prequel party the month before the birthday bash. Those in attendance would then vote on the best song. "It was one of the most outrageous times we've ever had at the Defender office," Packel recalled. "This was in the library. Maybe, there were eight individuals or groups who presented their anthems. I wrote one, needless to say, which I thought was the best, but it did not win. I don't remember which one won."[6]

Packel's anthem was a litany of the challenges that Defender lawyers faced daily, sung to the tune of "Bye, Bye, Blackbird":

> *Pack up all my files and go*
> *off to court singing low,*
> *"I'm your P.D.*
> *Judges hate me, D.A.'s, too,*
> *but most of all, my clients do*
> *hate this P.D.*
> *No one here can love or understand me;*
> *oh, what hard luck hardships they all hand me."*

More than thirty years later, not winning the competition still rankled Packel. Like all defenders, Packel hated to lose.[7]

The Defender's anniversary celebration also had a more serious side. The association used the occasion to reflect on its first half century, issuing a collection of reminiscences and reflections by Defender lawyers, volunteers, board members, and staffers on its growth and evolving mission. Among the most eloquent reflections was by Assistant Defender Jules Epstein, who would go on to become professor of law and director of advocacy programs at Temple University Beasley School of Law. Epstein began by identifying the kinds of lawyers who became public defenders: "Men and, more and more, women; former peace marchers, feminists, would-be businessmen, and ex-Green Berets; graduates of the Ivy Leagues and small, state-run law schools; more and more, attorneys making a career commitment to the office; those who came here for the thrill of trial work, and those who came with a commitment to help the poor."[8]

Defenders in 1984, he wrote, found themselves working in a judicial system that undermined the rights of the accused, denying them reasonable bail and compromising their right to a speedy trial and a presumption of innocence. Sentencing had become more severe. Appellate courts were finding less reversible error. The clients, poor and often illiterate, could be uncommunicative or mistrustful, suspicious that a public defender might not be as good as a private defender. Clients might fail to show up for pretrial conferences or provide information needed to locate witnesses. Defenders might handle fifty to one hundred cases per week if they were assigned to Municipal Court, thirty to forty cases if they were preparing cases for a nonjury trial, and fifteen or more cases a month if they were assigned to the Major Trials Unit. They did it by sticking together and supporting one another.[9]

Epstein wrote that "there is a M.A.S.H.-type support system—each of us having gone through the hell of having a judge as another prosecutor in the courtroom, of seeing a child committed to prison for more of his life than he has been free—so we are there to help when someone else comes back with the same burden." The Defender was the last line of defense for poor people accused of crime. "Their freedom is on the line," Epstein wrote. "Ensuring it, or guaranteeing that the loss is minimal, is the bottom line."[10]

The 1980s would prove to be a decade of personnel change at the top for the Defender, starting with Louis Natali's departure in 1983 and the appointment of David Rudovsky, a highly respected civil rights lawyer, to succeed him as first assistant. Like Lerner and Natali, Rudovsky had been one of the postgraduate fellows in the Amsterdam program in the late 1960s. After he had completed the two years of his fellowship, he stayed at the Defender as chief of the Motions Unit until he left in 1971 to form a private firm with another Amsterdam fellow, David Kairys, that would focus on civil rights and civil liberties litigation.

With Rudovsky as first assistant came a change in tone. Natali was a tough-talking, emotional motivator whose gruffness complemented Lerner's gregarious style. "They were like two halves of the same person," said Mary DeFusco, who was a young assistant defender at the time. "It was like Lou was the motivator and Ben was just, like, the rational guy. It was lots of fun."[11] Rudovsky brought a cerebral approach that turned down the volume on communications, and he replaced much of the Defender's middle management with people who reflected his style. Rudovsky's view was that high-decibel conversations were counterproductive, and his interactions with the staff were quiet.

Rudovsky's stay was relatively short. He had never intended to step permanently away from his law firm. He resigned as first assistant in 1986, the same year he was awarded a MacArthur Fellowship for his work as a civil rights lawyer.[12] He was succeeded by Ellen Greenlee, who had been chief of the Defender's Felony Waiver Unit. Women in the Defender were happy to have a woman as second in command. DeFusco recalled that their feeling was "Oh, at last, we have some representation. We're not going to get stepped on just because we're women."[13]

The biggest personnel change of all came in May 1990 when Lerner decided to retire from the Defender and return to private practice. Under his leadership, the Defender had grown from 90 to 145 lawyers. Common pleas court president judge Edward J. Bradley praised Lerner for "professionalizing" the Defender, while conceding that his activism on behalf of clients had ruffled the feathers of a few judges. Still, Bradley said, Lerner never sought confrontation for its own sake, and in the end his style helped improve the administration of justice in Philadelphia. Even Lerner's former opponents in the district attorney's office gave him his due. Ex–district attorney Rendell said that Lerner's tenure at the Defender "marked the turning point in that office" as it grew into a major force in the criminal justice system. Ronald D. Castille, then the incumbent district attorney, grudgingly praised Lerner as an advocate for the Defender's clients and for the justice system, although given to becoming involved in disputes in which he should not have been involved, in Castille's view.[14]

The board of directors named Greenlee, who had joined the Defender in 1973 and spent her entire legal career there, as interim chief defender early in 1990. After a national search, the board made the appointment permanent on October 30, 1990. Acting on Lerner's recommendation, the board also named Charles A. Cunningham as first assistant, making him the highest-ranking African American in Defender history. His appointment was a surprise, but a welcome one. Cunningham was highly respected among the Defender staff for his skills as a trial lawyer.[15]

Lerner called the appointment of Greenlee and Cunningham "the closest you could come to an iron-clad guarantee" that the Defender would continue its work on behalf of its clients and the courts.[16] With an eye, obviously, on recent complaints from some minority staff about the number of African Americans in supervisory positions, Greenlee said that among her first tasks would be bringing people together and increasing harmony in the Defender.[17]

15

GREENLEE STEPS UP

ELLEN GREENLEE was not only the Defender Association's first female leader; she was also its first homegrown chief. Unlike her predecessors, she had never practiced law anywhere else. Greenlee was appointed interim chief defender when Benjamin Lerner stepped down in June 1990. The Defender's Board of Directors made the job permanent four months later and appointed Charles A. Cunningham, one of the association's best trial lawyers, as first assistant defender. Greenlee and Cunningham had little prior experience working together, but they soon developed into an effective team—each a zealous advocate for the defense of the constitutional rights of their clients and dedicated to improving the Defender's quality and effectiveness. During their administration, the Defender Association not only grew but substantially broadened its services.

Greenlee joined the Defender in November 1973 after graduating from Villanova University School of Law the previous June and was hired as an assistant defender in April 1974 by Dennis Kelly, Vincent Ziccardi's deputy. Law was Greenlee's second career; she did not start law school until twelve years after graduating from Chestnut Hill College in 1958 with a degree in French. Greenlee studied as a Fulbright Scholar in France; taught high school French, Spanish, and English in Clifton Heights, Pennsylvania; and then worked as a public relations assistant in the International Division of Smith Kline Laboratories in Philadelphia.[1]

Like other Defender newcomers in the early 1970s, before Lerner and Louis Natali's training program, Greenlee made her legal debut with minimal preparation. She was handed a pile of case files and sent to represent Defender clients in preliminary hearings at the Eighteenth Police District at Fifty-Fifth and Pine Streets in West Philadelphia. "I still remember that first day at Fifty-Fifth and Pine," she would later recall. "I was handling a rape case. The victim was a seventy-two-year-old woman, with her two burly brothers standing behind her, and Rick DeMaio [a Defender supervisor] came in to kind of see what was going on, but at that point, you were on your own. When you went in, you prepared what little you had. There was not much in a file at a preliminary hearing."[2] It was the first of what would be many case files, representing many people who would benefit from Greenlee's representation before being handed off to another defender at another stage of the labyrinthine justice system.

In the sixteen years before she was appointed chief defender, Greenlee compiled a notable record. One of a handful of female assistant defenders in 1974, she spent six years as a Defender trial attorney, working in all the units except Juvenile, doing jury trial cases, bench trials, and appeals, but it was her administrative abilities that made her most valuable to the Defender. Lerner recognized Greenlee's abilities not only as a trial lawyer but also as a manager and supervisor. In 1980, he named her assistant chief of the Felony Waiver Unit and in 1984 promoted her to chief of the unit, one of the Defender's largest, representing clients in preliminary hearings before Municipal Court judges and in nonjury felony trials before common pleas judges, the majority of the felony cases the Defender Association tried. She not only supervised the large group of assistants working in Felony Waiver but also tried cases herself as needed.[3]

Greenlee was especially popular with the fast-growing number of female assistant defenders who would gather at her home for weekend potluck dinners and a discussion of office matters, including their impatience to have more women in managerial positions.[4] After David Rudovsky's return to private practice in 1986, the board, at Lerner's suggestion, made her first assistant defender and, with Lerner's retirement in 1990, elected her chief defender.[5]

The board also named the popular Charles Cunningham, a top-flight trial lawyer, as Greenlee's first assistant. Cunningham arrived as an experienced lawyer, nine years out of Temple University Law School when he signed on with the Defender. "Charlie certainly was an all star as a trial attorney," Greenlee said. "I remember at one point he tried either nine or fourteen jury trials in a row. He won most of his jury trials. He was extremely effective before a jury. He always looked good: sartorially splendent."[6]

With his appointment as first assistant, Cunningham became the first African American to reach the top tier of Defender management. The appointment came at a time when complaints of racial discrimination, originally voiced during the last years of Lerner's tenure, were still roiling the Defender. In recognition of the smoldering discontent, Greenlee told the *Philadelphia Inquirer* that she would give priority to "pulling people within the office together, and increasing the harmony in the office." Cunningham echoed those sentiments in the same *Inquirer* article, declaring that "one of the first things we are going to have to do is sit down, talk to everybody and work out any problems. This is a new administration and it should be a time where things are resolved."[7]

Greenlee led the Defender much as a head coach might after taking over a winning team. She encouraged and supported her lawyers, who numbered about 150 when she took over and 200 by the year 2000, and she brought to her new job a reputation for being supportive that stretched back to her earliest years as a supervisor. She continued Lerner's emphasis on recruitment and training. Not given to schmoozing, Greenlee did not spend much time walking around the Defender suite, talking to the staff, as Lerner had. She left that to the peripatetic Cunningham, remaining in the office throughout the day with the door open, more accessible than visible. She welcomed staff suggestions about broadening Defender services and helped find the funds to implement those suggestions. Some thought she should walk around more, while others were content knowing that they could always see her when necessary or reach her on the phone.

The list of new activities the Defender either initiated or embraced under Greenlee is long. The Defender began representing defendants in murder cases. The city started new special courts, called treatment courts, for defendants with special problems—drug addicts, prostitutes, and veterans—and these needed staffing by public defenders. The Defender embraced alternative sentencing to keep Defender clients out of jail by getting them into a broader range of rehabilitation and education programs. Greenlee's Defender intensified its efforts to track police misconduct and challenge convictions obtained on false evidence. Finally, the Philadelphia Defender Association pioneered the representation of juveniles in a program that would become the standard for other public defender offices around the country.

Greenlee also continued Lerner's efforts to increase the Defender's diversity, naming Robert Listenbee, an African American lawyer who was a rising Defender star, as director of minority recruiting.[8] Sure enough, recruitment increased under Listenbee's watch.[9] On the national level, Greenlee maintained the close ties that her predecessors had established with NLADA. Like Lerner, she served two terms as president of NLADA.

It was Greenlee's misfortune to become chief defender at a time of deteriorating relations between the Defender and the district attorney. Less than a year after Greenlee's appointment, common pleas judge Lynne Abraham became the district attorney and remained in office until 2009. Unlike earlier district attorneys, Abraham appeared to regard the Defender more as an annoyance than a partner in the criminal justice system. Her support for harsh sentencing, including the death penalty, raised the stakes for the Defender's clients even higher than it had been and complicated criminal defense work. Abraham also opposed pay parity between the district attorney and the Defender, making that goal ever more elusive.[10]

Greenlee's response to the district attorney's hostility was simply to keep the Defender on course, providing the best defense possible for its indigent clients. "I think that you kind of redouble your efforts to do the very best job that you can and try to get enough funding to keep the people that are good, the young lawyers who have done three or four years and want to leave to make money," she later recalled. "It's a constant struggle to upgrade the representation and try to keep the good people that you have."[11] It would be Greenlee's challenge for twenty-five years.

THE DEFENDER TAKES ON HOMICIDE

THE FIRST MAJOR EXPANSION of Defender services in the Ellen Greenlee administration came in 1993, when the Defender Association began representing clients charged with murder. Under an agreement between the Defender and the court system, the Defender would be randomly assigned the case of every fifth indigent charged with homicide in Philadelphia.[1] "We knew people would get better representation" if the Defender were allowed to take homicide cases, Greenlee said. "Also, it was kind of a prestige thing. There's no reason why a high-quality Defender office shouldn't do homicide. They did it in the other counties. The twenty percent figure was just because homicide had always been the moneymaker for private counsel and they did not want the Defender in the business."[2]

Philadelphia in the early 1990s was one of just two counties in Pennsylvania—and one of the few in the country—where public defenders were not assigned to murder cases. The Defender had been prohibited since its earliest days from representing accused killers, although Defender lawyers had long been itching to do it. However, the private bar had not wanted to give up the murder defense franchise, the most prestigious of all court appointments, and judges were not keen to take it away because it was a way to reward party loyalists. There was only so much compensation for court-appointed attorneys to go around.[3] In the view of the Philadelphia Bar Association, until early in 1991, allowing the Defender to represent murder defendants would cut into the livelihood of lawyers who had been getting the appointments.[4]

By the early 1990s, representation of murder defendants by court-appointed lawyers in Philadelphia had become shoddy enough to be scandalous. In September 1992, the *Philadelphia Inquirer* examined the status of murder defense in the city in a series of articles by Pulitzer Prize winner Fredric N. Tulsky, who reported that court appointments to defend indigent murder suspects usually went to lawyers with political connections. The *Inquirer*'s examination found that many of the court-appointed lawyers failed to prepare their cases adequately. Stuart Schuman, head of the Defender's Municipal Court Unit, told Tulsky that the system of appointing defense attorneys in murder cases was "a political device enabling judges with the opportunity to appoint favored lawyers to cases in which a decent appointment fee can be earned."[5] Since judges in Pennsylvania are elected, the implication was that they benefited politically from their choice of appointment just as the lawyer benefits in prestige and fee.

The court-appointed lawyers may have welcomed the money, but it was not enough to put on an adequate defense for a murder case, especially a capital murder case. In Los Angeles, a court-appointed lawyer could be paid as much as $60,000 for a murder case. In Philadelphia, court-appointed homicide lawyers averaged $6,399 per case, a testament to the difference in the politics of criminal defense in Pennsylvania.[6] The low compensation made it difficult to assemble the kind of defense team necessary to win a murder trial or avoid a death sentence in the event of a conviction—a second lawyer, investigators, social workers, psychologists, mitigation specialists, and jury selection consultants. In only one of twenty death penalty cases over a two-year span reviewed by the *Inquirer* did an indigent defendant have two lawyers, as the ABA recommended for capital cases.[7]

Louis Natali, the former first assistant defender, warned that Philadelphia needed to review its standards for trying homicide cases: "The floor has to be elevated seven or eight stories, from the bargain basement where it now exists."[8] The judges, much as they liked the prerogative of appointing homicide attorneys, were not blind to the problems of quality. In an effort to improve homicide representation, they decided in 1989 to appoint a panel that would certify lawyers they deemed experienced enough to represent murder defendants, but that failed to solve the problem because it used the number of cases tried as the yardstick for measuring experience. Some lawyers simply tried many cases badly.[9]

Tulsky's series "humiliated" the Philadelphia court system, said Marc Bookman, a Defender major trials attorney who was one of the first members of the association's Homicide Unit. The *Inquirer* editorial page called for reform.[10] A public defender in San Francisco declared that Philadelphia was "in the dark ages."[11] "I think [the series] shamed the city into saying, 'This is just beyond the pale,'" Bookman said.[12]

The *Inquirer*'s reporting may have put pressure on the courts, but reform would not have gone far without the powerful support of a newcomer to the Philadelphia justice system: Geoff Gallas, the executive administrator of the courts. "He was the one that pushed it through," Greenlee said.[13] The Pennsylvania Supreme Court appointed Gallas to the Philadelphia post in September 1991 and gave him extensive administrative power over the Court of Common Pleas and Municipal and Traffic Courts.[14] As an outsider, he had no political ties to Philadelphia and, consequently, no political debts to be paid off with patronage jobs. (Being an outsider eventually proved a grave liability for Gallas. In 1996, the Supreme Court demoted him to budget director and abolished the executive administrator post. Gallas claimed it was for resisting political patronage hiring and promotion, and he filed a federal lawsuit against several justices of the state Supreme Court, as well as state senator Vince Fumo and U.S. representative Bob Brady, both powerful Democrats, and several others. A U.S. judge dismissed the case in 1998, saying it had no merit.)[15]

In 1991, under prodding from Gallas, Philadelphia's judges agreed at last to allow the Defender to represent murder defendants. Greenlee said she thinks the Defender got 20 percent of the cases because Gallas believed that was a figure the private bar would accept. Trying to set it any higher would simply invite pushback.[16] However, even the bar was ready by this time to allow the Defender into homicide representation. In 1991, at the urging of Benjamin Lerner, who at that time was in private practice, the Philadelphia Bar Association's Board of Governors adopted a resolution supporting the idea of assigning 20 percent of homicide cases to the Defender. The board forwarded its resolution to the Board of Judges of the Court of Common Pleas, City Council, and the Defender's Board of Directors.[17]

Although a broad sentiment was developing in favor of the Defender taking murder cases, Greenlee was not about to rush into anything that would put her lawyers at a disadvantage. She wanted a pledge from the city to come up with the extra money, half a million dollars, that she estimated murder representation would cost the Defender.[18] The extra money was necessary because Greenlee and Cunningham insisted that the Defender would defend homicide cases only by adhering strictly to the ABA model.[19] The ABA called for two attorneys in murder cases, one for trial and one to argue for mitigation in the event of a conviction by presenting evidence that circumstances of life had lessened the defendant's culpability and hopefully convincing the jury not to impose the death penalty. The guidelines also called for the defense team to include an investigator and a social worker trained to probe the defendant's background for mitigating factors, "with at least one member of that team qualified by training and experience to screen for the presence of mental or psychological disorders or impairments."[20]

Greenlee and Cunningham wanted to establish a new unit within the Defender that would handle nothing but murder cases. "We had to get funding for those positions," Greenlee later said. In the meantime, common pleas judge Michael R. Stiles, who then oversaw the scheduling of murder cases, began appointing Defender lawyers as the second attorneys in some murder cases, anticipating the time when the Defender could begin accepting homicide appointments.[21]

Gallas proposed in December 1992 that the Defender receive 20 percent of the amount the city was spending on court-appointed lawyers in homicide cases. He reasoned that this was an appropriate figure since the Defender would take 20 percent of all indigent homicide cases. Greenlee initially balked, insisting that the Defender needed three hundred thousand dollars more, but relented.[22] Once the Defender and the court system reached agreement on murder representation, the Defender Association assembled a group of ten of its best lawyers—four teams of two lawyers, plus a chief, Paul Conway, and an assistant chief, Thurgood Matthews—to become the Homicide Unit. "They had to apply, and then we interviewed people and selected [the members of the unit]," Greenlee recalled. "There was a panel process for selecting the head of homicide, the assistant chief. Once we had them in place, then we did panel interviews for people who wanted to work in homicide."[23] Applicants had to have seven years of major trial experience. When the unit was finally in place, its least experienced member, Everett Gillison, had ten years of trial experience and had been a Defender social worker for ten years before going to law school. He would later become deputy mayor under Michael Nutter.[24]

Conway, the unit chief, exuded leadership skill. He had been with the Defender for twenty years and had extensive experience as a trial lawyer and supervisor. He had been the first chief of the Special Defense Unit when it was formed in 1979. Before beginning his law career, Conway had been a U.S. Army Green Beret and served in combat in Vietnam. (He had graduated from Villanova University School of Law in 1968 before going into the army but chose Special Forces over serving as an army lawyer.) He left the army in 1970, passed the bar exam, and worked with a small practice in northeastern Philadelphia but found it boring, so he decided to apply to both the district attorney's office and the Defender.[25]

Like so many lawyers hired by Vincent Ziccardi, Conway had an interesting story about his hiring. He stopped by the Defender office, hoping to set up an interview, and encountered Ziccardi: "I talked to Vince for a few minutes; he said, 'How about Monday?' I thought he meant, 'Come for an interview on Monday,' but what he meant was, 'Come to work on Monday.' He was good at picking people. He picked some of the best trial lawyers. He would pick these street fighters for trial lawyers and all these smart Ivy League guys for the appeals section." Conway was one of Ziccardi's best picks; his career with the Defender would last more than forty years.[26]

Greenlee and Cunningham knew the stakes for the new Homicide Unit would be high because the district attorney sought the death penalty in so many cases. "We knew going in that most of the cases we were going to be assigned to were going to at least start off as death penalty cases" since the district attorney's office sought so many death penalties, Cunningham said.[27] The Defender prepared to meet the challenge the way it always did—by training. It was "a huge amount of training," even though the lawyers were the most experienced the Defender had; it went on for at least six months, said Mary DeFusco, a top Defender lawyer who was involved in the training and would become the Defender's training director in 1995.[28] That was fine with Conway: "I worked with small units in the army, and one of the first things I always did was pick the best people, overtrain them, get them all the resources they needed, and then gave them their responsibility, and that's always worked."[29]

The Defender supplemented its own training programs by reaching out, with impressive humility, to lawyers across the country who had long experience trying death penalty cases. "We went to every conference we could go to with people who were doing this stuff," Conway said. "We didn't want to take the approach that we know how to do this. Sometimes, we went there and they were talking about how to negotiate death penalty cases and all this stuff, and at first our reaction was, 'Oh, man, we can win easily,' but sooner or later, you realized that death was different; there was a different way to handle death cases. That was the big mantra, 'Oh, sure, we know better than that,' but we still took the approach, 'We need to learn this.' We even shanghaied some of the experts. We got one guy who was coming to Philadelphia on a civil case, and we got him into a backroom at the White Dog at Penn and sat him down and just picked his brain all night."[30]

Everything the new homicide lawyers were learning pointed to the importance of mitigation in murder cases—how to explain the forces that shaped the defendant, such as childhood sex abuse or mental illness, with the aim of lessening the severity of punishment. "One of the things [the outside trainers] stressed was that you have to work on mitigation from the beginning," Cunningham said. "You don't work on mitigation after the person's been found guilty. You have to work on mitigation from the beginning."[31] The unit started with two mitigation specialists, later increased to four. Sometimes they were able to make a case for mitigation so strong that the defense was able to approach the prosecution before trial and get the charges reduced.[32]

On April 1, 1993, the Defender got its first appointment to represent an indigent murder defendant. When the Defender's homicide team finally got into court, they quickly began compiling a brilliant record. As of mid-2018, no Defender client accused of murder had ever been sentenced to death—in a jurisdiction where prosecutors were well known for zealously seeking the death penalty. However, it was not just success in avoiding death penalties that marked the Defender as a homicide defense trendsetter.

A study by the nonprofit RAND Corporation in 2011, "How Much Difference Does the Lawyer Make? The Effect of Defense Counsel on Murder Case Outcomes," validated the Defender's status as an elite office for homicide defense. The study's authors were James M. Anderson, a behavioral scientist and lawyer who had worked in the Defender's Federal Unit for eight years filing habeas corpus motions on behalf of death row inmates, and Paul Heaton, a RAND economist.[33] They discovered that murder defendants in Philadelphia fared better when represented by the Defender than by court-appointed private attorneys. In an effort to find out why, Anderson and Heaton tracked murder cases in Philadelphia from 1994 to 2005. They found that the "demographics, prior criminal involvement, and observable case characteristics" of defendants represented by court-appointed counsel and those represented by the Defender were about the same.[34] They also found that the guilty rate for the two groups on any charge was similar, about 80 percent. However, Anderson and Heaton found significant differences between the two groups in homicide case outcomes: "Compared to appointed counsel, public defenders in Philadelphia reduce their clients' murder conviction rate by 19 percent and lower the probability that their clients receive a life sentence by 62 percent. Public defenders reduce overall expected time served in prison by 24 percent."[35]

The RAND report highlighted the advantages Defender lawyers had over court-appointed counsel. They were salaried, so they did not have to give any thought to the amount of money they would make. They had the resources of the Defender behind them, so they knew they would have investigators and mitigation specialists to support them. Because they lacked financial incentives to go to trial, Defender lawyers were more likely than private counsel to suggest that their clients plead guilty. Unlike most court-appointed lawyers who had severe time and economic constraints because of the small compensation the courts paid them, Philadelphia's public defenders were free to devote as much time as they needed to engaging clients and their clients' families in repeated and difficult discussions about pleading guilty to avoid a potential death penalty.[36]

It was clear that the resources and incentives of the Defender gave its clients an advantage over those represented by other court appointees. Bookman was not content to write this up as a victory for the Defender but saw it as an issue in need of a remedy. The low fee structure for private court-appointed homicide attorneys led Bookman, who had left the Defender to found the Atlantic Center for Capital Representation, to file a petition with the Pennsylvania Supreme Court in 2011, arguing that inadequate fees were undercutting the efforts of defense lawyers and thus violated the constitutional right of their clients to effective counsel.[37] Court-appointed lawyers in capital cases received a flat fee of two thousand dollars for trial preparation, plus a daily fee of two hundred dollars for less than three hours in court and four hundred dollars for more than four hours, the lowest of any county in Pennsylvania. Co-counsel appointed to deal with the penalty phase received a flat fee of seventeen hundred dollars. Experienced defense lawyers estimated that capital cases actually required a minimum fee of thirty-five thousand to forty thousand dollars. About one-third of the nearly four hundred death penalties imposed in Pennsylvania since the state reintroduced the death penalty in 1978 had been reversed or sent back for retrial by 2011 because of ineffective counsel.[38] The Supreme Court appointed Lerner, by then a common pleas judge, to prepare a report on Bookman's petition.[39] Lerner concluded that the fees were "grossly inadequate."[40] In February 2012, the Philadelphia Court of Common Pleas raised the flat rate for capital murder representation to ten thousand dollars and to seventy-five hundred dollars for co-counsel handling the penalty phase.[41]

The Defender's team approach gave its lawyers a big advantage over court-appointed private attorneys. While most court-appointed attorneys were in solo practice, Defender lawyers were part of a unit whose only job was to defend murder cases. A Defender lawyer was never alone in a murder case; there would always be two lawyers, an investigator, and a mitigator. The RAND study concluded that the Defender, whether intentionally or inadvertently, had adopted an approach to homicide defense—"standardized preparation and a team approach"—that had been shown in other fields to minimize errors and boost efficiency. Defender lawyers were not necessarily better than court-appointed lawyers, but they were better prepared.[42]

The findings of Anderson and Heaton bore out the observations of Defender homicide lawyers on their work. Bookman said that having a unit dedicated solely to defending murder cases was key to the Defender's success. The Defender's experience also showed that "if you applied the ABA guidelines and you took the work seriously, you could avoid death sentences, and that idea has caught on dramatically."[43] From a trial attorney's point of view, having two attorneys working on a case is an enormous advantage, Bookman said. Both lawyers have to work the whole case, "not just one lawyer doing one part and one lawyer doing another. The idea of capital work is to synthesize the first phase, which is the guilt/innocence phase, and the second phase, which is sentencing, to put them together. The idea is to have two lawyers really working the whole case, not delegating it separately. Of course, it worked great."[44]

Having two lawyers also helped with voir dire, the process of examining potential jurors. "Good capital voir dire requires at least two lawyers, sometimes more," Bookman said. "The theory is you want the jury to get to know both lawyers, and you generally want the first phase of the trial to kind of be in sync with the second phase, so if your client had mental health problems, you're going to talk about those mental health problems in the first part of the case. It's called front loading, getting as much information in front of the jury that's going to be relevant to their life-and-death decision as early as you can so that they're more prepared to make this life-and-death decision and save your client's life, if need be."[45] The Defender's two-lawyer approach worked so well that in 2003 the Court of Common Pleas of Philadelphia started appointing two lawyers to every capital case.[46] However, just appointing two lawyers did not guarantee Defender-like success. "Coordination between the pair of appointed lawyers varies," Anderson and Heaton noted.[47]

An important element in the Defender's success at keeping its clients off death row and avoiding life sentences was getting to know the defendant and developing a strong relationship with the defendant's family. Anderson and Heaton emphasized the amount of time Defender lawyers spent "building trust" with the defendant's family. "This trust is important for developing an effective defense, particularly in the penalty phase of a capital case, which often requires the defendant to candidly discuss personal family background, including neglect and abuse," the report explained. "The trust also increases the ability of an attorney to convince a young defendant that the best course of action is to agree to a plea bargain or waive a jury."[48]

The RAND report's findings corroborated Bookman's experience. Homicide defendants can be very difficult clients, especially if they are mentally ill or have been badly traumatized. "Dealing with those clients is an art unto itself," Bookman said. A good defense attorney has to spend a lot of time talking to the client and the family, gaining their trust and exploring the defendant's backstory. The lawyer's goal is to arrive at "a vast understanding, to the point where you can reason with a client about taking a very big number to avoid a death sentence, or life without parole, even." It is hard work, and a lot of lawyers outside the Defender simply will not do it, in Bookman's view: "The reason that bad lawyers get a lot of death sentences is because they can't do what I've just said. They don't have the patience for it, they don't have the time for it, they don't have the resources for it, so at some point, it's easier just to throw up your hands and say, 'Okay, screw it, we're just going to go to trial.' That's not always the best answer."[49]

The Defender's success at defending murder cases depended not simply on the lawyer but on the work of investigators and mitigation specialists assigned to the unit. Mitigation is difficult work because it so often involves dark family secrets. "The real bad stuff is the good stuff in mitigation in capital cases," Conway explained. Some parents don't want to talk about what they did to their kids. Getting them to talk is an art. "Mitigators were good at relationship building," Conway said. "That is hard. The lawyers aren't good at that, generally. It's a whole different mind-set. It's different training; it's a different language, even, between social workers and lawyers. Lawyers need immediate gratification. This is the kind of stuff that takes time. You have to build up a relationship. You have to build up trust. This stuff you can't get just by asking questions."[50]

If anybody doubted the importance of mitigation to a defendant, the case of Abdul Malik El-Shabazz in 2004 made it plain. El-Shabazz, represented by two assistant defenders, was convicted of the rape and murder of six-year-old Destiny Wright. The evidence against him, including DNA evidence, was overwhelming, and El-Shabazz did nothing to help himself when he punched one of his two Defender lawyers in the face during the trial. He might easily have ended up on death row if not for the efforts of Danielle Scott, a Defender social worker and mitigation specialist. Scott told the *Philadelphia City Paper* that she spent at least one thousand hours talking with the twenty-year-old El-Shabazz, working past his deep mistrust of her, and she talked to members of his family more than one hundred times. Working up to fifteen hours a day, she dug deep into his past and found he had been born addicted to heroin, might have been sexually abused as a small child, was frequently in trouble at school, and was controlled by a mentally ill father. The jury split six to six on whether to impose the death penalty, so he got an automatic sentence of life without parole.[51]

Despite all the preparation work that the Defender's homicide lawyers, investigators, and mitigators did, they did not go to trial very often. One of the ways the Homicide Unit kept clients off death row was by avoiding trials. Bookman estimated that in his seventeen years representing homicide defendants, he took only forty to fifty cases to a jury, "a couple a year." While some criticized the Defender for the number of guilty pleas it negotiated, the more cautious approach worked better overall for the clients. Negotiating a plea was not a ploy to avoid capital juries, although juries qualified by the court for capital cases were more likely to convict than other juries, whether they impose a death sentence or not. Plea bargains are the result of "an extremely careful evaluation of the evidence and then an understanding of what a death-qualified jury is likely to do," Bookman explained. "There aren't that many whodunits in capital defense work."[52]

After the Defender had been handling homicide cases for a few years, other public defender offices around the country began to notice that no Defender Association of Philadelphia client had been sentenced to die. "In 1996, 1997, we were going to these national conferences, and national figures knew that we hadn't taken any death sentences," Bookman recalled. "It started to become big news that the Defender hadn't taken any death sentences. After three years, it wasn't maybe such a big deal, but after ten, it was. Some law review articles were written about it."[53] Public defenders from around the country began calling Conway, asking for advice.[54]

The Defender's success in avoiding death sentences was all the more remarkable in light of the Philadelphia district attorney Lynne Abraham's seeming determination to make nearly every murder case a death penalty case. So reflexive was the office's classification of homicides as death penalty cases that the New York Times in 1995 dubbed Abraham "the deadliest D.A." and reported that "no prosecutor in the country uses the death penalty more."[55] As a result of the district attorney's aggressive use of the death penalty, more than half the population of Pennsylvania's death row in the early years of the twenty-first century came from Philadelphia[56]—although no defendant sentenced to death under Abraham had been executed as of 2018.

Dealing with the district attorney's office during Abraham's years was difficult, but not impossible, according to Bookman. Most of the time, classifying a case as capital was a negotiating ploy. In all his years defending homicide cases, from 1993 to 2010, Bookman had only one case in which the district attorney refused to extend an offer of life in prison for a guilty plea, and that was under Abraham's successor, Seth Williams, in a case that involved the killing of two retired police officers. "Every case I ever had under Lynne Abraham, there was at least a life offer," Bookman said. The experience was the same for other Defenders doing homicide cases, except for killings of police.[57]

The Homicide Unit did its job so well that by 2004 the judges of Pennsylvania's First Judicial District, which comprises all the state courts of Philadelphia, were urging the Defender to take on more than the 20 percent of homicide cases they had been handling since 1993. The judges wanted the Defender to double, or nearly double, its homicide caseload to make up for a decline in the number of private attorneys accepting indigent homicide defendant appointments. Common pleas administrative judge James J. Fitzgerald III, a former assistant district attorney in Philadelphia, was the moving force behind the idea,[58] but common pleas president judge Frederica Massiah-Jackson embraced it enthusiastically. "All of our judges have tremendous respect for the Philadelphia public defender office," Massiah-Jackson told the *Philadelphia Inquirer*. "They're a model throughout the common-wealth."[59] However, words of praise got the judges nowhere, despite several years of trying. "The proposal has met resistance from the leadership of the Defender Association," the annual reports of the First Judicial District noted succinctly in 2005.[60]

The problem was money. Greenlee was not about to agree to the expansion unless the city came up with enough money to fund it. She figured that doubling the number of cases would mean doubling the size of the unit, which would mean doubling the unit's annual budget of two million dollars. "We're not going to do any expansion unless it is separately funded," she told the *Inquirer*. "We can't strap other services in order to do more homicide cases."[61] At the request of the First Judicial District, she did ask the city to double the Homicide Unit's budget. Former chief defender Lerner, by now a common pleas judge and the supervisor judge of the court's homicide program, thought that increasing the Defender's homicide budget would be money well spent. He told the *Inquirer* in 2004 that in the previous ten years, not a single Defender homicide case had to be retried on grounds of ineffective counsel, while eighty cases involving court-appointed lawyers were ordered to be retried.[62]

Others thought extra funding for the Defender a bad idea. The district attorney's office opposed giving the Defender more money, especially at a time when Mayor John Street had proposed cutting the district attorney's budget by 7 percent. Ed McCann, head of the district attorney's Homicide Unit, argued that while the Defender's eleven homicide lawyers handled only 20 percent of homicide cases, his nineteen prosecutors handled all the homicide cases.[63]

The leadership of the Philadelphia bar also did not have any enthusiasm for boosting the Defender's budget. George H. Newman, chairman of the Philadelphia Bar Association's Criminal Justice Section, described the Defender's Homicide Unit lawyers as "the elite" but thought that any additional money for indigent defense would be better spent helping court-appointed lawyers comply with ABA standards, as the Defender had done.[64]

In the end, a financially strapped city just did not want to spend as much money as the Defender was proposing. "The feedback we got was that the court experienced sticker shock," Greenlee told the *Philadelphia*

City Paper at the time. "They hoped we'd do it for $1.98 a case. They need to get serious about what representation in capital cases costs."[65]

Still, the idea of an expanded Defender homicide caseload lingered. A few years later, Mayor Michael Nutter's chief of staff, Everett Gillison, a former homicide public defender himself, had the Defender go through the numbers again, but still to no avail. "It did not get off the ground," Greenlee recalled. "There was a lot of talk with the Nutter folks, but no action."[66]

17

TREATMENT COURTS

HOMICIDE DEFENSE may have been the Defender's most dramatic new service in the 1990s, but the organization was expanding in other ways that affected a much larger portion of its clientele. In the late 1990s, the Defender became a major partner with the Philadelphia court system and the district attorney in establishing treatment courts to deal with nonviolent offenders, giving them a chance to straighten out their lives by placing them in rehabilitation programs instead of sending them to jail. It was something the Defender and the district attorney could agree on at a time when they agreed on little else.

In the 1980s and 1990s, jurisdictions across the country began establishing special courts to deal with the glut of drug arrests that were clogging the court systems and filling the prisons, creating the phenomenon of mass incarceration. The prototype was a drug court set up in Miami in 1989 under the leadership of Janet Reno, then the state's attorney for Dade County and later attorney general of the United States.[1] The courts were meant for low-level, nonviolent defendants with a drug dependency. Defendants waived their due process rights in return for the chance to enroll in a treatment program. The driving force behind the courts was research that had discovered that it was better, cheaper, and more effective to rehab drug offenders than to jail them.[2]

Benjamin Lerner had suggested in 1989 that Philadelphia copy the Dade County model. In a speech supporting efforts to relieve jail over-crowding in Philadelphia, Lerner suggested that a "drug crash court" could divert nonviolent, drug-dependent defendants into rehab and job training instead of prison. "You could take the case early—no more than one or two months from the arrest—and either divert it or give the defendants a chance to enter a plea with consent to a drug-treatment plan," he said. "Instead of just building more jail cells, build a facility for drug and alcohol addiction and for serious job training."[3]

Lerner's suggestion got no traction as the war against drugs raged on and drug arrests mounted, but it did not go away either. By the mid-1990s, the courts and even the district attorney's office, which had put so many people in jail, recognized that the swelling prison population was a major problem. Municipal Court president judge Louis J. Presenza wanted to establish a drug court in Philadelphia like the one in Dade County, but he could not do it without the cooperation of the public defenders and prosecutors. Late in 1995, a group that included First Assistant District Attorney Arnold Gordon, a powerful figure in the district attorney's office whose support would be crucial to setting up a drug court, and Defender training and recruitment chief Mary DeFusco traveled to Miami just before Christmas to observe the Dade County court. DeFusco was an accomplished trial lawyer with a commitment to social justice that transcended the courtroom. She joined the Defender in 1982 after graduating from Temple University Law School, and in 1988 Lerner appointed her assistant head of the Municipal Court Unit. Greenlee appointed her head of training in 1995.[4]

At first, DeFusco did not like what she was seeing when the Philadelphia delegation visited a Miami courtroom. A group of prisoners filed in and took up places in the jury box. They were first-time drug offenders who had agreed to waive their rights to a trial so they could enroll in an intensive rehabilitation program under court supervision that would allow them to avoid jail—as long as they complied with the rules set down by the court. The prisoners in the Miami courtroom had not complied with the rules; they had missed earlier court appointments, which were a crucial part of the process. The penalty was a short-term imprisonment, so the judge was about to send them to jail for two weeks, which would keep them behind bars over Christmas. DeFusco's defense attorney instincts told her the prisoners were being railroaded, but then something remarkable happened. One of the female defendants told the judge the prisoners wanted to give him a

Christmas present. This surprised DeFusco, but not as much as what happened next. The female defendant began to sing a hymn, "You Can't Hurry God." Soon all the prisoners were singing.[5]

"They knew they had violated the rules and they would have to do the two weeks," DeFusco said. "They were cool with it." The prisoners were grateful to the judge for helping them turn their lives around, even if they were going to spend Christmas in jail. The visiting lawyers were impressed, some of them moved to tears. "Gordon loved it," DeFusco recalled. He returned to Philadelphia and became a big booster for establishing a treatment court, selling the idea to his boss, Lynne Abraham.[6] The district attorney herself became a big fan of the Drug Treatment Court and argued on the program's behalf when its funding was threatened years later.[7]

Philadelphia Drug Treatment Court opened on April 1, 1997, the first such court in Pennsylvania, with DeFusco as a member of its Oversight Committee. To have their cases transferred to Drug Treatment Court, defendants had to be nonviolent offenders charged with felonies that were drug related or involved theft and who needed treatment. They were not eligible if they were facing any gun-related charges. To be eligible, defendants could not have more than two previous convictions, juvenile delinquency adjudications, or diversions into rehab or education programs as an alternative to prison. The result was that most of those in the program were first-time offenders. If the district attorney's office determined they were eligible, defendants were required to plead nolo contendere, which would be put on hold while they participated in a year-long rehab program and did not get rearrested or use drugs for a year. If they were successful, the nolo contendere plea would be erased. If not, they would go to jail.[8]

DeFusco and George D. Mosee Jr., the deputy district attorney for the Narcotics Unit, acted as gatekeepers, trying to keep the number of cases to a manageable level. They realized that the court's success would depend on not being overwhelmed by numbers. The court's caseload limit was supposed to be three hundred, so DeFusco and Mosee made sure it stayed around that number. "We had a pretty much hard-and-fast rule that it should be about fifty clients per case manager, because if those numbers grew, as they do in probation where you get two hundred fifty clients [per case manager], you don't know what the clients are doing," explained DeFusco. DeFusco went on maternity leave not long after Drug Treatment Court began operations, and Erica Bartlett replaced her as the Defender's drug court representative.[9]

By the time the court marked its twentieth anniversary in 2017, more than thirty-two hundred drug offenders had graduated from the program. "Of those, 92 percent were not convicted of a new crime within a year of graduation and 84 percent remained arrest-free during that same time period," common pleas judge Sheila Woods-Skipper testified before City Council in 2018.[10]

The success of Drug Treatment Court gave rise to other specialty courts within the Philadelphia justice system: Mental Health Court, Veterans Court, DUI Court, Juvenile Drug Court, and one that was the first, and still is among the few, of its kind in the country: Project Dawn Court, which deals with prostitutes. Project Dawn Court was DeFusco's idea, born out of her experience as a public defender representing women accused of prostitution. It exists because DeFusco managed to convince others in the justice system that such a court was necessary. She took as her model the Philadelphia Drug Treatment Court, in which she had been so deeply involved.

Prostitutes make up the second-largest group of women in Philadelphia jails, after those accused of violent offenses. Between 2000 and mid-2018, about nine hundred women from all over Pennsylvania served time at the women's state prison in Muncy for prostitution. "It was a population nobody could seem to do anything with, but something no one felt vindictive about," DeFusco said.[11] Helping prostitutes had become a mission for DeFusco. In 2007, she had joined with three Catholic nuns and Marissa Blustine, a former assistant defender, to create Dawn's Place, a shelter for women victimized by sex trafficking. Dawn's Place was named for a prostitute who had been murdered in Camden, New Jersey. It was also meant to evoke the idea of a new day dawning for women who used the shelter.

DeFusco brought the name "Dawn" from the shelter to the new court that she was proposing. Like the shelter, the court would try to help sex workers break out of prostitution. It would aim its efforts not at first-time offenders but at women who had prior arrests for prostitution and had been unable to shake free of the sex trade. As assistant chief of the Defender's Municipal Court Unit, DeFusco had noticed that the same women were being arrested again and again for prostitution. She concluded that the courts had been taking the wrong approach to dealing with prostitutes because judges and lawyers bought into the common belief that women turn to prostitution to support a drug habit. Even the women themselves would say they had a drug problem, which might have been true for many of them but, in DeFusco's opinion, most often was not the real reason for the prostitution. The way DeFusco saw it, prostitution led to drug abuse, not the other way around.

What DeFusco was observing in Municipal Court convinced her that prostitution actually "was all about sexual trauma. . . . I kept seeing the pattern over and over. For ten years or more, I'm trying to persuade people this is about sexual trauma," she said. The problem was that judges tried to deal with prostitutes by ordering them into drug rehab programs, which did nothing to address the long-lasting effects of sexual abuse. "There was no sexual trauma therapy in Philadelphia," DeFusco said. "There was nothing."[12] As a result, the women ended up back on the street, were arrested again, and went back to jail.

Finally, in 2010, the judges of the First Judicial District agreed to launch Project Dawn Court as a pilot program, with twenty-eight women participating. Going through the program took at least year. Everybody involved, including the judge, becomes part of the defendant's therapy team. Out of the first group of twenty-eight in 2010, 70 percent graduated. "You have to want to change your life if this program is going to work," said one participant. There was no way a defendant could fake her way through it.[13]

DeFusco had been a major participant in launching one specialty court and the driving force behind another, efforts far removed from her work as a trial advocate but nevertheless offering a way out of the justice system to Defender clients—and to others beyond the Defender client base. They were not the only programs the Defender pioneered under Greenlee to help indigents avoid future entanglements with the court system.

18

KEEPING THEM OUT OF JAIL

THE DEFENDER'S LONG-STANDING INTEREST in serving
its clients holistically for the better operation of the justice system led the organization in the direction of other new services
during the Ellen Greenlee years. A principal player in that effort was
Byron Cotter, who had joined the Defender in the early 1970s under
Vincent Ziccardi. Like most new assistant defenders, he wanted more
than anything to be a top trial lawyer, but years of trial work took their
toll: "You try enough back-to-back cases, and your stomach burns out,"
he recalled. "You're awake every night, thinking about what you're
going to say or you didn't say and wondering who on the jury is believing you. There's tremendous pressure."[1]

Fortunately, there was a way out that ended up benefiting Cotter,
the Defender, and thousands of Defender clients. In 1985, the head of
the Defender's Probation and Parole Unit, Len Lieberson, decided to
step down, and Benjamin Lerner named Cotter to replace him. Cotter
expanded the job far beyond its previous parameters. Instead of simply
handling violations of probation cases, Cotter focused on convincing
judges that there were better ways to deal with nonviolent guilty defendants than putting them in jail. He also made it part of his job to help
those who were sentenced to jail get out as soon as possible and try to
smooth their reentry into society.[2]

When Cotter started as probation and parole chief, conditions in Philadelphia's jails had been a matter of concern to the Defender for more than a decade. David Rudovsky, then an assistant defender, filed a habeas corpus petition in state court in 1970 on behalf of two Holmesburg Prison inmates, arguing that conditions in the jail were so bad that being confined there amounted to cruel and unusual punishment. The poor conditions at the jail were alleged to be the result of severe overcrowding. After prevailing in the 1970 case and leaving the Defender for private practice, Rudovsky filed a class-action lawsuit in 1971, again in state court, *Jackson v. Hendrick*, arguing that conditions at Holmesburg still had not improved. In 1982, Martin Harris, who was then in Graterford State Prison but had served time at Holmesburg, joined several Holmesburg inmates to sue the city in U.S. District Court. *Harris v. Pernsley* alleged that overcrowded conditions at the jail violated prisoners' rights under the Eighth and Fourteenth Amendments.[3]

The Defender did not represent the plaintiffs in either of the class-action suits (although Rudovsky did continue to litigate *Jackson* while serving as first assistant defender) but nevertheless ended up having an important connection to *Harris* through Cotter and other Defender personnel who became involved in implementing the lawsuit's remedial decrees.

The U.S. District Court assigned *Harris* to Judge Norma L. Shapiro, who originally declined to hear the case because it covered the same ground as *Jackson*. However, the lawyers for the plaintiffs appealed to the U.S. Court of Appeals for the Third Circuit, which directed Shapiro to proceed; the city appealed that decision to the U.S. Supreme Court, but the justices declined to review the circuit court's decision.[4] Harris's lawyers had the suit amended to include all inmates of Philadelphia city jails, not just Holmesburg. On December 30, 1986, the administration of Mayor W. Wilson Goode agreed to a consent decree, with Shapiro's approval, capping the city's jail population at 3,750. The city also promised to build a new detention center within four years that would ease the overcrowding.[5] Because of various delays, Shapiro did not formally impose the cap until June 1988. At the time the cap took effect, the city's prisons had housed an average of 4,000 inmates.[6] By 1990, despite the cap, it had risen to 5,000 inmates, part of the wave of mass incarceration sweeping a country stoked on fear of crime and determined to punish drug offenders.[7] In March 1991, Shapiro signed a second consent decree, committing the city to building a new prison, adding 250 drug-treatment beds to which inmates were to be diverted instead of prison and finding alternatives to prison for low-level offenders. According to the decree, 175 inmates per week would be nominated for early release.[8]

Cotter became involved in the case because he had gained a reputation as someone who cared about prisoners and was good at finding ways to get them early release. Shortly after Cotter took over the Probation and Parole Unit, some mothers of prisoners in city jails began asking him if he could get their sons and daughters out in time for Christmas. Cotter obliged, using student volunteers at the Defender to write letters to judges, asking them to grant early release to prisoners who were eligible for it. "We started to get a lot of people early parole with this one-page letter," Cotter said. "It worked really well."[9]

Word of the effectiveness of Cotter's Christmas letter-writing program eventually reached City Hall, where Mayor (and former district attorney) Edward G. Rendell, who took office in January 1992, was trying to figure out how to meet the prison cap he inherited from the Goode administration. "They called me up and said, 'We hear you're getting people out early. We want you to do this on a regular basis,'" Cotter recalled. "They said, 'What do you need?' I said I needed drug and alcohol programs that were reliable and were going to be monitored so I could say they were good, excellent programs, state of the art."

Cotter asked Greenlee to let him write up a proposal to have the city fund an early parole project—for the benefit of all prisoners, not just those who were Defender clients—in which Cotter would play a major role. Greenlee gave him the go-ahead, and the city came through with the money. Cotter would work not just with his own staff to get prisoners released but also with the Philadelphia Health Department, the district attorney's office, and the Defender's own Social Service Unit.

Soon, Linda Mathers, director of addictive services for the Philadelphia Department of Parole and Probation, began working with Cotter's group. "It was the first time we had a team concept in the criminal justice system," Cotter recalled. Cooperation became the norm, at least in regard to keeping prison numbers under control. "The D.A. would fight me tooth and nail in the courtroom, but they understood that this could help the clients and help reduce recidivism and would keep the city safer, and that was always my argument: 'It saves the city money, reduces recidivism, but the bottom line is it makes the city safer. The guy gets off drugs; he's not going to rob you or burglarize your house.'"

And if all that was not reason enough for cooperation, Shapiro stood ready to fine the city if it did not decrease the number of prisoners.

Filing early parole petitions was a huge task. Cotter's mission was to get an early release for any nonviolent offender he could, whether or not the person had originally been a Defender client. "I got the prisons to buy into it, to give me adjustment reports from the judges," he recalled. "The problem was, when I started to do it full-time, everybody [with any responsibility for the prisoner] wanted more information, so I had to get adjustment reports, Lock and Tracks [reports from the software system for keeping track of prisoners], court histories, a parole plan, what the client was going to do once he was released."

To help him, Cotter had two staff assistants, Val White and Terri Messing. "The prisons would let Teri and Val—and as my staff increased, my whole staff—go up into the record room and pull the jackets to go through the records to see that time credit was correct, to get the judicial orders, which we had to attach in the petitions. We had carte blanche in that file room, and we knew all the guards in there. We had very close relationships. Correctional officers would call us all the time, and social workers: 'Why aren't you getting John out of jail? This guy is a great guy; he should be out,' so we had a very close working relationship with the prisons. It just blossomed." If "John" happened not to be a Defender client, no problem. Cotter would help all prisoners who did not have a lawyer working on their parole.

Getting prisoners out of jail did not mean simply releasing them into the community; it meant getting them into rehabilitation programs that would help them stay out of jail. But which rehab programs were good? Cotter took it on himself to find out. He did not know much about drug rehab, and he was skeptical about whether drug programs really worked, so he set himself a mission of visiting every drug program doing business with the Philadelphia court system. His visits included private talks with clients to see if they felt the programs were really helping them. What he found was that a lot of the clients really did like the programs and thought they were helpful.

Because Cotter was playing a major role in getting early release for prisoners, he regularly appeared as a witness for the city in hearings before Shapiro. Cotter's thoroughness earned him some scoldings from the judge, who wanted to hear that the prison population was shrinking quickly in accordance with the consent decree. "She would scream at me, 'I want more people out, Byron!' And I said, 'We're going slow because I wanted to visit the programs to make sure.' She said, 'Well, I want you to get one hundred out a week,' and we were getting, like, ten, fifteen. I said, 'We're not ready; we're just not ready.' So I can't go before the judge and tell her, 'Your Honor, let this guy out; we're sending him here' and not have seen it, not feel comfortable with it."

One key to reducing the prison population was to address the issue of how long a judge could take to rule on probation detainers, filed to keep someone in custody who has been arrested for a crime while on probation until the new issue can be resolved. When someone was held on a detainer for violating the terms of probation, a judge would have to decide whether to lift the detainer or keep the defendant in jail, even if the defendant had been acquitted of all other charges. When Cotter became head of Probation and Parole in 1985, defendants waited three or four months behind bars for a resolution of their status. Shapiro asked Cotter to suggest time limits on how long those prisoners could be held. Cotter told Shapiro that the situation was a ridiculous waste of time and that detainer hearings should be held within ten days after a defendant was found not guilty. Shapiro agreed.

In April 1993, Cotter got a new ally in his early-release efforts when Mayor Rendell appointed Dianne Granlund, a former assistant district attorney under Rendell, to be the city's director of criminal justice population management. Granlund told the *Inquirer* that she would cooperate with the Defender in identifying prisoners who could be released. "I hope we all recognize there is a common goal and that it's beneficial for the city to resume control of its own fate," she said.[10] That, however, was not the sentiment Cotter picked up at the beginning of their relationship. Granlund, he said, "first hated me. She finally came around and became a criminal justice partner and was on my side at meetings because she saw that it was right; these people were sitting for no reason at all." The time limits that Cotter suggested had an impact. "In the late nineties, I was probably getting three hundred people released a month because they didn't hit the time limits after the open case was done," Cotter said.

Shapiro finally closed the books on the *Harris* case in 2000, but that was not the end of Cotter's efforts to keep defendants out of jail.[11] In the mid-1990s, Greenlee had given him the title "Director of Alternative Sentencing." It was a job for which Cotter's experience implementing the consent decree in *Harris* had prepared him well. He had learned a lot of things, but perhaps most important, that it was not a good idea to release a prisoner to a rehab program without making sure that prisoner would have a place to stay. Cotter discovered that inmates often faced a catch-22: Being jailed made them homeless, and being homeless made them ineligible for programs that could get them released. "We could get a lot more inmates released both pretrial and after sentencing if they had appropriate housing available," Cotter said. "Inmates don't qualify for alternative programs like electronic monitoring if they're returning to a shelter or to the street. The fact is, the city can't implement alternatives without supportive housing."

Cotter's experience with *Harris* also made clear to him how important it was that his office be well organized. The stakes were too high. "You have to be organized," he said. "If you make a mistake, you hurt a person. If we make a mistake, a guy sits in jail when he doesn't have to. If a judge says, 'Immediate parole upon getting him into a drug treatment program,' you can't just say, 'Okay, you're paroled; go to this program at Tenth and Diamond or something.' A third of our clients don't have a place to go when they're released, so we got housing for them, recovery housing. A lot of judges want inpatient, but we can't afford inpatient, so a recovery house is just as good. Go to treatment during the day, recovery house at night; the recovery house staff is monitoring your urine, so they know you're not high. Those are the things that we learned when we started with Shapiro. She would throw these programs out there, but you have to get a system [for evaluating the programs]. We slowly developed that system, and it works very well."

Cotter's work expanded the Defender's range of concern. Until then, the Defender's involvement with clients usually ended after acquittal or sentencing, except for dealing with appeals and parole violations. That was no longer true. "Trying the case is extremely important, but that's not the end of it," Cotter explained. "Sentencing and reentry and alternative sentences are extremely important and save more people's lives in the end than one case. Some clients win the case, most you lose, and the client would go out in handcuffs. You would never see those clients again; you never get an opportunity to help them."

How long is somebody a client? That is a tough question, according to Cotter: "If a person comes in and asks me for help and he was a former client, I'm going to try to help him. If he's sentenced, and he's given a state sentence of five to ten years, then the parole board can only parole him. I can't enter into it, so we would end there, unless there was a time credit problem. Then I would look into it. When he's paroled, if he violates [parole], we'll step in and help him."

Cotter and his staff—which by 2018 had grown to twenty-five, including five other attorneys—became the advocates for all Defender clients whose cases did not end in acquittal. Their mission was to convince judges to sentence the clients to probation and rehabilitation rather than jail. They tried to get those they could not keep out of jail freed as quickly as the law would allow, with sufficient support for successful reintegration into society. In addition, Cotter and his staff still had the responsibility for representing clients on violations of probation charges, more than sixty thousand a year. Of those, probably forty thousand actually had hearings. Cotter himself averaged between 450 and 550 contacts with clients a month. The lawyers in his unit handled about thirty-four thousand cases a year.

As of mid-2018, the Defender had compiled a list of eighty programs throughout the city and the surrounding counties that it could confidently recommend to the court as alternatives to prison. In addition to steering clients toward drug and alcohol programs, Cotter and his staff began working with other programs, such as "New Leash on Life," a prison dog-training program that trained prisoners to care for dogs rescued from shelters.[12] After parole, many of the inmates used the training to find paid internships in animal care. Cotter's group also collaborated with the Pennsylvania Horticultural Society on a program called "Roots to Re-entry," designed to provide inmates with the skills they needed to find work in the landscape and horticulture industries after release.[13]

The Defender joined forces with the University of Pennsylvania School of Social Policy and Practice in the Goldring Reentry Initiative (GRI), a program that Penn began in 2011 to help prisoners overcome the obstacles they encountered when returning to life outside prison. Students pursuing a master's degree in social work at Penn met with Cotter and his staff to select about one hundred clients to participate in GRI each year. The grad students worked with the program participants for six months: three months while the clients were still behind prison walls and three months after they were released. Once the GRI student and the client agreed to a discharge plan, the Defender acted as the mediator between GRI, the district attorney, and the sentencing judge. GRI credited the Defender with playing "a crucial role [in GRI programs]; their support and guidance are integral to our success."[14] The collaboration has been "very effective," Cotter said.

Cotter and his staff became significant figures for Philadelphia's prisoners. They kept track of every prisoner's time served, whether a Defender client or not, and made sure that no prisoner served too much time by getting lost in the system. "I work with any client where the private attorney is not working on their parole," Cotter said. "If a client gets eleven and a half to twenty-three [months], I'm looking to get that client out within six months," Cotter said. "I'm trying to get him out at half."

Cotter and his team handled about three thousand calls a month from prisoners—or the families of prisoners—seeking their help. The courts sent every sentencing order to Cotter's team, who entered it into the Defender's case management system. Cotter's staff then checked the docket to see whether the prisoner had a lawyer working on parole. If not, the Defender became the prisoner's lawyer. "We have three people we call communicators review these sentencing orders and then write to the client," Cotter said. "They review what the judge said, like 'I want him to do anger management; I want him to do this or that,' and we try to make sure he does what the judge wanted him to do behind the walls. We'll also communicate with the prison social workers to make sure they're on track. We'll write to the client and tell him what to do and ask the client to send us back this parole plan form. We also ask for what they call 'an adjustment report' from the prison to make sure that the prison social worker is recommending early parole also."

So important a part of the prisoner release process did Cotter become that he and his staff were listed in the prison system's "Inmate Handbook," as if they were employees of the prison system. If prisoners were held in jail because of detainers filed against them for technical violations of probation, the handbook informed them that Cotter's office would seek to have the detainer lifted. They were supposed to contact Cotter if they did not have a hearing on their detainer within the prescribed time: ten days from the time the detainer was lodged or thirty days for a second hearing if the detainer was not lifted at the first hearing.[15] The handbook also informed prisoners that Cotter and his staff would send them a letter within forty-five days of sentencing. "All sentenced inmates will receive this letter," the handbook assured them. Cotter's office would review every inmate's record and decide whether early parole or work release was advisable.[16] Cotter became well known among the prison population. "I get people out of jail, so I'm known," he said. "I'll go inside and talk to a whole block about early parole, drug treatment."

While the tension may not have been the same as being on trial, Cotter and his staff still face tension from their work. "We now have a detainer hotline, where a client can just call and say, 'I haven't had my hearing,' and now throughout the prison, they all know the time frames," Cotter said. By mid-2018, only ten inmates a month, at most, did not have detainer hearings within the required time, thanks to the vigilance of Cotter and his staff. "The biggest complaint I get [from staffers] is, 'Byron, I can't sleep at night because I wake up at three in the morning and think, "I forgot to do this for John Doe."' I do the same thing; I keep a pad, and now I keep my cell phone and email near. You couldn't go back to sleep because you know you'll forget it in the morning, and my whole staff does that."

By 2018, Cotter could look with satisfaction at what his unit had accomplished since Lerner named him to head the Probation and Parole Unit more than thirty years earlier. More defendants were being diverted to rehabilitation or probation. Sentences were more enlightened. Judges were more likely to listen to arguments for diversion. "It's the new thinking," Cotter reflected. "The judge-run programs without probation are the best because the judge becomes the parental figure in the client's life, either the mother or father. The clients will say, 'I don't want to upset the judge, my judge.' The recidivism rate in these programs is much lower. It's totally different than what I thought about when I started, but it's made me stay."

It also brought Cotter something that Defender lawyers were not used to getting: expressions of gratitude from clients and from their families. "I got so much contact from the parents thanking me," he said. "That makes an impression on you. And slowly the clients would come back and thank me. It's why I continue to work. I love what I do. I tried one hundred jury trials. You won the case, maybe you get a thank you, and then they walk out the door; you never see them again. These clients, I see them once they get in prison, and then I follow them. They come in five years later, or they'll see me on the street, and they'll thank you. I have thank-you letters. I never got a card in my life for winning a jury trial. Every day, I get an opportunity to help someone. You don't know how happy that makes me. All my staff knows if you don't feel that way, you don't work with me."

19

JUVENILE DEFENDERS AND
CHILD ADVOCATES

ROBERT LISTENBEE JR., like Byron Cotter, joined the Defender to try criminal cases. And like Cotter, Listenbee became more interested in changing lives than in trying cases. While Cotter concentrated on alternative sentencing and getting people out of jail, Listenbee would find his niche in the Juvenile Unit. The Defender hired Listenbee in 1986, and like other Defender newcomers, he went through the rotation that would take him to every area of the Defender's practice, including Juvenile. After three years and about a dozen jury trials, Listenbee wanted to go back to Juvenile: "It's the one place where you can do something on any given day that could change the life of a child," he said.[1] He remained with the Juvenile Unit until 2013, when President Barack Obama named him to be administrator of the U.S. Justice Department's Office of Juvenile Justice and Delinquency Prevention, a position he held until the end of the Obama administration in January 2017.

Juveniles have been part of the Defender Association's client base since its earliest days. The Defender's mission, as laid out in its charter in 1934, was to represent indigents charged with crime and juvenile delinquency, but until 1968, the bulk of the Defender's practice was in adult court. That changed in the wake of the U.S. Supreme Court ruling in May 1967 in the case *In re Gault* that juvenile criminal defendants were entitled to the same representation and procedural protections as adults.[2] And, like adults, they had a right to free counsel if they were indigent. That meant the states—or, in Pennsylvania's case, the counties—would have to expand their responsibility for providing indigent defense to juveniles.

In Philadelphia, representation of juveniles became another issue in the back and forth between the city and the Defender over funding in the late 1960s. In July 1968, Acting Chief Defender Martin Vinikoor said that the Defender Association would take over representation of juveniles accused of crime if the city would agree to provide $300,000 annually.[3] Community Legal Services (CLS), a program funded by Congress, had been representing juveniles, but Congress ordered CLS to end all criminal representation, adult and juvenile, by September 1, 1968. That meant the city would have to find someone else to represent juveniles charged with crime. The Philadelphia Bar Association recommended that the city turn the task over to the Defender. That idea also had the support of Judge Frank J. Montemuro Jr., one of five judges then hearing juvenile cases. Montemuro warned that Juvenile Court might have to shut down if the city could not get the Defender involved. The judge believed that appointing private attorneys to represent indigent juveniles would be too expensive. He reckoned that the private attorneys would cost the city $22 million, while the Defender could handle the same work for $350,000.[4]

The math was persuasive, and representation became part of the deal between the city and the Defender. The contract with the city took effect in January 1969, and the Defender began representing juveniles on March 10, 1969. The new unit was staffed by the four former CLS lawyers who had handled juvenile cases, led by Paula Gold, a graduate of New York University Law School who had worked for the district attorney's office for four years, becoming chief of the Family Court Division before she joined CLS in April 1968.[5] She would later earn a master's degree in sociology from Temple University.[6] Newspaper articles described Gold as having a "fiery" disposition,[7] and her passion for juvenile justice could lead her to emotional public critiques of Family Court judges. At a law fraternity gathering honoring three retiring judges in 1969, Gold declared that Philadelphia's Juvenile Court needed better-qualified judges and that the attitude at Juvenile Court was one of "pushing kids around, punishing them instead of helping them."[8]

While the Defender was representing an increasing number of minors facing criminal charges, it also began representing children in dependency cases, in which the child had not committed a crime but was often a victim and in which it needed to be determined whether it was in the best interest of the child to remain at home or be removed from the family. A new Defender department, the Child Advocacy Unit, created in 1976, handled dependency cases under the leadership of Alice Margaret "Peg" O'Shea, who had passed the bar a quarter of a century after finishing law school and taken up the cause of protecting dependent children. Politically well connected—her husband, John J. O'Shea, had been treasurer of the Philadelphia Democratic City Committee— she put together a pilot project in 1974 with a $107,000 federal grant, supplemented by $26,000 from the state and Philadelphia Family Court, to provide independent counsel for neglected children and children whose parents had nominated them to donate organs to a sibling. It was the first such unit in the United States, and Family Court judge Nicholas Cipriani, who helped O'Shea set up the project, described her as a "pioneer." In 1975, *Family Circle* magazine named her one of twenty-five Americans who changed a community for the better.[9]

O'Shea's child advocacy group, which was not yet part of the Defender, had a staff of two lawyers, a social worker, and a secretary. When the federal funding ran out, city officials asked the Defender to give the unit a home. Lerner agreed, and the O'Shea project became the Defender's Child Advocacy Unit (CAU), operating independently of the Juvenile Unit. With the arrival of CAU, the Defender added civil law to its practice, a move none of the Defender's original incorporators ever anticipated.[10] Peg O'Shea remained head of the CAU through 1981. "She was a tough-minded, tenacious Irish grandmother who didn't shrink from standing up for children," Ellen Greenlee said when O'Shea died in 2005.[11]

The CAU grew under the Defender, and its importance became clear when the American Civil Liberties Union and the Juvenile Law Center, a nonprofit, public-interest law firm for youth in the justice and welfare systems, filed a class-action lawsuit against the city of Philadelphia and its Family Court in U.S. District Court in 1989. The suit asked that all children in dependency proceedings be guaranteed counsel, alleging that children were being put at risk when they were assigned to foster homes or institutions without the help of a lawyer. The plaintiffs contended that four thousand of the five thousand minors then under the supervision of the welfare system were not being represented by counsel. The city responded that it did not have to appoint lawyers because the social workers from the Department of Human Services (DHS) would be the children's advocates. Nevertheless, in April 1990, the city—while still arguing that it had no obligation to guarantee each child a lawyer—agreed to a settlement that did just that. Under the terms of the settlement, each child under the care of DHS would be represented by a lawyer from the CAU. The city would increase the Defender's funding, then $700,000 a year, by $200,000 for the following four years, bringing it to $1.5 million by mid-1993. The Defender would double the number of its CAU lawyers to represent all the children in the welfare system—about eight thousand at the time.[12]

Eventually, Child Advocacy would grow into one of the Defender's largest units, with as many as seventy-six hundred clients. By 2015, at the end of Greenlee's term as chief defender, the CAU included twenty-six lawyers and forty social workers. Every case was assigned a social worker. Administrative staff brought the total number of personnel working in the unit to more than seventy.[13] The CAU's early days with the Defender were much smoother than the Juvenile Unit's. As it began operations, the Juvenile Unit had to overcome some obstacles that went beyond Gold's penchant for poking judges. The unit initially had to limit the number of appointments it could accept. However, the Defender quickly added more lawyers until, by mid-1970, there were twelve. As a result, the unit was able to handle sixty-five hundred cases—85 percent of the city's juvenile defendants—in its first year of operation.[14]

The work environment was not especially pleasant: two small rooms in the cavernous Family Court building at 1801 Vine Street. The offices—one of them thirty by twenty feet and the other twenty by twenty feet—were located at either end of a long corridor. They were so small and crowded that it was nearly impossible to accomplish much there. By the early 1970s, the two rooms were used by ten to twelve attorneys, seven social workers, five investigators, and eight or nine secretaries, augmented occasionally by twenty student volunteers from Bryn Mawr College. Lawyers not working in one of the building's five courtrooms were supposed to be conducting interviews, either in the office or at the nearby Youth Study Center, where juveniles were held.[15]

Some of those lawyers were less than enthusiastic about being assigned to Juvenile. Experienced attorneys viewed the unit as the Defender version of Siberia and being assigned there as a form of punishment; young lawyers thought of it as spending time in the minor leagues on the way to the majors, an easy post until a better opportunity came along. NLADA's 1971 evaluation of the Defender found that supervision in Juvenile was lax and staff lawyers were "openly critical" of their supervisors. The study also found that while the lawyers were capable, none seemed to know much about developments in constitutional law that affected juveniles. The unit seemed disorganized, with staff frequently sitting around as if they had nothing to do, especially after two o'clock in the afternoon. Disdain for the assignment itself and for the supervision created a morale problem in the Juvenile Unit. As a result, NLADA evaluators found that "the juvenile office exhibits a non-professional attitude and inefficiency."[16]

The evaluators suggested that the Defender could do better by assigning one lawyer to each of four Family Court courtrooms, three more to the pretrial courtroom, and three to special litigation. They recommended that Defender social workers expand their focus beyond runaways and truants and continue to work with clients after the disposition of the case instead of ceding responsibility to probation officials. NLADA also recommended that the Juvenile Unit move to larger quarters. The offices were too crowded, and there were not enough desks. "The appearance is that of wall-to-wall people," the evaluators concluded. "Under such circumstances, no law office can operate efficiently."[17]

The NLADA team also found a flaw in the relationship between lawyers and social workers in Juvenile. The Defender recognized early on that social workers would play an important role in Juvenile and that their young clients had different social-service needs from those of adult clients. Some of the offenses juveniles were charged with were unique to their status as minors, such as incorrigibility, truancy, and running away. Juvenile Unit social workers, often at the order of the court, investigated the charges and made recommendations for dealing with them after researching the young client's court records and consulting with social-service agencies, school officials, and the family. As part of preparing a recommendation for treatment, the Defender social workers sometimes brought the child and the family in for counseling. However, the evaluators concluded that the social workers were operating "too independently of the lawyers" and recommended closer collaboration.[18]

Even so, the Juvenile Unit elicited some praise from the NLADA study, which concluded that its representation was "as competent as any in the country."[19] This was faint praise because juvenile justice in America was changing rapidly, discarding a paternalistic approach in favor of due process and access to counsel, as the U.S. Supreme Court required in *Gault*. Philadelphia may have had problems, but NLADA thought Philadelphia was dealing with them better than other cities.

Local press coverage of the unit was more enthusiastic than NLADA had been. An article in the *Philadelphia Inquirer* in October 1970 described the unit's work as "aggressive" and "hard-hitting."[20] Defender leadership made an effort to solve the supervision problem by transferring Gold out of the unit on October 19, 1970. Vincent Ziccardi, who had just been named chief defender the previous month after serving as acting chief for more than a year, said he was transferring Gold in an effort to standardize procedures. He said he was not happy with the unit's filing and office procedures. Gold claimed that the transfer amounted to firing because the Juvenile Unit was her sole area of interest.[21] She left the Defender soon afterward. The Juvenile Unit would have several leaders over the next decade and would grow, adding lawyers, social workers, psychologists, and support staff, but the Defender's juvenile representation really took off in the 1980s under the leadership of Darnell Jones.

In 1984, Benjamin Lerner appointed Jones, who had been one of the Defender's preeminent trial lawyers, to be assistant chief in the Juvenile Unit and then quickly promoted him to chief. "I put Darnell in because I wanted 'oomph' in the unit," Lerner said. Jones's "oomph" plus the quality of the Defender's training program raised the Defender's level of juvenile representation to the same quality that adult clients were getting. Lerner also wanted Jones to make the Defender's voice heard in the community discussion that was developing around juvenile justice reform. Jones did just that, speaking frequently to and quoted by reporters, speaking out on behalf of a probation program that would keep juvenile offenders from Philadelphia from being sent to state institutions, questioning the methods of a prominent delinquency program, blaming increased incarceration of minors on the demands of a public determined to punish juveniles, and criticizing the juvenile justice system for holding children with mental health problems in detention instead of getting help for them quickly. "He did a pretty spectacular job with it," Lerner said.[22]

Jones left the Defender in 1987 when Governor Bob Casey Sr. appointed him to the Philadelphia Court of Common Pleas bench.[23] Jones was succeeded first by Gerald Stanshine and then in 1991 by Mingo Stroeber. The unit continued to grow. By 1989, it numbered seventeen lawyers (including Listenbee, who had returned to the unit for good from his rotation among the units), two interns, and five social workers.[24] In addition, the Defender had created a new Juvenile Special Defense Unit the year before, with the aid of federal funding, to deal with the most serious and complicated cases, including those in which the district attorney was attempting to have a defendant charged as an adult rather than a juvenile. "In handling those juvenile special defense cases, every child had a social worker, and we hired a psychologist in every case to do a report on the kid to try to get him out of the adult system," Greenlee said. "We got more than fifty percent of the kids sent back to Juvenile [Court]. That was a significant achievement."[25] The Juvenile Special Defense Unit was also the first step in a process of specialization that continued after Listenbee returned.

Listenbee was named assistant chief of the unit in 1992, replacing Stroeber, who had become the chief. At that time, each lawyer in the unit was handling a mix of serious and routine cases while contending with the legal requirement that juvenile cases in Pennsylvania be disposed of within ten days. The ten-day rule was honored in the breach and was more likely to stretch to twenty days, but that was little relief for lawyers who might be dealing with thirty or forty cases at a time. If those cases included any that involved rape; aggravated or indecent assault; armed robbery, especially if a gun was involved; or attempted homicide, the lawyer would not have much time for the less serious cases. In a new approach, which the Juvenile Unit leadership worked out in conversations with Greenlee, the unit moved to a new level of specialization. Some assistant defenders would handle only certain kinds of charges. One might take all the cases in which someone was shot, another all the cases in which someone was raped, and a third all the cases in which someone was paralyzed. Lawyers would be assigned to those cases from the very beginning and stay with them all the way through the process rather than simply handling any case on the docket in whichever courtroom they were assigned. Specialized assignment raised the level of representation, according to Listenbee. And it allowed the more experienced lawyers in Juvenile to handle some of the cases that had been going to Juvenile Special Defense, taking some of the pressure off that unit.[26]

The Juvenile Unit also began to focus on raising the level of investigation. Previously, much of the Defender's investigation work had centered on adult court, and there was no specialized investigation effort for the Juvenile Unit. In the late 1980s and early 1990s, lawyers from the Juvenile Unit began working more closely with investigators, assigning them to find witnesses and generally do the sorts of things that they would do for an adult criminal case but had not been doing for juveniles. "Our standard was we wanted to be better than anybody in the city and have as good a preparation in legal representation as what happened in any adult case, so using that standard, we began to transform the unit," Listenbee said.[27]

Enthusiasm of Defender lawyers for working in the Juvenile Unit had grown, but not because the work was easy. Far from it, as Charles Cunningham, Greenlee's first assistant, explained. Some lawyers are better than others at building rapport with children, and there were parents to deal with. "Your duty is to the child, not to the parents," Cunningham said. "As a matter of fact, many times I asked the parent to leave the room because I wanted to be able to have a free conversation with the kid, and I wanted him or her to know that whatever [the child] told me, I wasn't necessarily going to go back and tell the parents. That is without a doubt a question that would come up, and in the end the answer is that you are responsible for the child; you are his or her attorney and only his or her attorney."[28]

In an adult case, the lawyer's goal was simple: get the client off or at least spared from going to jail. In a juvenile case, things were not so clear. The lawyer might be able to win a motion to suppress evidence and get the young defendant off, but what kind of lesson would the defendant take away from that? "Will he figure he can do whatever he wants as long as he has a smart enough lawyer?" Cunningham asked. "Those are questions that I found myself asking when I was in the juvenile rotation that I didn't ask myself when I was on the adult side." The only answer he could come up with was that he had done his job as a lawyer and hoped things would work out well for the youngster. However, he also could rely on the Juvenile Unit's social workers to help steer juvenile clients away from future trouble.[29]

One of the more difficult aspects of working in Juvenile was that it could sometimes involve representing adults accused of violence toward children. Juvenile Court was only one branch of the Family Division of the Court of Common Pleas in Philadelphia. There were two others: Orphans' Court, which dealt with wills, estates, and trusts and thus was out of the Defender's purview, and Domestic Relations, which dealt with domestic violence, among other things, and was very much in the Defender's purview. In addition to representing minors, the Defender had to represent indigent adults charged with a crime of violence when the complainant was a child. Those cases were heard in Courtroom B of the Family Division, and some assistant defenders tried to avoid being assigned there. An assistant defender working in Courtroom B might end up defending someone who had done horrible things to a child. Listenbee once had to defend a client who was charged with using a cigarette to burn a little girl's back. "A little girl, just like my little daughters, and I had to figure out how to defend my client," Listenbee said. "How do I reduce the charges so that he has a chance of getting out of jail one day? That's my job. It's not pretty. How do I try and talk to the little girl as I cross-examine her in a way so that she says things that are beneficial to my client? That's what we do; that's the job of a criminal defense attorney. It's not pleasant. It's not nice and kind, but that's what our job was."[30]

Another courtroom that some assistant defenders would have preferred to avoid was the so-called Love Court, where domestic abuse cases were heard. The Defender was responsible for representing defendants accused of domestic violence. "We'd go in there and represent the guys that were beating up their wives," Listenbee said. "I hated to go there."[31]

In 1997, Listenbee became chief of the Juvenile Unit, succeeding Stroeber. Listenbee's work as unit chief would be greatly and unexpectedly influenced by a lawyer from outside the Defender Association—George Mosee Jr., the deputy district attorney overseeing juvenile cases. Mosee became chief of the district attorney's Juvenile Unit in 2002. He was already well regarded at the Defender because of his work with Mary DeFusco in Drug Treatment Court, and he and Listenbee began to cooperate on improving some of the practices in juvenile justice. Mosee made the first move. Listenbee was devoting the bulk of his time to trying cases, but Mosee thought the quality of the juvenile justice system would be improved if he and Listenbee worked together. In 2004, Mosee approached Greenlee and asked that she free up Listenbee to spend more of his time working with Mosee on reshaping juvenile justice in Philadelphia. Greenlee, who trusted Mosee, agreed. "Now think about that," Listenbee said. "The prosecutor is coming to my boss to get her to tell me how to work with him." Listenbee agreed. He and Mosee became a juvenile reform team.[32]

Mosee wanted to see a juvenile drug court established, something that Listenbee had been trying to do unsuccessfully for several years. Working together, Listenbee and Mosee got it done, with the help of strong backing from Judge Myrna Field, then the administrative judge of the Family Division. Field took a personal interest in the juveniles who were appearing in court. She also insisted that a school district representative come to court to help keep track of the educational credits juvenile defendants were getting in whatever program they were placed so they could graduate from high school. "She had the educational representative going out to the high school, working with the kids on papers to make sure that they got their papers done so that they could graduate," Listenbee said. He described Field, who died in 2007 of a rare blood disorder, as "a phenomenal person."[33]

The drug court that Listenbee, Mosee, and Field created made it possible for juveniles charged with felony drug offenses to get appropriate treatment as an inpatient or outpatient. After the juvenile's successful treatment, the case would be discharged and the records expunged. (Several years later, when Listenbee began working at the U.S. Justice Department, he found that there were 450 juvenile drug treatment courts across the country, but they "were very poorly run, and they were not achieving very good results." Based on his experience setting up the juvenile drug treatment program in Philadelphia, Listenbee was able to restructure the entire drug treatment court system nationally and produce better results.)[34]

Listenbee and Mosee also began to focus on diversion, finding ways to deal with juvenile offenders other than locking them up. Mosee began agreeing to consent decrees, which placed an allegedly delinquent juvenile under the supervision of a juvenile probation officer as an alternative to adjudication. The juvenile was spared the possible stigma that goes with being judged delinquent. The district attorney and the Defender also worked on expunging juvenile records. "What's significant about that is that we would work through and come up with a list of maybe fifty to one hundred cases," Listenbee said. "We would go to court and the D.A.'s office, under George's direction, would look at them in advance, and by the time we got to court, we could handle a list of fifty to one hundred cases in half an hour."[35] Judges responded positively to the changes because it helped them close cases more quickly. "Their stats were going up dramatically," Listenbee said.[36]

As part of their effort to improve juvenile justice, Listenbee and Mosee tried to improve relations between police and teenagers. They started by organizing programs that would bring together police, probation officers, social workers, and adolescents, first at a hotel and later at the Bible Way Baptist Church on Fifty-Second Street in West Philadelphia. Listenbee and Mosee used the conversations as a basis for a one-day curriculum on cops-kids relations that they taught at the Philadelphia Police Academy. In 2008, every new class of police recruits began taking the curriculum, which included material on adolescent development, childhood trauma, and trauma-informed care to police officers. The program also brought juveniles to the academy to tell their stories to the police in training. In response, the recruits were asked to tell the youngsters about their fears and anxieties. The sessions even included role-playing. The curriculum was so successful that Listenbee and Mosee used it to develop a nonprofit corporation, the Pennsylvania DMC Youth Law Incorporation, funded by the Pennsylvania Commission on Crime and Delinquency. The organization's mission, according to its brochure, was "to eliminate the overrepresentation of youth of color in the Pennsylvania juvenile justice system by advocating strategies for policy changes, education programs, funding and technical assistance at the local and state levels." To carry out that mission, the organization conducted forums in southeastern Pennsylvania, Harrisburg, Lancaster, Reading, Allegheny County, and even Florida.[37]

Listenbee's efforts to educate police about juveniles was not always easy, but he persisted. In 2005, the International Association of Chiefs of Police (IACP) invited him to speak about developing a curriculum for them. He consulted Greenlee, who encouraged him to go. When he walked into the room, "everybody turned their head." He figured that they did not want him there, but even so, he won them over. IACP named him a consultant on juvenile training, and he implemented the Philadelphia curriculum throughout the country. Over the next decade, Listenbee would help train thousands of police officers through the IACP.[38]

Listenbee gave credit to Greenlee for much of his success in Juvenile. "What Ellen did was meet with me, usually for about half an hour or forty-five minutes, two to three times a week," he said. "It came out to over a thousand meetings. That was how I came to work effectively. I knew what she wanted me to do." In 2012, when U.S. attorney general Eric Holder called Listenbee and asked him to be cochair, along with New York Yankees manager Joe Torre, of the National Task Force on Children Exposed to Violence, Listenbee was taken aback. "I took a big swallow," he said, but Greenlee told him to go ahead, saying, "It's a good idea." Greenlee told him to serve. When the first draft of the thirteen-member committee's report seemed inadequate and a deadline loomed, Listenbee went to Greenlee for advice, and she told him to use whatever Defender resources he needed to get the report done on time. Listenbee asked that the Juvenile Unit's policy analyst, Rhonda McKitten, be detached to work with him. Greenlee agreed and even sent McKitten to Los Angeles, where the committee was based, to work on the report for several weeks. "None of that stuff was stuff that other public defenders were doing," Listenbee said. The 256-page report was released in December 2012. The report's fifty-six recommendations charted a pathway for federal, state, and local governments to reduce children's exposure to violence, which research showed hampered their development.[39]

The work the Defenders did on the report raised the association's national reputation even more, but that was not the purpose. "It helped kids," Greenlee said. "It helped the representation of children. It wasn't so much that it highlighted our office or Bob's national profile. It all looked toward elevating the representation of children who were caught up in the system."[40]

The Defender fought the George W. Bush administration's effort to have juvenile sex offenders register. Greenlee authorized policy analyst Nicole Pittman to travel across the country to talk about why juvenile sex offender registration was not a good idea. Pittman and her assistant, Quyen Nguyen, also compiled a book-length survey, *A Snapshot of Juvenile Sex Offender Registration and Notification Laws*, on what registration looked like from state to state. "This was the only publication of its type in the nation that was like that," Listenbee said. "We shared it with people all over the country and said, 'This is what you need to be doing; this is what you need to know about representation in your state and how you need to follow through.' We set some national standards on that."[41] The Pennsylvania Supreme Court ruled in 2014 that juvenile sex offender registration was unconstitutional because the requirement of lifetime registration violated the due process clause of the Fourteenth Amendment. The court also pointed out that "juvenile sexual offenders exhibit low levels of recidivism." Two Defender lawyers were part of the legal team that argued the case.[42]

The Juvenile Unit also fought to shield young defendants from Pennsylvania's Act 21, which makes every child accused of a sex offense subject to the possibility of civil commitment to a mental health facility in western Pennsylvania. Act 21, passed in 2003, is aimed at juvenile sex offenders who have aged out of the juvenile justice system but have a "mental abnormality" that makes them unable to control violent sexual impulses. Under Act 21, such offenders must be referred to the Pennsylvania Sexual Offenders Assessment Board ninety days before their twentieth birthday. The board determines whether the offender has "serious difficulty in controlling sexually violent behavior." If the board concludes the person does have difficulty with control, then a mental health hearing will determine whether to commit the offender to the Sexual Responsibility and Treatment Program at Torrance State Hospital in Westmoreland County.[43]

The Defender has fought Act 21 as unduly harsh and punitive because it subjects minors to the prospect of indefinite confinement beyond their twenty-first birthday, along with the possibility of being listed on a registry of sex offenders for life. Those who go into the program do not get out easily, according to Listenbee. The commitment is renewable yearly, for an indefinite number of years, and the patients stay well beyond their twenty-first birthday. The Defender has fought hard to keep its clients from being assigned to the program, and none had gone there as of mid-2018. "We litigated it," Listenbee said. "We'd hire experts from other parts of the country to come in and litigate the civil commitment of a child, and we won, over and over and over again, because we had our best lawyers and we focused on it."[44]

The Juvenile Unit under Listenbee developed a special subunit that focused on sex assault cases and found ways to have charges against juvenile defendants changed so juveniles would not have to register as sex offenders, which public defenders regarded a violation of due process because it predicted a likelihood of future offense without evidence. Defender lawyers negotiated with prosecutors to get their clients placed in "carve-outs" that would not require registration. "We could put them in misdemeanor sex assaults, so that typically they didn't have to register, and certain kinds of felony sex assaults didn't have to register," Listenbee said.[45]

The Juvenile Unit took the Defender's preoccupation with training one step further, establishing a training program of its own for lawyers joining the team as juvenile advocates. "We did a notebook on how to handle juvenile cases, a two hundred–page, in-depth notebook, which we spent two hundred thousand dollars developing," Listenbee said. "There [are] only two of them in the whole nation. The notebook had every nuance of the juvenile practice, and it had the three hundred most frequently used cases, which we put on a disc. It had resources for all sixty-seven counties in Pennsylvania."[46]

The purpose of the notebook and disc was to build up the practice of juvenile defense all across Pennsylvania. Any lawyer representing a juvenile anywhere across Pennsylvania "would then be able to use that notebook. You could just pull it up at night because we had a flash drive, you put it in, and you could prepare your cases on your computer at home, file your motions the next morning in court. And we did a lot of training, starting in 2004, across the state. There's nobody we know who has done this. There's nobody who has done it nationally."[47]

One of the challenges the Juvenile Unit faced under Listenbee was a wave of sentiment across the country that began in the mid-1990s to impose more severe punishments on juveniles, especially on those deemed to be superpredators—thought to be incorrigible and ruthless juvenile criminals who would continue to prey on society once they reached adulthood. The thinking was that they had to be tried and punished as adults, even if they were still minors. The result was a wave of legislation throughout the United States that allowed prosecutors to file charges against minors directly in adult court without going through juvenile court.[48] The Defender found the practice of direct file abhorrent. "We were getting five hundred, six hundred direct-file cases a year," Listenbee said. "There were enormous numbers. There were four hundred, maybe five hundred, six hundred new direct-file cases—felony cases where there was violence involved: aggravated assault, attempted murder, rape with weapons. All those cases were direct file." In response, Greenlee converted the Special Defense Unit to the Direct-File Unit, staffing it with top-flight lawyers and adding an important psychological component: Every child had to have an in-depth psychological evaluation. The psychological exam meant spending thousands and thousands of dollars, and Philadelphia may have been the only public defender office in the country to take that course. It was another element in making the Defender's juvenile justice program cutting edge.[49]

Listenbee's innovative leadership of the Juvenile Unit led to his appointment (along with Mosee of the district attorney's office) to the Interbranch Commission on Juvenile Justice, set up by the state government in August 2009 to address the "Kids for Cash" scandal in Luzerne County. Two judges there had been pressuring juveniles to waive their rights to counsel and plead guilty to whatever charges, often petty, had been filed against them. The judges then steered the young defendants into one of two for-profit detention facilities in return for kickbacks from the owners. Both judges were tried for their actions in federal court and sentenced to long prison terms. The task of the Interbranch Commission was to find out what went wrong and suggest ways of keeping it from ever happening again, not just in Luzerne County but throughout Pennsylvania.[50]

Listenbee was an active member of the panel, according to Darren Breslin, an attorney on the staff of the Administrative Office of Pennsylvania Courts who worked with the Interbranch Commission. "The interplay between him and George [Mosee] was fantastic and vital to the report," Breslin recalled. "Bob took the laboring oar on some of the [commission's] recommendations, notably those dealing with defense counsel." Recommendation G of the group's final report declared that "all juveniles should be deemed indigent for the purposes of appointment of counsel."[51] The Pennsylvania Supreme Court made that requirement part of the "Rules of Juvenile Court Procedure" in Pennsylvania. It meant that all juveniles were entitled to free counsel and did not have to rely on their parents to hire a private attorney for them. Since parents no longer had the leverage that footing the bill brings, it also meant that decisions would be made by the lawyer and the juvenile, not by the lawyer and the parents. "That was a huge step," Greenlee said.[52]

Listenbee's accomplishments did not go unnoticed. Before Obama tapped him for the Justice Department post, the John D. and Catherine T. MacArthur Foundation in 2011 honored Listenbee with a Champion for Change Award for his leadership in juvenile justice reform.[53]

The Defender's deepening involvement with juvenile justice was every bit as important to Greenlee as its entry into homicide defense. "I think that actually in the juvenile area, there were more revolutionary things done," she said. "Homicide was simply a matter of taking on homicide representation, but this was cutting-edge stuff."[54]

20

THE FEDERAL DEFENDER

THE DEFENDER ALREADY HAD all it could handle in Pennsylvania's state courts when the federal judges came calling. What the judges of the U.S. District Court for the Eastern District of Pennsylvania wanted was a reliable source of counsel for indigents facing charges in their court, which covered Philadelphia, Montgomery, Delaware, Chester, Lehigh, Berks, Bucks, and Northampton Counties. They needed defense attorneys because the right to counsel was mandated by law in the federal court system and it kept order in the court, avoiding the inefficiencies and breaches of decorum that often went along with self-representation.

Until 1946, the court had been appointing private attorneys as needed to represent indigents, who were usually charged with such crimes as bank robbery, interstate transportation of stolen vehicles, or sex trafficking across state lines. Chief Defender Herman Pollock had duly noted the federal court's need but kept his distance because he thought the association could not handle the work without hiring another assistant.[1] However, when the judges' invitation came, Pollock concluded that the time had arrived to hire that extra assistant, so he accepted. The Community Chest, which funded the Defender, agreed to supply funds to cover the added expense, and the Defender started appearing in federal court in 1947, furnishing its services to the court free of charge. In the early days, the Defender's involvement with the federal system was small, far less than with the state courts. In 1951, five years after agreeing to work in U.S. District Court, the Defender was involved in only 182 cases there, compared with 2,820 in state courts.[2] A few years later, in 1957, the association handled 163 cases in federal court and 3,157 in state court.[3]

The day would come, though, when the Defender would do much more than represent clients accused of moving hot cars or knocking over banks. As the twentieth century ended, the Defender would become a major player in death penalty appeals, scouring trial records for constitutional flaws to save prisoners from the ultimate penalty and compiling a record of success in doing it that would please some and anger others, state prosecutors and some powerful judges among the latter.

The Defender's path to becoming a major player in federal court began with *Gideon*. While the U.S. Supreme Court's *Gideon* decision was aimed at state courts, it had a significant indirect impact on the federal courts. Spurred by the spirit of *Gideon*, Congress passed and President Lyndon B. Johnson signed the Criminal Justice Act (CJA) in 1964, as groundbreaking at the federal level as *Gideon* was at the state level.[4] The CJA established a procedure for appointing and compensating lawyers to represent penniless defendants in federal criminal proceedings, including habeas corpus challenges to state and federal convictions and sentences. Under the CJA, each federal district court had to come up with a plan to provide adequate representation for its indigent criminal defendants.[5] After enactment of the CJA, the Defender's federal appointments swelled in number. Pollock responded by appointing a staff lawyer as "federal defender" with the responsibility of coordinating the office's federal court work. The job went first to Leonard Packel and then to Carolyn Temin, to be assisted as necessary by the Amsterdam fellows.[6]

Crucially for the Defender, Congress amended the CJA in 1970 to provide that representation for indigent federal defendants come either from a federal public defender organization—a kind of counterpart to the U.S. attorney for the district—or by a nonpublic, nonprofit defense counsel service known as a "community defender organization" (CDO).[7] The judges of the Eastern District of Pennsylvania named the Defender as a CDO, to take effect in 1971. It was the only CDO operating as a division of a larger public defender organization, in this instance, the Defender Association of Philadelphia.[8]

The federal government paid for the Defender's services through a series of one-year grants; the Defender would now be reimbursed for its federal court work. Since the caseload had increased beyond the capacity of one lawyer to handle, Defender leadership decided to assign five full-time lawyers to federal court. To avoid any concern over having an agency supported by the city managing a federal court program, the Defender created a board of trustees to oversee the federal court division, which came to be known formally as the Federal Community Defender Office. The ten members the Defender was allowed to appoint to its own board of directors would also serve on the board of the federal division. The Federal Defender and the Defender Association would keep separate books and occupy different office space, although the Federal Defender would remain under the supervision of the chief defender and the first assistant. Under the CJA plan for eastern Pennsylvania, the Federal Defender did more than represent indigent defendants. The federal office also had to recommend and train private criminal defense lawyers, who would represent about 25 percent of the court's indigent criminal defendants.[9]

The Defender Association named Mark Schaffer the first chief federal defender in 1971 but demanded his resignation in 1983, after federal investigators accused him of accepting cash and construction of a patio from a client. A federal judge found him guilty of criminal contempt and fined him $2,000 but suspended a six-month jail sentence. He was succeeded by Edward Weis and later by Maureen Rowley (1989) and Leigh Skipper (2009).[10]

At its inception in 1971 and for the next twenty-five years, the federal division's principal function was simply to represent impoverished defendants charged with federal offenses, so the division was able to function with a small staff. When Lerner appointed Rowley chief federal defender in 1989, the unit had a staff of twelve, including eight lawyers, three secretaries, and an investigator. That would soon change. Rowley was an uncommonly skillful administrator and an equally skilled advocate, and she used those talents to engineer the growth of the Federal Community Defender Office. She formed an Appeals Unit to complement the Trial Unit and opened a branch office in Allentown. When she retired in 2008 because of the illness that would end her life, her office of 12 had grown to 138, including sixty-one lawyers and a nonlawyer staff that included investigators, social workers, and mitigation specialists.[11]

Rowley also distinguished herself in the courtroom. She was part of a team that litigated *Rompilla v. Beard* in which the U.S. Supreme Court upheld a lower-court decision granting a new trial to Ronald

Rompilla, who had been convicted of the murder of an Allentown tavern owner and sentenced to death. In so doing, the justices expanded the standard for effective assistance of counsel.[12] The defense team argued that Rompilla's court-appointed counsel had failed to investigate mitigating evidence that might have spared him the death penalty. Rompilla himself had told his trial attorney that he had nothing extraordinary in his background to mitigate the crime, so his lawyer dug no further. That turned out not to be true, and the Supreme Court ruled that his counsel at trial should have dug deep enough into his past to test the assertion, no matter what Rompilla said. Rompilla did have some significant mitigating issues related to his childhood, mental capacity, overall health, and alcoholism. Defense attorneys henceforth would have to seek mitigating evidence even if the defendant and the defendant's family said there was none.[13]

In 2006, Rowley expanded the division's reach a little further, accepting appointments from the District Court for the District of Columbia for her lawyers to represent detainees held on charges or suspicion of terrorism at the military prison at Guantanamo Bay, a politically as well as legally charged assignment.[14] Rowley's peers within the Federal Defender community and the Administrative Office of the U.S. Courts recognized her achievements by appointing her to serve on national committees dealing with Federal Defender services. Locally and nationally, she received a legion of awards for her contributions to criminal justice.[15] She won the admiration of her staff, too. One former federal defender, L. Felipe Restrepo, who later became a judge of the U.S. Third Circuit Court of Appeals, described her as "one of my mentors, absolutely. She was great."[16]

Rowley's successor, Leigh Skipper, who had been a supervisor in the Federal Defender's Trial Unit, built on and defended what Rowley had created. He steered the office through the 2013 sequestration, which required automatic cuts in federal programs and hit federal public defender offices hard.[17] The Federal Defender office in Philadelphia saw its budget drop 20 percent during the sequestration, forcing it to close the Allentown branch, lay off five people, and have the rest of the staff take ten unpaid furlough days.[18] While he was still a supervisor with the Trial Unit, Skipper had worked with judges of the Eastern District, including Restrepo and U.S. magistrate judge Timothy R. Rice, as well as the U.S. Probation Office and the U.S. Attorney's Office to create one of the country's first Reentry Courts, also known as the Supervision to Aid Reentry (STAR) program. The purpose of STAR is to help ex-convicts reenter society after many years in federal prisons. "These are guys with violent histories, and we help them readjust as returning citizens," Restrepo said. "The program has had a good bit of success in terms of recidivism rate. The recidivism rate is much lower for guys that are in the program and for graduates than a comparable demographic that's not participating in the program. STAR provided its participants housing, education, employment, family services."[19]

Around the time Rowley became the chief of the Federal Defender office, the federal government was beginning to recognize, if belatedly, that America had a burgeoning death-row population with an acute need for adequate representation. Before 1988, indigent federal defendants had a right to appointed counsel at trial, but not at the postconviction stage. Applicants for federal habeas corpus relief, whether state or federal prisoners, could ask to have counsel appointed for them, but that was up to the judge. On occasion, Federal Division lawyers had been appointed to represent defendants who petitioned on their own for federal habeas corpus relief and convinced a judge they might have a claim plausible enough to warrant a lawyer's assistance. In 1988, Congress recognized the unique importance of counsel in postconviction death penalty litigation and, for the first time, mandated the appointment and compensation of counsel for both state and federal indigent defendants seeking relief from a death sentence in federal habeas corpus proceedings.[20]

In Philadelphia, a high number of gang and drug-related killings each year, along with willingness of district attorneys in the late 1980s and through the 1990s to routinely seek the death penalty, helped make federal habeas corpus review of state capital cases a practice of major proportions. Each death sentence spawned a lengthy and intense process of judicial review that could go all the way from the trial court to the U.S. Supreme Court. In 1989, the federal government made funding available for "death penalty resource centers" in states that had a death penalty. Through the centers, lawyers experienced in capital cases could assist attorneys assigned to represent prisoners on death row filing habeas corpus petitions. The Pennsylvania Capital Case Resource Center opened in July 1994, but in 1995 Congress adopted a budget that eliminated funding of such resource centers and did away with federal postconviction defense organizations. A diminished Resource Center managed to survive until 1999.[21]

The Federal Defender stepped into the gap when Rowley proposed a pilot project establishing a capital habeas unit within her office. The

Administrative Office of the U.S. Courts approved the pilot project in 1995, and Rowley promptly hired three lawyers from the Capital Case Resource Center who made up the original Capital Habeas Unit (CHU) of the Federal Community Defender Office.[22]

Between 1995 and 1999, CHU and the Capital Case Resource Center operated concurrently. The Resource Center had a broader reach because it was authorized to represent clients in both state and federal postconviction proceedings. When the Resource Center shut down in 1999, its remaining funds went to CHU, which, along with the Defender Association and the Federal Defender, created a new entity, the Pennsylvania Capital Representation Project. The Representation Project raised money from private sources to fund the work of CHU lawyers in state court when those services fell outside the scope of the unit's federal grants. Actors Danny Glover and Ossie Davis headlined a fundraiser for the project in November 2000 that raised twenty thousand dollars. "A society should not be executing its own citizens," Glover told those attending the $150-per-ticket affair. "Somewhere, we have to rescue our morality."[23]

From its original three lawyers in 1996, CHU grew within a dozen years to a staff of thirty-six lawyers and forty-seven nonlawyers. As of 2018, the number of lawyers had stabilized at thirty-four. The U.S. District Courts for the Middle and Western Districts of Pennsylvania designated CHU as eligible for appointments in capital habeas corpus proceedings in their respective districts.[24]

CHU lawyers set out to raise every question they could about whether their clients' constitutional rights had been violated, looking for any constitutional flaw. The impact of their efforts was striking. Between 1978, when Pennsylvania reinstated the death penalty, and the end of 2017, Philadelphia judges or juries sentenced 155 defendants to die. (The district attorney's numbers did not include prisoners whose capital cases were resolved after Larry Krasner, a death penalty opponent, took office on January 1, 2018; a small number of inmates who died in prison while awaiting the disposition of their appeals; and Gary Heidnik, who waived his right to further appeals and was executed. Two other condemned prisoners from outside Philadelphia also gave up their appeals and were executed.) Of those 155 murder convictions in Philadelphia, 72 percent were overturned, and 91 percent of those, 102 people, ended up not being sentenced to death a second time, according to Krasner, who asked the Pennsylvania Supreme Court in July 2019 to declare the death penalty unconstitutional.[25] Not all of the death-row occupants who secured relief from the death penalty were represented by CHU; some were represented by the Pennsylvania Capital Case Resource Center, and others, by private, pro bono counsel.

To some prosecutors and state court judges, it seemed perverse that the federal government had enabled this state of affairs with its funding of capital postconviction litigation brought by state prisoners. Making matters worse, from their point of view, CHU lawyers were appearing with disturbing frequency at postconviction proceedings in state courts to preserve constitutional claims for later assertion in a federal habeas corpus petition. Those smoldering feelings burst into the open in 2011 in an opinion by Chief Justice (and former Philadelphia district attorney) Ronald D. Castille in *Commonwealth v. Spotz*, a case from Cumberland County in which CHU lawyers had represented Mark Spotz in an unsuccessful challenge to his murder conviction and death sentence. The six justices who heard the appeal were unanimous in upholding the conviction and death penalty, but the chief justice had something else he wanted to say.[26]

In a separate opinion, joined by two other justices, Castille wrote that he wanted "to note and address broader issues implicated by the role and performance of federal counsel in purely state court collateral proceedings in capital cases, such as this one." From that measured beginning, he proceeded to castigate CHU for what he called "abusive appellate tactics" and for following a strategy that "had taken a substantial and unwarranted toll on the state courts." He complained that CHU was overwhelming underresourced county prosecutors, a bit of irony given the chronic funding problems that regularly beset public defenders. Castille observed disapprovingly that "[CHU's] commitment of federal manpower alone is beyond remarkable, something one would expect in major litigation involving large law firms." In the chief justice's view, CHU's practices were calculated to "obstruct capital punishment in Pennsylvania at all costs." Castille speculated that it was possible that federal authorities were unaware of CHU's state court activities apparently underwritten with federal funds, a state of ignorance he meant his opinion to dispel.[27]

Castille's *Spotz* opinion engendered a campaign by the Philadelphia district attorney's office, the attorney general of Pennsylvania, and a handful of other county prosecutors to oust CHU lawyers from representing federal clients in state court postconviction relief proceedings. In a series of motions filed in state court postconviction proceedings, prosecutors requested that judges rule that CHU's "federally funded lawyers" were not authorized to appear in state court and were violating federal law and, by implication, state ethical requirements. On those grounds, the motions argued, they should be excluded from appearing in state court.[28]

The campaign to keep CHU lawyers out of state courts seriously threatened the welfare of CHU's clients. After the enactment of the Antiterrorism and Effective Death Penalty Act of 1996, federal habeas practice had become a minefield for the unwary. Procedural obstacles, including rigid time bars, lay everywhere. Without knowledgeable, sophisticated counsel, a litigant had slim chance of ever securing relief in federal court. The barely disguised aim of the campaign waged against CHU was to rid Pennsylvania's prosecutors of a formidable and determined adversary and to insulate death sentences decreed by Pennsylvania courts against meritorious challenges.[29]

Leigh Skipper led the Defender's effort to fight off the attack on CHU. To beat back the attacks, the Defender Association invoked a rarely used federal law enacted to protect federal officers and those acting under them from hostile state courts. First, the Defender removed the state court motions to federal district court and then immediately asked for dismissal of the commonwealth's disqualification motions. The Defender argued that federal law preempted the motions because Congress had given supervisory authority over CJA grantees, including federal community defender organizations, exclusively to the Administrative Office of the U.S. Courts, the judicial branch agency that provides support services for the federal courts.[30]

In 2015, after four years of litigation, the U.S. Court of Appeals for the Third Circuit ruled for the Defender on both counts. First, it upheld the validity of the removal of the disqualification motions to federal court. Then it sustained the Defender's argument that federal law preempted the commonwealth's attempts to disqualify CHU's Pennsylvania lawyers from appearing in Pennsylvania courts based on their supposed violation of federal law.[31] What was really at stake in the disqualification cases did not escape the notice of the Third Circuit. In a concurring opinion, Chief Judge Theodore McKee pithily characterized the marrow of the dispute: "The Commonwealth is obviously not objecting [to CHU's appearances in state court] because the Federal Community Defender is providing inadequate representation and thereby denying the petitioners the constitutional rights that all parties seek to respect. Rather, the objection seems to be that the Federal Community Defender is providing too much defense to the accused."[32]

If Pennsylvania authorities were embittered by CHU's unbroken record of success and its excursions into state courts, the national Federal Defender community did more than admire the work of CHU at its home base. In case after case, the "Philly CHU" was asked and agreed to serve as co-counsel on federal habeas corpus petitions filed in courts around the country on behalf of a death-row inmate. As of 2018, CHU lawyers had appeared by request or judicial appointment in fifteen federal judicial districts as far away as Texas, in addition to the Eastern, Middle, and Western Districts of Pennsylvania. CHU had come to be known to the Administrative Office of the U.S. Courts as a "crisis office" to be summoned wherever and whenever a particular capital habeas petition posed a unique challenge requiring the services of lawyers with CHU's rare expertise and resourcefulness under the most stressful circumstances to which a lawyer can be subjected—life and death.[33]

21

THE DEFENDER IN THE
TWENTY-FIRST CENTURY

THE FIRST DECADE of the twenty-first century brought several major challenges for the Defender. Philadelphia's prison population, which had fallen to about seven thousand as a result of Judge Norma Shapiro's orders in the prison overcrowding case, increased once the federal lawsuit ended in 2000.[1] The rise caused headaches for everyone connected with the justice system, including the Defender, and took a significant chunk out of the city's tax revenues. Mayor Michael Nutter complained in 2009 that he did not want to allocate more funds for the prisons, which already took up 7 percent of the city's tax revenue, but said he had no choice.[2] The recession of 2008 made matters worse, biting into the city's tax base. Money for housing the growing jail population was tight, as was money for defending the indigents who continued to make up more than 70 percent of those accused of crime in the city.

The surging prison population was part of a wave of mass incarceration that had been building across the nation for four decades, dating back to the 1960s. The national tough-on-crime attitude took on a special intensity in Philadelphia, where the "lock-'em-up" philosophy of District Attorney Lynne Abraham, Philadelphia's chief prosecutor from 1991 to 2010, contributed to the rise in jail population as prosecutors routinely filed the most serious charges possible even for minor offenses.[3] Police were making more arrests for drug possession and drunk driving.

At the same time, Philadelphia bail commissioners began imposing higher bails, which meant that even fewer defendants would be able to get out of jail while awaiting trial.[4]

The Defender was a strong proponent of reducing the number of inmates. More than 60 percent of the prisoners in Philadelphia jails were awaiting trial on misdemeanor and minor felony charges and were behind bars simply because they could not make bail.[5] If they could not afford bail, then they probably could not afford a lawyer, making them part of the Defender's client base. In the Defender's view, keeping them locked up contributed nothing to public safety but cost the prisoners their jobs and rents, making them more likely to commit more crimes, more dependent on social services, and less likely to be able to support their children and families. "For justice and for economic reasons, we can't continue to jail everyone we're now jailing," Ellen Greenlee said at the time. "We have to find a better way."[6]

For years, the search for a better way led to federal court, as, for example, when David Rudovsky, joined by Angus Love of the Pennsylvania Institutional Law Project and David Richman of the Pepper Hamilton law firm, sued on behalf of eleven city inmates in U.S. District Court in July 2006, arguing that the conditions under which the inmates were held amounted to cruel and unusual punishment and thus violated their constitutional rights[7]—the same argument he had used successfully in earlier lawsuits aimed at compelling the city to improve conditions in its jails.

By mid-2006, Philadelphia's prison population had climbed to about eighty-eight hundred,[8] well above the city's prison capacity of about sixty-five hundred.[9] So many defendants were behind bars that some were being housed three to a cell and others were being kept in common areas never intended for overnight habitation. Still others were being held at police districts or in the Police Administration Building instead of one of the city's jails.[10] The situation had been exacerbated by record-keeping lapses in the court system that led to inmates being held too long. Rudovsky had already filed a federal lawsuit in 2001 aimed at making sure prisoners were released on time. Pursuant to provisions in the settlement agreement, the staff of the Defender was able to compile a daily list of prisoners due for release. Defender staff then checked to make sure the day's prisoners really were going to be released. That was fortunate for the inmates, because by 2009, when the prison population was at its peak, Senior Assistant Defender Thomas J. Innes III, supervisor of the Defender's In-Prison Services Unit, counted twenty cases in a single month in which defendants got out on time only because he reminded jail authorities that the defendants' time was up.[11]

In January 2007, U.S. District Judge R. Barclay Surrick ruled on Rudovsky's 2006 suit, agreeing that conditions in the city's jails were so bad that they violated the prisoners' rights. He ordered the city to correct the situation at once, but the problems persisted.[12] By April 2008, the prison population was still about eighty-eight hundred and by 2009 had reached an all-time high of nearly ninety-four hundred—the fourth highest of any city or county in the United States.[13]

Faced with those stubbornly high numbers and jail conditions that were not improving, Rudovsky (who by this time had become president of the Defender's Board of Directors) sued again in 2008 but suspended the suit in 2011 when the jail census dropped below seventy-seven hundred.[14] The number decreased in part because the Philadelphia prison system benefited from a state law, enacted at the city's urging in 2008, that required prisoners sentenced to two to five years in jail to serve their time in a state prison rather than a county jail. The transfer resulted in the immediate removal of several hundred inmates from the Philadelphia prison system to the state system.[15]

Then the prison population started to increase again, in part because bails were higher than many defendants could afford and the courts began a crackdown on bail skippers and defendants who missed court dates. Some court officials thought the space that had been freed up should be used to imprison fugitives.[16] In 2012, the First Judicial District of Pennsylvania, which covers Philadelphia, even created a Bench Warrant Court to deal with defendants who had not appeared for court dates.[17] The increase in prison numbers convinced Rudovsky to reopen the 2008 suit, declaring that whenever the court stopped applying pressure, the numbers started increasing.[18] Other important figures in the Philadelphia justice system also arrived at the same conclusion as Greenlee and Rudovsky: There had to be a better way. Imprisonment was necessary only "to keep the monsters away," said Pamela Pryor Dembe, president judge of the Court of Common Pleas.[19]

In 2010, R. Seth Williams succeeded Abraham as district attorney and acknowledged that the prisons were overflowing with inmates who were there because of "junk" offenses.[20] Williams initiated a few salutary changes that the Defender applauded. Instead of using "probable cause" as the standard for charging specific criminal offenses, as Abraham had done, Williams changed the charging standard to "reasonable doubt." "Probable cause" allowed a prosecutor to charge a suspect if the police report indicated a likelihood that the defendant had committed a crime, usually the most serious crime the investigation would support. "Reasonable doubt" allowed the prosecutor to bring a charge only if convinced it was possible to prove beyond a reasonable doubt that the suspect had committed a crime.[21] The Defender also welcomed Williams's decision in 2010 to reduce the charge for possession of marijuana from a misdemeanor to a summary offense—a defendant would receive a citation but would not be subject to further prosecution.[22]

The district attorney also began sending more cases to "Crash Court," a special program within Municipal Court for defendants charged with low-level misdemeanors. Crash Court had been around for decades as a vehicle for moving minor cases speedily through the system. The Defender and the city's director of prisons identified prisoners eligible for Crash Court, and then the Defender and the district attorney worked out a plea bargain. If the defendant accepted the plea deal, the case went onto the Crash Court docket and was completed within two or three weeks. In 2009, prosecutors and defenders alike saw Crash Court as a way to resolve even more cases. Prosecutors began bringing cases to Crash Court that they had not brought before, including those involving domestic violence and warrants. The introduction of videoconferencing made it possible for Crash Court to operate every day instead of just twice a week as it had previously. Greenlee welcomed the changes, which she said were "making a big difference." Plea offers were coming earlier, which made the whole process move more quickly. "It's taken a lot of effort, and all of the stakeholders working together," she said. "But it's paying off."[23]

Just as it found itself reliving the old problem of prison overcrowding into the twenty-first century, so too did the Defender find itself dealing yet again with a familiar troubling issue: police misbehavior. Once again, accusations against the police would lead to convictions being overturned or charges dropped for hundreds of Defender clients.

In May 2013, Jeffrey Walker, a veteran narcotics officer, was arrested and charged with stealing money and drugs from drug dealers. He had been the subject of an FBI investigation for more than a year. When arrested, Walker was found to have fifteen thousand dollars in cash and drugs. He had planned to frame a known drug dealer by planting cocaine in his car.[24] Walker confessed to the charges, and in 2013, Philadelphia common pleas supervising judge Sheila Woods-Skipper tossed out fifty-three drug convictions of Defender clients he had arrested.[25] The following month, she tossed another dozen.[26]

After his arrest, Walker informed on six fellow narcotics officers he claimed also had been stealing drugs, money, and personal belongings from drug dealers and using force to do it. The six were fired from the police force and tried in federal court. Walker testified against them at a trial in 2015 before U.S. District Judge Eduardo Robreno. While prosecutors praised Walker for breaking "an institutional code of silence," the jury acquitted the six officers. Because of his cooperation, Walker eventually was sentenced to only three and a half years in prison. The acquitted officers got their jobs back.[27]

Nevertheless, the Philadelphia courts, with the agreement of the district attorney's office, began overturning drug cases in which the officers had been involved. By February 2016, the number of convictions overturned for defendants arrested by Walker and the other six officers stood at 699, with several hundred more still to be examined.[28] Some of the drug defendants also began suing the city and received settlements. By the end of 2017, the city had paid out more than two million dollars to settle the wrongful conviction claims. Prosecutors by that time had dropped charges against more than one thousand defendants convicted on evidence developed by the six. Nearly 250 more cases were still under review.[29]

AS THE NEW CENTURY WORE ON, Philadelphia's prison population remained stubbornly high. By early 2015, it had climbed back up to eighty-three hundred, giving Philadelphia the highest per capita incarceration rate of any of the country's ten largest municipalities. Inmates spent an average of ninety-five days behind bars, four times the national average. Racial imbalance was also a concern: 72 percent of Philadelphia's jail population was African American, while 54 percent of the general population was African American.[30]

Despite the continuing problems, Greenlee had not been wrong about the spirit of cooperation among the stakeholders in the justice system. It was there, and it enabled Philadelphia to take advantage of an opportunity for help that came from outside the city. In 2014, the Chicago-based John D. and Catherine T. MacArthur Foundation had become convinced that mass incarceration was a major social issue in the United States. The foundation's approach would be to place "a few big bets" on proposals from local jurisdictions for alleviating mass incarceration in their communities. MacArthur officials announced a

"Safety and Justice Challenge," inviting municipalities to submit plans for solving the problem.[31]

Philadelphia was one of 191 municipalities vying for MacArthur money. The city's proposal to reduce its prison population by one-third in three years made the challenge's first cut in May 2015, when Mac-Arthur named the city as one of twenty that would receive $150,000 to help them go forward with their planning. From the twenty finalists, the MacArthur Foundation would select ten to receive major grants.[32] In what many considered an example of unprecedented cooperation, representatives of the Defender, the district attorney's office, the city managing director's office, the prison system, the police, and the court system collaborated on an ambitious detailed strategy. Over a period of seven months, the planning team met weekly to develop all of the "deliverables" of the planning phase with technical assistance by the Vera Institute of Justice, a nonprofit organization based in New York that seeks to reform the justice system. The city presented its plan to the MacArthur Foundation in January 2016. Just three months later, Mac-Arthur awarded the city $3.5 million, the largest criminal justice grant it made that year. Laurie Garduque, director of MacArthur's justice reform program, praised the Philadelphia plan as "bold and ambitious" but also "sound, practical and reasonable." The plan called for changes that included continuing efforts to reduce the pretrial jail population, make greater use of diversion to get defendants into rehab instead of jail, move away from cash bail, process cases more efficiently, use electric monitoring as an alternative to probation detainers, reduce racial disparities by providing bias training for personnel in all phases of the justice system, and do a risk assessment at arraignment to identify nonviolent defendants who are likely to show up for a court date if released.[33]

The Defender had been an enthusiastic partner in developing the plan. Innes, of the Defender's In-Prison Services Unit, hailed the proposed changes as a real effort to reform the justice system rather than just tweak it. "We were spending so much money on jailing people, we never had the opportunity to go back and look at the process from the beginning of the pipeline," Innes said. "What we're looking to do now is to prevent people from going into that jail pipeline."[34]

THE DEFENDER LAWYERS also found themselves early in the twenty-first century trying to free people who been in the jail pipeline for quite a while: prisoners who were serving mandatory life terms without the possibility of parole for crimes they had committed as juveniles. In 2012, the United States ruled in *Miller v. Alabama* that it was a violation of the Eighth Amendment's prohibition of cruel and unusual punishment to sentence a juvenile to life without parole.[35] Four years later, in *Montgomery v. Louisiana*, the court ruled that *Miller* was to be applied retroactively.[36] That meant that more than 500 prisoners across Pennsylvania would have to be resentenced, including about 300 juvenile lifers from Philadelphia, more than from any other city in the United States. The Defender would represent about 225 of them.[37]

"I went to my bosses and suggested to them that we should set up a unit in our office to do this," Bradley Bridge said. "We made a proposal to the city to handle about seventy-five percent of the resentencings."[38] Bridge was one of the cochairs of the unit, along with Paul Conway, the former head of the Homicide Unit, and Helen Levin.

The work was tedious and time-consuming, Conway said. The Defender was not involved in most of the cases originally. "We have no records on these cases," he said. "There were only a few that our office did that were juvenile lifers. First thing I did, I went through a lot of these names and tried to put files together for them—one hundred forty of them. I read newspaper articles, dockets, letters to Brad Bridge. Brad was one of the champions of this whole issue for years. He was writing letters to a lot of these guys, and they were writing letters, so we've got all the letters that they wrote to him with information about their case. We put that together, and then we started to assign cases. We started in July [2016], and the first month, we saw two hundred–some people in twenty-six different prisons."[39] The hard work was worth it. Conway found the first lifers they represented, those who had been behind bars the longest, to be "amazing—the most mature group of people I've ever met in my life. They were just so thankful for the work we're doing." Prisoners could get out if their time served qualified them for parole. Those who were paroled made a determined effort to stay out of trouble. "Every one of these juvenile lifers believe that they have an obligation to the others coming behind them to do well when they get out," Conway said.[40]

The state Department of Corrections reported that as of May 2019, 416 of Pennsylvania's 523 juvenile lifers had been resentenced and 189 had been released on parole; 75 percent of those who applied for parole had gotten it. Three of the inmates had died in prison.[41] By about the same time, the Defender had disposed of about 150 cases, Conway said.[42]

The juvenile lifers had an impact on their lawyers. A group of paroled juvenile lifers met every month in Bridge's office. "They just talk about whatever they want to talk about," he said. "It's a big support group. You can't just wave good-bye to the juvenile lifers after they're released. I can't emotionally, and I can't because I want to make sure that they succeed. This is a group of clients that are unlike other clients. These clients are a potential model in their success for changing the way the entire Commonwealth of Pennsylvania and the United States deal with incarceration."[43] If the juvenile lifers can come out of prison after thirty, forty, or fifty years and do well, Bridge reasoned, then maybe people would conclude they should not have been imprisoned for so long: "Maybe it should have been ten, fifteen, twenty years, and they wouldn't have wasted the extra incarceration time when these people would have succeeded after twenty years."[44]

WHILE THE DEFENDER PLAYED a major role in obtaining money to reform the criminal justice system, money to support the Defender itself lagged. The economic crisis of 2008 hit Philadelphia city government hard. "From 2008 to 2013, there was no pay increase [for Defender staff] whatsoever," said Rudovsky. "That was somewhat across the board. [Mayor] Nutter came in at the start of the recession." In 2012, the city asserted that the economic climate was "the worst . . . that any administration had to deal with" and they could not respond to the Defender's needs, either for salary relief or funding twenty-two additional attorneys. The salary differential between those in the district attorney's office and the Defender was severe: An assistant district attorney with seven years' experience could make sixty-five thousand dollars annually, while an assistant defender with similar experience would make about fifty-one thousand dollars.[45]

Ironically, the city official the Defender had to deal with the most on funding issues was a former assistant defender, Everett Gillison, who had joined the Defender in 1976 as a social worker in the Social and Psychiatric Services Unit after graduating from the University of Pennsylvania with a degree in political science. He left the Defender in 1982 to attend Syracuse University Law School but returned as a staff lawyer after receiving his law degree in 1985. He tried cases for the Defender for the next two decades and was one of the original members of the Homicide Unit.[46]

In 2008, the newly elected Mayor Nutter appointed Gillison deputy mayor for public safety and in 2011 promoted him to chief of staff. He was involved in developing the mayor's budget and was acutely aware of the Defender's need for parity. For several years, discussions involved the concept of an integrated public-service pay schedule for the district attorney's office, the city's Law Department, and the Defender Association. Unfortunately, there was little progress over the eight years of the Nutter administration, and although the Defender got money for a 3 percent pay raise in 2013, that still did not get staff salaries to parity with those in the district attorney's office. The gap remained sizable.[47]

The lack of pay parity impacted morale and enhanced turnover. "I think more people left the office than we usually see," Rudovsky said. "We generally see a ten percent attrition each year."[48] In 2013, the Defender hired thirty new attorneys; by 2016, fourteen of them had left—47 percent.[49] As Bridge explained, Defender staffers began to feel the lack of parity more acutely as their legal experience grew. "It's two things," he said. "They get a little trial experience, and they feel a little bit more marketable, and also now they're a little older. They graduated law school at twenty-five; they're now twenty-eight. People are more likely to be married, more likely to have children, more likely to see a need to worry more about income. 'I want to be able to buy a house; I worry about my kids.' That becomes clearer as time goes by."[50]

Faced with a city administration that was not budging on funding, the Defender at one point—as it had at times of financial crisis in the past—considered cutting the scope of its coverage. The Defender Board of Directors advised the city that, without some fiscal relief, the Defender could no longer staff four courtrooms that collectively processed charges against 655 defendants. Replacing the Defender with private lawyers would cost the taxpayers as much as $229,000 per week, twenty times the cost of staffing by the Defender. The city still did not provide funding to eliminate the salary differential but did come up with money for the Defender to hire the necessary attorneys to provide adequate representation in all the courts.[51]

The fight for parity carried over from the administration of Ellen Greenlee to that of her successor, Keir Bradford-Grey. The cooperation that marked the application for the MacArthur grant seemed to create an atmosphere in which the Defender's need for parity might be looked on more kindly. "Right now is our time," Bradford-Grey said in 2017. "It's reform time, and you need the Defender's vantage point and expertise more than ever, so I have made it my business to raise awareness about our services and what we do. We've actually got a commitment from the city to increase the wages of our staff, and we were able to do that in an increment. We're still not where we need to be in terms of showing our value to our counterparts in the D.A.'s office, but we're climbing up. We still have discussions with city council, who are now understanding the value of having us at the table."[52] In 2019, under Mayor Jim Kenney, the city agreed in principle to parity, opening the way at last to equal pay for Philadelphia's prosecutors and public defenders.

IN DECEMBER 2014, Ellen Greenlee announced that she would retire as chief defender the following March. She had been with the association for forty-one years, twenty-five of them as chief defender. "It's time to get some new blood in here," she said. "I've had a good run."[53] Indeed, she had. Under her leadership, the Defender had been recognized as a vital partner in Philadelphia's criminal justice system, made invaluable contributions to justice, and saved the city of Philadelphia millions of dollars. During her tenure, the Defender expanded to meet the needs of its clients and fulfill its fundamental mission of providing competent, effective legal defense services consistent with the Constitution. Her leadership had been recognized nationally by NLADA, which twice chose her to serve as its president, and by Philadelphia's criminal justice community.

The Defender's Board of Directors aptly described her in a resolution at her retirement as "a committed and fierce advocate for those without power in our community and for those whose status leaves them vulnerable to the somewhat arbitrary exercise of state power. Her exemplary career has truly been a light in the all too often dark corner of the criminal justice system and we join in celebrating her accomplishments and well-earned retirement."[54]

EPILOGUE

THE CRIMINAL JUSTICE SYSTEM of Philadelphia entered a period of dramatic change not long after Ellen Greenlee stepped down in 2015. The unprecedented cooperation among all the partners in the system—courts, prosecutors, defenders, police, mayor, city council, prison officials—that began in the latter years of Greenlee's tenure lasted beyond her retirement, and the Defender continued to be a major player in reform efforts.

Greenlee's successor, Keir Bradford-Grey, was one of three cochairs of a seventeen-member Special Committee on Criminal Justice Reform that Philadelphia City Council established in February 2016. The mission of the group—which included representatives from the council, the mayor's office, the courts, and community groups—was to work with the community and with leaders in the criminal justice system to find ways of overhauling the system. "We should struggle and strive to understand, when are we making people more desperate?" Bradford-Grey said after she was named to the panel. "Are our policies hurting more people than protecting the safety of the individuals in the community?"[1]

In Bradford-Grey's view, reforming the justice system was "the civil rights movement of our time," and she welcomed the opportunity that the MacArthur grants offered to include grassroots communities, such as local churches and community organizers, as part of the reform process.[2] Engaging with the community was an important part of

Bradford-Grey's vision of the Defender's mission as it began expanding its purview to include not just criminal defense but also social-service activities aimed at ameliorating the conditions that gave rise to crime. "We're really looking to understand not only what's going on in our clients' lives but what's happening in their communities so that we can empower people to come up with some of their own solutions to their problems," she said in 2018. "When we see trends and patterns, we start to work with community advocacy groups, churches, to understand what we're seeing and how they can prevent these things from happening."[3] Under Bradford-Grey, the Defender launched a "participatory defense" initiative, which a Defender report in 2018 described as an effort "to show the community how the justice system operates so they can better assist in the defense of their own case or assist family/ community members who may be behind bars."[4]

If deep involvement in criminal justice reform efforts were not enough to validate the Defender's place at the cutting edge of serving Philadelphia's needs, an unexpected turn of events brought a former public defender to the post of district attorney. In June 2017, District Attorney R. Seth Williams resigned after pleading guilty to a federal bribery charge and was sentenced to five years in jail.[5] Williams's fall from grace came at time when calls for reform were increasing across the country, especially in major cities where minorities had been targeted by the wars on drugs and mass incarceration and justice reform had become became a political issue. Williams, who succeeded Abraham as district attorney in 2009, had come to office vowing reform, but anyone who had expected major reforms ended up disappointed. "When Seth Williams came in, [the district attorney's office] changed less than I thought it would," said David Rudovsky, who was president of the Defender board during Williams's term. "He ran as a kind of reform, progressive D.A. He didn't perform that way. He kept a lot of the old guard there from the Abraham administration."[6] However, the Defender did find some good in Williams's time as district attorney. "This is the one thing that Seth Williams did which I think was credible and useful," Rudovsky said. "More diversion of cases, more specialty courts, focus on getting the least serious cases out of the system, one way or the other."[7] The emphasis on diversion led to more cooperation between Defender and district attorney "because those specialty courts are really a joint enterprise whether it's a drug court or a mental health court or a veterans' court."[8]

In the 2017 election to choose Williams's successor, several left-leaning, reform-minded groups from across the country supported the candidacy of Democratic candidate Larry Krasner, a civil rights lawyer and former assistant defender. Krasner was elected with substantial financial backing from George Soros, an outspoken advocate for justice reform. Although not supported by either party in the primary, Krasner won the Democratic nomination and easily won the election. Similar calls for reform also resulted in the election of progressive prosecutors with views similar to Krasner's in other jurisdictions, including Boston, Dallas, and southern Virginia.

When he took office in January 2018, Krasner brought several other prominent former public defenders into the district attorney's office in leadership roles, including Carolyn Temin, Robert Listenbee, and Charles Cunningham. Krasner asked the Pennsylvania Supreme Court to declare the death penalty unconstitutional and directed his prosecutors to request shorter prison terms, limit the term of supervised release, and decline to prosecute some minor crimes, such as prostitution and possession of marijuana.

While Krasner was viewed as a transformational leader in some quarters, he faced strong opposition in others. In his first week in office, he forced more than thirty assistant district attorneys to resign. Opponents claimed that Krasner's actions were devastating and detrimental to the morale of the district attorney's office. For the Defender, Krasner's initiatives were a welcome change from the policies of some of his predecessors. Though the relations between a district attorney and a chief defender are inherently adversarial, Bradford-Grey welcomed many of Krasner's initiatives and the opportunity to work together in "a commonality of approach and understanding of what our system should be."[9]

NOTES

INTRODUCTION

1. Virginia Commonwealth Libraries Social Welfare History Project, "Pennsylvania Prison Society," https://socialwelfare.library.vcu.edu/corrections/pennsylvania-prison-society/ (accessed March 3, 2020).

2. Negley K. Teeters, *They Were in Prison: A History of the Pennsylvania Prison Society, 1787–1937* (Chicago: John C. Winston), 443.

3. "Prison Society Backs Public Defender Move," *Philadelphia Inquirer*, March 29, 1930, p. 3; Teeters, *They Were in Prison*, 443.

4. Herman I. Pollock, "Francis Fisher Kane: Philadelphia's Lance of Justice," *Prison Journal* 35, no. 2 (1955): 2–3.

5. Teeters, *They Were in Prison*, 443.

6. Defender Association of Philadelphia Board of Directors, *Defender Association of Philadelphia, 1934–1984: A Report on the First Fifty Years* (Philadelphia: Packard Press, 1984), ii.

7. John M. McCullough, "Francis F. Kane Named Winner of Phila. Award," *Philadelphia Inquirer*, February 6, 1936, p. 13.

8. Pollock, "Francis Fisher Kane," 3.

9. A. A. DiS. and I.P.T., "Legal Aid to Indigent Criminal Defendants in Philadelphia and New Jersey," *University of Pennsylvania Law Review* 107, no. 6 (1959): 820.

10. Webb v. Baird, 6 Ind. 13 (1854).

11. James Park Taylor, "Bespeaking Justice: A History of Indigent Defense in Montana," *Montana Law Review* 68, no. 2 (2007): 364–365.

12. Barbara Babcock, "Women's Rights, Public Defense, and the Chicago World's Fair," *Chicago-Kent Law Review* 87, no. 2 (2012): 492–497.

13. Los Angeles County Public Defender, "About Us," https://pubdef.lacounty.gov/about-us (accessed May 18, 2020).

14. Sara Mayeux, "What *Gideon* Did," *Columbia Law Review* 116, no. 1 (2016), https://papers.ssrn.com/sol3/papers.cfm?abstract_id=2724830.

15. Geoff Burkhart, "Public Defense: The New York Story," *Criminal Justice* 30, no. 3 (2015): 23.

16. The text of the Constitution of Pennsylvania is available at https://avalon.law.yale.edu/18th_century/pa08.asp.

17. "Frazer [*sic*] Urges Post of Public Defender," *Philadelphia Inquirer*, March 17, 1928, p. 2.

18. Ibid.

19. "End Death Penalty and Sale of Arms, Prison Body Urges; Society Also Asks State to Adopt Public Defender System," *Philadelphia Inquirer*, January 20, 1929, p. 2.

20. "Frazer [*sic*] Urges Post of Public Defender," 2.

21. Teeters, *They Were in Prison*, 443.

22. Pollock, "Francis Fisher Kane," 3.

23. "Plan $45,000 Fund to Defend Poor," *Philadelphia Inquirer*, May 26, 1929, p. 11.

24. Pollock, "Francis Fisher Kane," 3.

25. Defender Association of Philadelphia Board of Directors, *Defender Association of Philadelphia*, v.

26. "Public Defender Fund to Be Sought," *Philadelphia Inquirer*, March 28, 1930, p. 11.

27. "'Public Defender' Named for Phila.," *Philadelphia Inquirer*, March 19, 1934, p. 2.

28. Pollock, "Francis Fisher Kane," 4.

29. McCullough, "Francis F. Kane Named Winner of Phila. Award," 13.

30. Keir Bradford-Grey, interview by the authors, April 26, 2017, Philadelphia.

31. Ibid.

CHAPTER 1

1. "'Public Defender' Named for Phila.," *Philadelphia Inquirer*, March 19, 1934, p. 2.

2. "T. E. Cogan, Public Defender," *Philadelphia Inquirer*, February 17, 1951, p. 5.

3. Defender Association of Philadelphia Board of Directors, *Defender Association of Philadelphia, 1934–1984: A Report on the First Fifty Years* (Philadelphia: Packard Press, 1984), 2–3.

4. "Innocent Convict Revealed at Prison by Public Defender," *Philadelphia Inquirer*, April 19, 1934, p. 3.

5. Ibid.

6. "Free Innocent Man," *Philadelphia Inquirer*, May 19, 1934, p. 29.

7. "'Framed' Youth Freed after Jail Term," *Wilkes-Barre Times Leader*, April 24, 1934, p. 2.

8. Defender Association of Philadelphia Board of Directors, *Defender Association of Philadelphia*, 4.

9. Eleanor Morton, "How the Voluntary Defender Frequently Prevents Tragic Injustice to Those Wrongly Accused," *Philadelphia Inquirer*, December 6, 1934, p. 16.

10. "A Day in the Life of the Public Defender Who Sees That Justice Is Done the Forlorn and the Penniless," *Philadelphia Inquirer*, January 25, 1936, p. 12.

11. "Justice Does Not Miscarry When the Voluntary Defender Sets Out to Help the Poor and Bewildered," *Philadelphia Inquirer*, December 17, 1936, p. 20.

12. "Cardinal Indorses [*sic*] Aid," *Philadelphia Inquirer*, October 26, 1934, p. 15.

13. Defender Association of Philadelphia Board of Directors, *Defender Association of Philadelphia*, 10.

14. Sixth Amendment Center, "Understanding Gideon's Impact, Part 2: The Birth of the Public Defender Movement," https://sixthamendment.org/understanding -gideons-impact-part-2-the-birth-of-the-public-defender-movement/ (accessed March 4, 2020).

15. Defender Association of Philadelphia Board of Directors, *Defender Association of Philadelphia*, 10.

16. "Annual Report of the Directors of the Philadelphia Voluntary Defender Association, April 26, 1935," in Defender Association of Philadelphia Board of Directors, *Defender Association of Philadelphia*, 5–6.

17. Ibid., 3, 8.

18. "Curtis Bok Named Acting Defender," *Philadelphia Inquirer*, July 6, 1934, p. 10.

19. "Annual Report," 3.

20. Ibid., 10.

21. Ibid., 9.

22. Ibid., 11.

23. Ibid.

24. A. A. DiS. and I.P.T., "Legal Aid to Indigent Criminal Defendants in Philadelphia and New Jersey," *University of Pennsylvania Law Review* 107 (1959): 836.

25. Powell v. Alabama, 287 U.S. 45 (1932).

26. Commonwealth v. Richards, 111 Pa. Super. 129 (Pa. Super. Ct. 1933); "Sixth Annual Report of the Directors of the Philadelphia Voluntary Defender Association," June 21, 1940, p. 1, Defender Association of Philadelphia Records, Special Collections Research Center, Temple University Libraries.

27. Johnson v. Zerbst, 304 U.S. 458 (1938).

28. "Sixth Annual Report," 1.

29. Ibid., 1–2.

30. Ibid., 6.

31. Ibid., 2.

32. Ibid.

33. Ibid., 3.

34. Ibid.

35. "Ninth Annual Report of the Directors of the Philadelphia Voluntary Defender Association, for the Year June 1, 1942 to May 31, 1943," p. 6, Defender Association of Philadelphia Records, Special Collections Research Center, Temple University Libraries.

36. "Justice Does Not Miscarry When the Voluntary Defender Sets Out to Help the Poor and Bewildered," *Philadelphia Inquirer*, December 19, 1936, p. 9.

37. "Justice Does Not Miscarry When the Voluntary Defender Sets Out to Help the Poor and Bewildered," *Philadelphia Inquirer*, December 16, 1936, p. 17.

38. "Ninth Annual Report," 6.

39. Ibid., 2.

40. "Twelfth Annual Report of the Directors of the Philadelphia Voluntary Defender Association, for the Year June 1, 1945 to May 31, 1946," p. 1, Defender Association of Philadelphia Records, Special Collections Research Center, Temple University Libraries.

41. Ibid., 2.

42. Ibid., 3.

43. Ibid., 4–5.
44. "Ninth Annual Report," 7.
45. "Twelfth Annual Report," 5.

CHAPTER 2

1. Powell v. Alabama, 287 U.S. 45 (1932).
2. Commonwealth v. Richards, 111 Pa. Super. 124 (Pa. Super. Ct. 1933).
3. Johnson v. Zerbst, 304 U.S. 458 (1938).
4. "Volunteer Defenders Praised by Judge," *Philadelphia Inquirer*, April 3, 1941, p. 1.
5. "Free Aid for Only 1 in 10," *Courier-Post*, August 13, 1964, p. 16.
6. Robert M. Landis, quoted in Defender Association of Philadelphia Board of Directors, *Defender Association of Philadelphia, 1934–1984: A Report on the First Fifty Years* (Philadelphia: Packard Press, 1984), 42.
7. "Twelfth Annual Report of the Directors of the Philadelphia Voluntary Defender Association, for the Year June 1, 1945 to May 31, 1946," p. 8, Defender Association of Philadelphia Records, Special Collections Research Center, Temple University Libraries.
8. Ibid., 3.
9. "Defenders Give Aid to 3002 in Year," *Philadelphia Inquirer*, June 11, 1951, p. 19.
10. "Defender Group Changes Name," *Philadelphia Inquirer*, March 30, 1958, p. 25.
11. "Young Lawyers to Help Defenders," *Philadelphia Inquirer*, October 27, 1947, p. 21.
12. "Thirteenth Annual Report of the Board of Directors of the Philadelphia Voluntary Defender Association, for the Year June 1, 1946 to May 31, 1947," p. 3, Defender Association of Philadelphia Records, Special Collections Research Center, Temple University Libraries.
13. A. A. DiS. and I.P.T., "Legal Aid to Indigent Criminal Defendants in Philadelphia and New Jersey," *University of Pennsylvania Law Review* 107 (1959): 839.
14. Defender Association of Philadelphia Board of Directors, *Defender Association of Philadelphia*, 21.
15. Ibid., 16.
16. Ibid., 30–31.
17. A. A. DiS. and I.P.T., "Legal Aid to Indigent Criminal Defendants in Philadelphia and New Jersey," 842.
18. Defender Association of Philadelphia Board of Directors, *Defender Association of Philadelphia*, 13.
19. Ibid., 31.
20. Ibid., 12–13.
21. Ibid., 31.
22. Ibid., 18–19.
23. Ibid.
24. Dave Racher, "Court Case Lost by Pre-DA Specter Pops Up Mysteriously," *Philadelphia Daily News*, November 2, 1967, p. 4.
25. Defender Association of Philadelphia Board of Directors, *Defender Association of Philadelphia*, 19.
26. Ibid., 20.

27. "Defender Association of Philadelphia: 37th Annual Report of the Directors, for the Year July 1, 1970–June 30, 1971," p. 23, Defender Association of Philadelphia Records, Special Collections Research Center, Temple University Libraries.

28. Philip R. Goldsmith, "Bar Says Volunteer Lawyers Will Help Ease Court Backlog," *Philadelphia Inquirer*, February 17, 1972, p. 21; "Unwanted Defender Help on Way, Bar Says," *Philadelphia Daily News*, February 29, 1972, p. 20; Dave Racher, "Bar Association Vetoes Free Work to Cut Court Backlog," *Philadelphia Daily News*, March 28, 1972, p. 20.

29. "34th Annual Report of the Directors of the Defender Association of Philadelphia for the Year June 1, 1967 to June 30, 1968," pp. 1–6, Defender Association of Philadelphia Records, Special Collections Research Center, Temple University Libraries.

30. A. A. DiS. and I.P.T., "Legal Aid to Indigent Criminal Defendants in Philadelphia and New Jersey," 851.

31. "Defender Group Changes Name," 25.

32. A. A. DiS. and I.P.T., "Legal Aid to Indigent Criminal Defendants in Philadelphia and New Jersey," 852–853.

33. Herman I. Pollock, "Equal Justice in Practice," *Minnesota Law Review* 45, no. 737 (1961): 749–752.

34. Robert I. Greenberg, "'Tax' on Lawyers Proposed by Judge," *Philadelphia Inquirer*, September 25, 1960, p. 37.

CHAPTER 3

1. Johnson v. Zerbst, 304 U.S. 458 (1938).

2. Powell v. Alabama, 287 U.S. 45 (1932).

3. Betts v. Brady, 316 U.S. 455 (1942).

4. Eleanor Morton, "How the Voluntary Defender Frequently Prevents Tragic Injustice to Those Wrongly Accused," *Philadelphia Inquirer*, December 6, 1934, p. 16.

5. Betts v. Brady, 456, 471–472.

6. Bruce Green, "Gideon's Amici: Why Do Prosecutors So Rarely Defend the Rights of the Accused?," *Yale Law Journal* 122, no. 2336 (2013): 2338.

7. William M. Beaney, "The Right to Counsel: Past, Present and Future," *Virginia Law Review* 49, no. 6 (1963): 1153.

8. Gideon v. Wainwright, 372 U.S. 335 (1963).

9. Mapp v. Ohio, 367 U.S. 643 (1961).

10. Escobedo v. Illinois, 378 U.S. 478 (1964).

11. Miranda v. Arizona, 384 U.S. 436 (1966).

12. Wife of Defender Association volunteer, conversation with Edward Madeira, 1961, Philadelphia.

13. Argesinger v. Hamlin, 407 U.S. 25 (1972).

14. Benjamin Lerner (Philadelphia Court of Common Pleas judge), interview by the authors, May 13, 2018, Philadelphia.

15. Strickland v. Washington, 466 U.S. 668 (1984).

16. Herman I. Pollock, "Equal Justice in Practice," *Minnesota Law Review* 45, no. 737 (1961): 737.

17. Anne Selby, "Gideon Decision on Appeals of Prison Inmates Haunts Many Courts," *Philadelphia Inquirer*, September 15, 1963, p. 5.

18. Public Defender Act, December 2, 1968, Pub. L. 1144, No. 358 C.L. 16.

19. "Pennsylvania," *Gideon at 50*, http://gideonat50.org/in-your-state/pennsylvania (accessed May 19, 2020).

20. "In Your State," *Gideon at 50*, http://gideonat50.org/in-your-state/#state -funding-level (accessed May 19, 2020).

21. Grace Toohey, "Judge Advances Louisiana Public Defense Lawsuit, Calls Funding Woes Bad Excuse for Violating Rights," *Acadiana Advocate*, January 24, 2019, https://www.theadvocate.com/acadiana/news/courts/article_2ba286b6-2021 -11e9-b60e-1f8f0c190611.html.

22. See the Federal Bureau of Investigation's *Uniform Crime Reporting Statistics* database, at https://www.ucrdatatool.gov/Search/Crime/State/RunCrimeStatebyState.cfm.

23. Richard H. Rovere, "The Campaign: Goldwater," *New Yorker*, September 26, 1964, https://www.newyorker.com/magazine/1964/10/03/the-campaign-goldwater.

24. Cheryl Corley, "President Johnson's Crime Commission Report, 50 Years Later," National Public Radio, October 6, 2017, https://www.npr.org/2017/10/06/542487124/president-johnson-s-crime-commission-report-50-years-later.

25. John A. Martin and Michelle Travis, "Defending the Indigent during a War on Crime," *Cornell Journal of Law and Public Policy* 1, no. 69 (1992): 69–70.

26. Bill Fidati and Bob Williams, "3 Obstacles Barred Specter from Victory Path," *Philadelphia Daily News*, November 8, 1967, p. 4.

27. Frank Clifford, "Voters Repudiate 3 of Court's Liberal Justices," *Los Angeles Times*, November 5, 1986, p. 8.

28. Gregory A. Huber and Sanford C. Gordon, "Accountability and Coercion: Is Justice Blind When It Runs for Office?," *American Journal of Political Science* 48 (2004): 247–248.

29. Elizabeth Duff, "Jubilant Judge Richette Assails Rizzo," *Philadelphia Inquirer*, November 7, 1973, p. 18.

30. Vera Institute for Justice, "Incarceration Trends: Philadelphia County, PA," http://trends.vera.org/rates/philadelphia-county-pa?incarcerationData=all (accessed March 16, 2020).

31. "Defender Association of Philadelphia, 32d Annual Report of the Directors for the Year June 1, 1965–June 30, 1966," p. 3, Defender Association of Philadelphia Records, Special Collections Research Center, Temple University Libraries, Philadelphia; "Defender Association of Philadelphia 35th Annual Report of the Directors for the Year July 1, 1968–June 30, 1969," pp. 7, 27, Defender Association of Philadelphia Records, Special Collections Research Center, Temple University Libraries.

32. "34th Annual Report of the Directors of the Defender Association of Philadelphia for the Year June 1, 1967 to June 30, 1968," p. 2, Defender Association of Philadelphia Records, Special Collections Research Center, Temple University Libraries.

33. A. A. DiS. and I.P.T., "Legal Aid to Indigent Criminal Defendants in Philadelphia and New Jersey," *University of Pennsylvania Law Review* 107 (1959): 842.

34. "31st Annual Report of the Directors of the Defender Association of Philadelphia for the Year June 1, 1964–May 31, 1965," p. 8, Defender Association of Philadelphia Records, Special Research Collection Center, Temple University Libraries.

35. "34th Annual Report," 8–9.

36. Harry J. Karafin and Leonard J. McAdams, "3 Agencies Provide Legal Guidance to 20,000 Families Each," *Philadelphia Inquirer*, December 13, 1964, p. 8; "Defender Association of Philadelphia 36th Annual Report of the Directors for the Year July 1, 1969 to June 30, 1970," p. 20, Defender Association of Philadelphia Records, Special Collections Research Center, Temple University Libraries; "Defender

Association of Philadelphia 39th Annual Report of the Directors for the Year July 1, 1972–June 30, 1973," p. 31, Defender Association of Philadelphia Records, Special Collections Research Center, Temple University Libraries.

37. Lerner, interview by the authors.

38. "Defender Association of Philadelphia 35th Annual Report," 2.

39. Letter from Vincent Carroll to James H. J. Tate, May 27, 1968, Defender Association of Philadelphia Records, Special Collections Research Center, Temple University Libraries.

40. "Defender Association of Philadelphia 35th Annual Report," 7.

41. "Defenders Fill Post," *Philadelphia Inquirer*, May 6, 1968, p. 15.

42. "Defender Works Overtime to Save Agency; 2,000 Criminal Cases Pending," *Philadelphia Inquirer*, November 4, 1968, p. 42.

43. Rem Rieder, "Defender Unit to End Criminal Trial Work," *Philadelphia Inquirer*, November 19, 1968, p. 5.

44. Rem Rieder, "Defenders Are Broke, Will Refuse Cases," *Philadelphia Inquirer*, November 2, 1968, p. 5.

45. "$76,000 Given Defender Unit to Ease Crisis," *Philadelphia Inquirer*, November 22, 1968, p. 14.

46. Letter from Richard Tilghman to Joseph N. DuBarry IV, November 19, 1968, Defender Association of Philadelphia Records, Special Collections Research Center, Temple University Libraries.

47. Letter from Martin Vinikoor to Mercer D. Tate, November 19, 1968, Defender Association of Philadelphia Records, Special Collections Research Center, Temple University Libraries; letter from Martin Vinikoor to Louis Sherman, November 1968, Defender Association of Philadelphia Records, Special Collections Research Center, Temple University Libraries.

48. "Defender Association of Philadelphia 35th Annual Report," 2.

49. Ibid.

50. Letter from Theodore Voorhees to members of the Board of Judges, November 25, 1968, Defender Association of Philadelphia Records, Special Research Collection, Temple University Libraries.

51. Rem Rieder, "Mayor Proposes City Take Over Duties of Defender Association," *Philadelphia Inquirer*, December 6, 1968, p. 9.

52. "New City Office Needed at Time Like This?," *Philadelphia Daily News*, December 9, 1968, p. 29.

53. Dave Racher, "Board of Judges Opposes Plan for Public Defender," *Philadelphia Daily News*, December 10, 1968, p. 5.

54. Rem Rieder, "City May Drop Plans for Public Defender," *Philadelphia Inquirer*, December 17, 1968, p. 41.

55. Ibid.

56. "Compromise Plan on Public Defender Draws Criticism," *Philadelphia Inquirer*, January 1, 1969, p. 27.

57. Ibid.

58. Frank McDevitt, "Defender Fires Farewell Blast at Tate's Rule," *Philadelphia Inquirer*, January 15, 1969, p. 14.

59. Acel Moore, "Martin Vinikoor, Law Professor, Defender," *Philadelphia Inquirer*, March 6, 1976, p. 8-A.

60. "Defender Association of Philadelphia 35th Annual Report," 2.

61. Louis M. Natali Jr., interview by the authors, October 11, 2017, Philadelphia.

62. "Defender Association of Philadelphia 35th Annual Report," 3.

63. Ibid., 7.

64. Letter from Louis B. Schwartz to Joseph N. DuBarry IV, December 30, 1968, Defender Association of Philadelphia Records, Special Research Collections Center, Temple University Libraries.

65. Defender Association of Philadelphia Board of Directors, *Defender Association of Philadelphia, 1934–1984: A Report on the First Fifty Years* (Philadelphia: Packard Press, 1984), 25–26.

66. Defender Association of Philadelphia Amendment of Articles of Incorporation, 453 Pa. 353 (1973).

67. Defender Association of Philadelphia Board of Directors, *Defender Association of Philadelphia*, 29.

68. Natali, interview by the authors.

CHAPTER 4

1. "Defender Association of Philadelphia 36th Annual Report of the Directors for the Year July 1, 1969 to June 30, 1970," p. 2, Defender Association of Philadelphia Records, Special Collections Research Center, Temple University Libraries, Philadelphia.

2. "38th Annual Report of the Directors, Defender Association of Philadelphia, for the Year July 1, 1971–June 30, 1972," p. 30, Defender Association of Philadelphia Records, Special Collections Research Center, Temple University Libraries; "Defender Association of Philadelphia 39th Annual Report of the Directors for the Year July 1, 1972–June 30, 1973," p. 36, Defender Association of Philadelphia Records, Special Collections Research Center, Temple University Libraries.

3. "Violent Crimes Rise Slightly in Phila., but U.S. Boost Is Greater," *Philadelphia Inquirer*, June 23, 1970, p. 30.

4. Pew Charitable Trusts, "Philadelphia's Poor: Who They Are, Where They Live, and How That Has Changed," November 2017, https://www.pewtrusts.org/-/media/assets/2017/11/pri_philadelphias_poor.pdf.

5. Defender Association of Philadelphia Board of Directors, *Defender Association of Philadelphia, 1934–1984: A Report on the First Fifty Years* (Philadelphia: Packard Press, 1984), 41–42.

6. "Defender Association of Philadelphia: 37th Annual Report of the Directors, for the Year July 1, 1970–June 30, 1971," p. 22, Defender Association of Philadelphia Records, Special Collections Research Center, Temple University Libraries.

7. Ibid.

8. National Legal Aid and Defender Association, "Evaluation Report on the Defender Association of Philadelphia," September 1971, included in "Public Defender Representation in Pennsylvania: A Report from Vincent J. Ziccardi, Esq., to the Honorable A. Evans Kephart, Court Administrator of Pennsylvania, Project Director," June 1974, p. 47 (in authors' possession).

9. Vincent Ziccardi, conversation with Edward Madeira, 1973, Philadelphia.

10. "Sixth Annual Report of the Directors of the Philadelphia Voluntary Defender Association, June 21, 1940," p. 3, Defenders Association of Philadelphia Records, Special Research Collections Center, Temple University Libraries.

11. Jim Nicholson, "Public Defenders Are Soft on Crime (That's What They Get Paid For)," *Philadelphia Inquirer Magazine*, March 26, 1972, p. 10.

12. Frank DeSimone, telephone interview by the authors, January 29, 2018.

13. Benjamin Lerner, interview by the authors, October 13, 2017, Philadelphia.

14. Nicholson, "Public Defenders Are Soft on Crime," 10.

15. "Today's Mail, Public Defenders," *Philadelphia Inquirer Magazine*, April 23, 1972, p. 38.

16. "Defender Association of Philadelphia 39th Annual Report," 3.

17. Andy Wallace, "Vincent Ziccardi, 63, Well Known as Caring Criminal Defense Lawyer," *Philadelphia Inquirer*, June 14, 1996, p. R4.

18. Nicholson, "Public Defenders Are Soft on Crime," 15.

19. Ibid.

20. Philip R. Goldsmith, "Public Defenders Seek Court Sanctions against D.A. Specter," *Philadelphia Inquirer*, May 19, 1972, p. 4.

21. Jon Katz, "D.A. Assailed on Conviction Rate," *Philadelphia Inquirer*, December 27, 1972, p. 21.

22. Lerner, interview by the authors.

23. Ibid.

24. DeSimone, interview by the authors.

25. "Jesuit Who Serves as Lawyer Marks 25 Years as Priest," *Wilkes-Barre Times Leader*, June 23, 1973, p. 5.

26. Paul Conway, interview by the authors, September 11, 2018, Philadelphia.

27. Dennis Kelly, interview by the authors. November 14, 2018, Philadelphia.

28. David Kairys, *Philadelphia Freedom: Memoir of a Civil Rights Lawyer* (Ann Arbor: University of Michigan Press, 2008), 10.

29. "Defender Association of Philadelphia 39th Annual Report," pp. 3–4.

30. Lerner, interview by the authors.

31. Ibid.

32. DeSimone, interview by the authors.

33. Ibid.

34. Ibid.

35. Ibid.

36. Conway, interview by the authors.

37. Abbe Smith, "Defending Those People," *Ohio State Journal of Criminal Law* 10, no. 1 (2012): 288.

38. Louis M. Natali Jr., interview by the authors, October 11, 2017, Philadelphia.

39. Jonathan Rapping, telephone interview by the authors, May 8, 2017.

40. Natali, interview by the authors.

41. Kelly, interview by the authors.

42. David Rudovsky, interview by the authors, July 5, 2017, Philadelphia.

43. Abbe Smith, "Too Much Heart and Not Enough Heat: The Short Life and Fractured Ego of the Empathic, Heroic Public Defender," *UC Davis Law Review* 37, no. 5 (2004): 1212.

44. Ibid.

CHAPTER 5

1. "Defender Association of Philadelphia: 37th Annual Report of the Directors, for the Year July 1, 1970–June 30, 1971," p. 2, Defender Association of Philadelphia Records, Special Research Collection, Temple University Libraries, Philadelphia.

2. Dorothy Lynch Posel, quoted in Defender Association of Philadelphia Board of Directors, *Defender Association of Philadelphia, 1934–1984: A Report on the First Fifty Years* (Philadelphia: Packard Press, 1984), 38.

3. Ibid.

4. "Defender Association of Philadelphia: 37th Annual Report," 2.

5. Ibid., 2–3.

6. Posel, quoted in Defender Association of Philadelphia Board of Directors, *Defender Association of Philadelphia*, 39.

7. National Legal Aid and Defender Association, "Evaluation Report on the Defender Association of Philadelphia," September 1971, p. 7 (in authors' possession).

8. Ibid., 9.

9. "Sixth Annual Report of the Directors of the Philadelphia Voluntary Defender Association, June 21, 1940," p. 7, Defender Association of Philadelphia Records, Special Collections Research Center, Temple University Libraries.

10. "34th Annual Report of the Directors of the Defender Association of Philadelphia for the Year June 1, 1967 to June 30, 1968," p. 2, Defender Association of Philadelphia Records, Special Collections Research Center, Temple University Libraries.

11. In re Gault v. Arizona, 387 U.S. 1 (1967).

12. "Juvenile Trials Threatened," *Philadelphia Inquirer*, June 23, 1968, p. 18.

13. Donald A. McDonough, "Specter Advocates More Judges to Try Phila. Criminal Cases," *Philadelphia Inquirer*, September 7, 1968, p. 11.

14. "Defender Association of Philadelphia 35th Annual Report of the Directors for the Year July 1, 1968 to June 30, 1969," p. 7, Defender Association of Philadelphia Records, Special Collections Research Center, Temple University Libraries.

15. Ibid.

16. Ibid.

17. "Defender Association of Philadelphia: 37th Annual Report," 14.

18. "Defender Association of Philadelphia 35th Annual Report," 8.

19. Ibid.

20. "Defender Association of Philadelphia 36th Annual Report of the Directors for the Year July 1, 1969 to June 30, 1970," p. 3, Defender Association of Philadelphia Records, Special Collections Research Center, Temple University Libraries.

21. National Legal Aid and Defender Association, "Evaluation Report," 42.

22. Benjamin Lerner, interview by the authors, October 13, 2017, Philadelphia.

23. Jim Nicholson, "The Public Defenders Are Soft on Crime (That's What They're Paid For)," *Philadelphia Inquirer Magazine*, March 26, 1972, p. 14.

24. Dave Racher, "Psychiatrist Hired to Examine Clients of Defender," *Philadelphia Daily News*, October 2, 1972, p. 10.

25. Edward Eisen and James S. Lintz, "80 Inmates, 25 Guards Injured as 400 Riot at Holmesburg; Police Quell 2½-Hour Melee," *Philadelphia Inquirer*, July 5, 1970, p. 1-A.

26. Thomas Ferrick and Elliot Brown, "Ex-Holmesburg Inmates Tell of Beatings," *Philadelphia Inquirer*, July 19, 1970, p. 1.

27. Mike Willman, "Holmesburg Uprising Not Racial, D.A. Says," *Philadelphia Inquirer*, August 11, 1970, p. 1; Dave Racher and Lou Antosh, "2 at Holmesburg Ordered Transferred," *Philadelphia Daily News*, August 11, 1970, p. 4.

28. Mike Willmann, "3 Probers Refuse to Step Aside in Case of Holmesburg Prisoner," July 18, 1970, p. 7.

29. David Rudovsky, telephone interview by the authors, June 19, 2019.

30. Ferrick and Brown, "Ex-Holmesburg Inmates Tell of Beatings," 1.

31. Ken Shuttleworth and Mike Willmann, "3 Judges Call Holmesburg 'Cruel Place,'" *Philadelphia Inquirer*, August 12, 1970, p. 1.

32. Ibid.

33. Mike Willmann, "Overcrowding at Holmesburg Slowly Easing," *Philadelphia Inquirer*, September 11, 1970, p. 20.

34. Rudovsky, interview by the authors.

35. Jackson v. Hendrick, 457 Pa. 405 (Pa. 1974).

36. Rudovsky, interview by the authors.

37. Maxwell King, "City Prisons Ruled 'Cruel,' 'Inhuman' by 3 Judges," *Philadelphia Inquirer*, April 8, 1972, p. 1.

38. Rudovsky, interview by the authors.

39. Harris v. Pernsley, 755 F.2d 338 (3rd Cir. 1984).

40. Rudovsky, interview by the authors.

41. Fredric N. Tulsky, "Prison Suit Reported Settled," *Philadelphia Inquirer*, November 26, 1986, p. 1.

42. Ibid.

43. Rudovsky, interview by the authors.

44. Bowers v. Philadelphia, Civil Action No. 06-CV-3229 (E.D. Pa. September 28, 2006).

45. Williams v. Philadelphia, 2:08-cv-01979-RBS (E.D. Pa. 2008).

46. Rudovsky, interview by the authors.

47. Ibid.

CHAPTER 6

1. Mike Leary, "Bicen Restaurant in the Park?," *Philadelphia Inquirer*, November 8, 1974, p. 1-B.

2. Dave Racher, "Ziccardi Quits Defender Post," *Philadelphia Daily News*, November 7, 1974, p. 15.

3. Ibid.

4. Benjamin Lerner, interview by the authors, May 13, 2017, Philadelphia.

5. Ibid.

6. Ibid.

7. "34th Annual Report of the Directors of the Defender Association of Philadelphia for the Year June 1, 1967 to June 30, 1968," p. 14, Defender Association of Philadelphia Records, Special Collections Research Center, Temple University Libraries.

8. Lerner, interview by the authors.

9. Louis M. Natali Jr., interview by the authors, October 11, 2017, Philadelphia.

10. Ibid.

11. New York University School of Law, "Anthony G. Amsterdam: Biography," https://its.law.nyu.edu/facultyprofiles/index.cfm?fuseaction=profile.biography&personid=19743 (accessed March 17, 2020).

12. Furman v. Georgia, 408 U.S. 238 (1972).

13. Lerner, interview by the authors.

14. David Rudovsky, interview by the authors, July 5, 2017, Philadelphia.

15. Ibid.

16. Andrea B. Wapner, "The Peter Pan of Appellate Practice," *Philadelphia Lawyer* 55, no. 1 (1992): 56.

17. Lerner, interview by the authors.

18. Ibid.

19. Anthony G. Amsterdam, email interview by the authors, April 4, 2019.

20. "34th Annual Report," 14.

21. Amsterdam, interview by the authors.

22. Rudovsky, interview by the authors.

23. Ibid.
24. Ibid.

CHAPTER 7

1. National Legal Aid and Defender Association, "Evaluation Report on the Defender Association of Philadelphia," September 1971, p. 47 (in authors' possession).
2. Argersinger v. Hamlin, 407 U.S. 25 (1972).
3. "Defender Association of Philadelphia 39th Annual Report of the Directors for the Year July 1, 1972–June 30, 1973," p. 3, Defender Association of Philadelphia Records, Special Collections Research Center, Temple University Libraries, Philadelphia.
4. In re Gault v. Arizona, 387 U.S. 1 (1967).
5. "Defender Association of Philadelphia 35th Annual Report of the Directors for the Year July 1, 1968–June 30, 1969," p. 7, Defender Association of Philadelphia Records, Special Collections Research Center, Temple University Libraries.
6. "Defender Association of Philadelphia 36th Annual Report of the Directors for the Year July 1, 1969 to June 30, 1970," 3, Defender Association of Philadelphia Records, Special Collections Research Center, Temple University Libraries.
7. Louis M. Natali Jr., interview by the authors, October 11, 2017, Philadelphia.
8. Benjamin Lerner, interview by the authors, October 13, 2017, Philadelphia.
9. Paul Messing, interview by the authors, October 22, 2017, Philadelphia.
10. Jim Nicholson, "The Public Defenders Are Soft on Crime (That's What They're Paid For)," *Philadelphia Inquirer Magazine*, March 26, 1972, p. 28.
11. Lerner, interview by the authors.
12. Donald L. Barlett and James B. Steele, "Findings Don't Match Specter Statements," *Philadelphia Inquirer*, February 20, 1973. p. 9A.
13. Donald L. Barlett and James B. Steele, "D.A. Churns Out Indictments . . . but Many Are Weak," *Philadelphia Inquirer*, February 20, 1973, p. 1A.
14. Stephen J. Schulhofer, "Is Plea Bargaining Inevitable?," *Harvard Law Review* 97, no. 5 (1984): 1096–1097.
15. Bradley S. Bridge, interview by the authors, June 22, 2018, Philadelphia.
16. Ibid.
17. Abbe Smith, telephone interview by the authors, October 20, 2017.
18. Ibid.
19. Marc Bookman, interview by the authors, May 20, 2018, Philadelphia.
20. Defender Association of Philadelphia Amendment of Articles of Incorporation, 453 Pa. 353 (1973).
21. Natali, interview by the authors.
22. Ibid.
23. "Research the System," *Presumed Guilty: Tales of the Public Defender*, PBS, https://www.pbs.org/kqed/presumedguilty/3.2.1.html (accessed March 17, 2020).
24. Lerner, interview by the authors.
25. Bookman, interview by the authors.
26. Lerner, interview by the authors.
27. Ellen Greenlee, interview by the authors, March 20, 2017, Philadelphia.
28. Lerner, interview by the authors.
29. Defender Association of Philadelphia Board of Directors, *Defender Association of Philadelphia, 1934–1984: A Report on the First Fifty Years* (Philadelphia: Packard Press, 1984), 45.

30. Phyllis Subin, interview by the authors, September 13, 2018, Philadelphia.

31. Ibid.

32. Ibid.

33. Ibid.

34. Ibid.

CHAPTER 8

1. "Annual Report of the Directors of the Philadelphia Voluntary Defender Association, April 26, 1935," in Defender Association of Philadelphia Board of Directors, *Defender Association of Philadelphia, 1934–1984: A Report on the First Fifty Years* (Philadelphia: Packard Press, 1984), 5–6.

2. Thurgood Matthews v. The Defender Association of Philadelphia, No. 94-CV-2442 (1997).

3. Benjamin Lerner, interview by the authors, August 1, 2018, Philadelphia.

4. Reggie B. Walton, interviews by Harold L. Talisman, March 16, April 11, and May 8, 2007, Oral History Project, Historical Society of the District of Columbia Circuit, https://dcchs.org/sb_pdf/complete-oral-history-walton/.

5. Ibid.

6. C. Darnell Jones II, interview by the authors, December 4, 2017, Philadelphia.

7. Ibid.

8. Steven Church, "Sleet Often Sought for Leadership," *Wilmington News Journal*, November 30, 1998, p. 1.

9. U.S. District Court for the District of Columbia, "Senior Judge Reggie B. Walton," https://www.dcd.uscourts.gov/content/senior-judge-reggie-b-walton (accessed March 17, 2020); Fredric N. Tulsky, Daniel R. Biddle, and Henry Goldman, "Casey Names 10 to City's Court," *Philadelphia Inquirer,* February 25, 1987, p. 1; Lerner, interview by the authors; Church, "Sleet Often Sought for Leadership," 1.

10. Mike Willmann, "City's Black Lawyers' Corps Charges Racism in Profession," *Philadelphia Inquirer*, September 20, 1970, p. 1.

11. Charles L. Mitchell, "The Black 'Philadelphia Lawyer,'" *Villanova Law Review* 20, no. 2 (1975): 399.

12. Acel Moore, "Black Judges, Police—but Few Prosecutors," *Philadelphia Inquirer*, July 21, 1974, p. 1-B.

13. Mitchell, "The Black 'Philadelphia Lawyer,'" 387.

14. Jones, interview by the authors.

15. Matthews v. Defender.

16. Michael Matza, "Disputing the 'Darden Dilemma' Theory," *Philadelphia Inquirer*, March 24, 1997, p. B5.

17. Lerner, interview by the authors.

18. Linda Loyd, "Minority Lawyers Allege Bias," *Philadelphia Inquirer*, June 7, 1989, p. B1.

19. Ibid.

20. Ibid.

21. Ibid., B1, B6.

22. Lerner, interview by the authors.

23. Matthews v. Defender.

24. Ibid.

25. Ibid.

26. Jules Epstein, *Legal Intelligencer*, October 30, 1990, quoted in "VLS Alumna Becomes Chief Defender," *The Docket* 28, no. 3 (1990): 4, https://digital commons.law.villanova.edu/cgi/viewcontent.cgi?article=1156&context=docket.

27. Ibid.

CHAPTER 9

1. Carolyn Temin, interview by Senior Judge Oral History Program, First Judicial District of Pennsylvania, August 10, 2011, https://www.philacourts.us/sjhistory/.

2. Ibid.

3. Ibid.

4. Ibid.

5. Ibid.

6. Ibid.

7. Phyllis Subin, interview by the authors, September 12, 2018, Philadelphia.

8. Ibid.

9. Ibid.

10. Linda Loyd, "Obituaries: Rita Levine, 39, Bus-Attack Victim," *Philadelphia Inquirer*, July 19, 1989, p. 10-E.

11. Mental Health Procedures Act, Pub. L. 817, No. 143 C.L. 50 (July 9, 1976).

12. Donald C. Drake, "11 Anguished Days, Shackled and Unwanted," *Philadelphia Inquirer*, July 19, 1982, p. 1-A.

13. Loyd, "Obituaries," 10-E.

14. Ellen Greenlee, interview by the authors, March 20, 2017, Philadelphia.

15. Lerner, interview by the authors.

16. Greenlee, interview by the authors.

17. Ibid.

18. Fredric N. Tulsky, "Defender Association Appoints First Woman Chief in 56 Years," *Philadelphia Inquirer*, October 31, 1990, p. 4-B.

19. Edward Colimore and Fredric N. Tulsky, "Breaking Down Legal Bastions," *Philadelphia Inquirer*, December 6, 1986, p. 1-B.

20. Lerner, interview by the authors.

21. Greenlee, interview by the authors.

22. Cynthia Grant Bowman, "Women in the Legal Profession from the 1920s to the 1970s: What Can We Learn from Their Experience about Law and Social Change?," *Maine Law Review* 61, no. 1 (2009): 15.

23. American Bar Association, "A Current Glance at Women in the Law," July 2014, https://www.americanbar.org/content/dam/aba/administrative/women/current_glance_statistics_july2014.pdf.

24. Susan Bozorgi, "Women Criminal Defense Attorneys: Interview with Claire Rauscher," *Women Criminal Defense Attorneys Blog*, https://womencriminalde fenseattorneys.com/women-criminal-defense-attorneys-interview-with-claire-rauscher/ (accessed March 17, 2020).

25. Ibid.

26. Susan Bozorgi, "Women Criminal Defense Attorneys: Interview with Abbe Smith," *Women Criminal Defense Attorneys Blog*, https://womencriminaldefense attorneys.com/women-criminal-defense-attorneys-interview-with-abbe-smith/ (accessed March 17, 2020).

27. Ibid.

28. Abbe Smith, telephone interview by the authors, October 20, 2017.

29. Ibid.

30. Mary DeFusco, interview by the authors, April 19, 2018, Philadelphia.

31. Ibid.

32. Ibid.

33. Lerner, interview by the authors.

CHAPTER 10

1. Abbe Smith, "Too Much Heart and Not Enough Heat: The Short Life and Fractured Ego of the Empathic, Heroic Public Defender," *UC Davis Law Review* 37, no. 3 (2004): 1212.

2. John Packel, interview by the authors, January 26, 2018, Philadelphia.

3. Ibid.

4. "3-Man Board Holds Inquiry into Police-Magistrate Feud," *Philadelphia Inquirer*, April 30, 1958, p. 37.

5. Packel, interview by the authors.

6. Ibid.

7. Ibid.

8. "Public Defender Representation in Pennsylvania: A Report from Vincent J. Ziccardi, Esq., to the Honorable A. Evans Kephart, Court Administrator of Pennsylvania, Project Director," June 1974, p. 31 (in authors' possession).

9. A. A. DiS. and I.P.T., "Legal Aid to Indigent Criminal Defendants in Philadelphia and New Jersey," *University of Pennsylvania Law Review* 107, no. 6 (1959): 842.

10. "30th Annual Report of the Directors of the Defender Association of Philadelphia for the Year June 1, 1963–May 31, 1964," p. 15, Defender Association of Philadelphia Records, Special Research Collection Center, Temple University Libraries, Philadelphia.

11. A. A. DiS. and I.P.T., "Legal Aid to Indigent Criminal Defendants," 842.

12. Ibid., 843.

13. Ibid., 842.

14. "31st Annual Report of the Directors of the Defender Association of Philadelphia for the Year June 1, 1964–May 31, 1965," p. 15, Defender Association of Philadelphia Records, Special Research Collection Center, Temple University Libraries.

15. "34th Annual Report of the Directors of the Defender Association of Philadelphia for the Year June 1, 1967 to June 30, 1968," p. 18, Defender Association of Philadelphia Records, Special Research Collections Center, Temple University Libraries; "Defender Association of Philadelphia: 37th Annual Report of the Directors for the Year July 1, 1970–June 30, 1971," p. 29, Defender Association of Philadelphia Records, Special Research Collections Center, Temple University Libraries.

16. National Defender Project, "Client Service in a Defender Organization: The Philadelphia Experience," *University of Pennsylvania Law Review* 17, no. 448 (1969): 466; Fairhurst v. United States, 388 F.2d 825 (3d Cir.), cert. denied, 392 U.S. 912 (1968).

17. Carolyn Temin, interview by Senior Judge Oral History Program, First Judicial District of Pennsylvania, August 10, 2011, https://www.philacourts.us/sjhistory/.Temin.

18. "34th Annual Report," 8.

19. Temin, interview by Senior Judge Oral History Program.

20. Ibid.

21. Commonwealth v. Daniels, 210 Pa. Super. Ct. 156 (1967).

22. Temin, interview by Senior Judge Oral History Program.

23. Commonwealth v. Daniel [*sic*], 430 Pa. 642 (1968).

24. Temin, interview by Senior Judge Oral History Program.

25. Gabriel Ireton, "Woman Offenders Jailing Changed," *Pittsburgh Post-Gazette*, October 18, 1974, p. 9.

26. Temin, interview by Senior Judge Oral History Program.

27. Commonwealth v. Hall, 451 Pa. 201 (1973).

28. Ibid.

29. Packel, interview by the authors.

30. Commonwealth v. Hall, 210.

31. Ibid., 208.

32. Packel, interview by the authors.

33. Commonwealth v. Matos, 543 Pa. 449 (1996).

34. Marc Kaufman, "Pa. Ruling Adds to Uproar over Chases and Evidence," *Philadelphia Inquirer*, March 24, 1996, p. A-1.

35. Commonwealth v. Matos.

36. Kaufman, "Pa. Ruling Adds to Uproar," A-1.

37. Joseph P. Fried, "Harold Baer Jr., Judge Whose Civil Liberties Rulings Drew Fire, Dies at 81," *New York Times*, May 29, 2014, https://www.nytimes.com/2014/05/29/nyregion/harold-baer-jr-judge-whose-civil-liberties-decisions-drew-criticism-dies-at-81.html.

38. Kaufman, "Pa. Ruling Adds to Uproar," A-1.

39. Packel, interview by the authors.

40. Ibid.

41. Ibid.

42. Ibid.

43. Pennsylvania v. Finley, 481 U.S. 551 (1987).

44. Packel, interview by the authors.

45. Commonwealth v. Benjamin Walker, No. 28 EAP 2011, brief for amicus curiae, American Psychological Association in support of appellant, https://www.apa.org/about/offices/ogc/amicus/walker.pdf.

46. Richard A. Leo, "False Confessions: Causes, Consequences, and Implications," *Journal of the American Academy of Psychiatry and the Law* 37, no. 3 (2009), http://jaapl.org/content/37/3/332.

47. Katherine Reamy, "Pennsylvania Stacks the Deck against Defendants in *Commonwealth v. Alicia*, Leaving False Confession Assessments to the Jury," *Villanova Law Review* 61, no. 2 (2016): 323–326.

48. Commonwealth v. Benjamin Walker.

49. Commonwealth v. Alicia, No. 27 EAP (2012).

50. Joseph A. Slobodzian, "When 'Yes, I Did It' Isn't True," *Philadelphia Inquirer*, June 8, 2014, p. 1-A.

51. Commonwealth v. Benjamin Walker.

52. Ibid.

53. Mark Scolforo, "Pa. Supreme Court Allows Expert Testimony on Eyewitness ID," *Associated Press*, May 29, 2014, p. 4.

54. David Rudovsky, interview by the authors, March 26, 2017, Philadelphia.

55. Slobodzian, "When 'Yes, I Did It' Isn't True," 1-A.

56. Ibid.

57. Ibid.

58. Joseph A. Slobodzian, "Man Sentenced in '05 Olney Murder," *Philadelphia Inquirer*, May 9, 2015, p. 1-B.

59. Slobodzian, "When 'Yes, I Did It' Isn't True," 1-A.

60. David DeMatteo, Jaymes Fairfax-Columbo, and Daniel A. Krauss, "Making Sense of a Court's Two Cents," *Judicial Notebook* 45, no. 11 (2014): 24, https://www.apa.org/monitor/2014/12/jn.

61. Paula Reed Ward, "Pa. Court Rulings Differ on Expert Witnesses," *Pittsburgh Post-Gazette*, June 15, 2014, p. A-13.

CHAPTER 11

1. Leonard Sosnov, interview by the authors, July 22, 2019, Philadelphia.

2. Ibid.

3. McMillan v. Pennsylvania, 477 U.S. 79 (1986).

4. Alleyne v. United States, 570 U.S. 99 (2013).

5. Sosnov, interview by the authors.

6. Apprendi v. New Jersey, 530 U.S. 466 (2000).

7. Harris v. United States, 536 U.S. 545 (2002); Julie L. Hendrix, "Harris v. United States: The Supreme Court's Latest Avoidance of Providing Constitutional Protection to Sentencing Factors," *Journal of Criminal Law and Criminology* 93, no. 4 (2003): 947.

8. Commonwealth v. Hopkins, 117 A.3d 247 (Pa. 2015).

9. Commonwealth v. Sorrell, 319 Pa. Super. Ct. 103 (1982), 465 A.2d 1250.

10. Commonwealth v. Lovette, 498 Pa. 665 (1982), 450 A.2d 975.

11. Commonwealth v. Bernhardt, 359 Pa. Super. Ct. 413 (1986), 519 A.2d 417.

12. Peter Rosalsky, email interview by the authors, July 25, 2019.

13. Commonwealth v. McClintic, 909 A.2d 1241 (Pa. 2006).

14. Commonwealth v. Dickson, 918 A.2d 95 (Pa. 2007).

15. Rosalsky, interview by the authors.

16. Ibid.

17. Commonwealth v. Weigle, 997 A.2d 306 (Pa. 2010).

18. Commonwealth v. Wolfe, 140 A.3d 651 (Pa. 2016).

19. Commonwealth v. Sessoms, 532 A2d 775 (Pa. 1987); Commonwealth v. Ludwig, 594 A.2d 281 (Pa. 1991).

20. David Rudovsky, interview by the authors, May 15, 2017, Philadelphia.

CHAPTER 12

1. Mike Leary and William K. Marimow, "False Arrests by Squad Alleged," *Philadelphia Inquirer*, February 1, 1981, p. 1-A.

2. Ibid.

3. Ibid.

4. Ibid.

5. Ibid.

6. Ibid.

7. Ibid.

8. Mike Leary and William K. Marimow, "Charges Dropped in Phila. 'Grandpop Squad' Arrest," *Philadelphia Inquirer*, March 24, 1981, p. 3-B.

9. Christopher Hepp, "City Pays $30,000 to Settle Suit in Decoy-Squad Arrest," *Philadelphia Inquirer*, January 15, 1987, p. 6-B.

10. Mike Leary and William K. Marimow, "Philadelphia D.A. Drops 2 'Grandpop' Cases," *Philadelphia Inquirer*, June 12, 1981, p. 3-B.

11. Mike Leary, "Judge Frees 'Grandpop' Case Suspect," *Philadelphia Inquirer*, July 9, 1981, p. 5-B.

12. William K. Marimow, "Suit over Police Grandpop Squad Settled for $15,000," *Philadelphia Inquirer*, April 9, 1986, p. 4-B.

13. Mike Leary and William K. Marimow, "'Grandpop' Squad Is Ordered off Street," *Philadelphia Inquirer*, February 3, 1981, p. 2-B.

14. Ibid.

15. William K. Marimow and Mike Leary, "Suspect in 'Grandpop' Case Acquitted," *Philadelphia Inquirer*, May 12, 1981, p. 1-A.

16. William K. Marimow and Mike Leary, "U.S. Grand Jury Indicts Four on 'Grandpop' Team," *Philadelphia Inquirer*, September 11, 1981, p. 1-A.

17. Phyllis Subin, interview by the authors, September 12, 2018, Philadelphia.

18. Tim Weiner, "Civil Rights Case against 'Grandpop' Squad Is Dropped," *Philadelphia Inquirer*, January 22, 1985, p. 1-B.

19. Dave Racher, "11 Nabbed by Decoys Sentenced," *Philadelphia Daily News*, March 27, 1985, p. 29.

20. Jim Smith, "U.S.: No Case against 'Grandpop' Cops," *Philadelphia Daily News*, January 22, 1985, p. 6.

21. Subin, interview by the authors.

22. Paul Messing, interview by the authors, October 22, 2017, Philadelphia.

23. Mark Fazlollah, "39th District Problem Seen in '89," *Philadelphia Inquirer*, May 3, 1995, p. 1-A.

24. Joseph A. Slobodzian, "5 City Officers Indicted on Corruption Charges," *Philadelphia Inquirer*, March 1, 1995, p. 1-A.

25. Joseph A. Slobodzian, "More Drug Convictions Tossed," *Philadelphia Inquirer*, November 22, 2015, p. 10-B.

26. Bradley S. Bridge, interview by the authors, April 25, 2018, Philadelphia.

27. Messing, interview by the authors.

28. Bridge, interview by the authors.

29. Ibid.

30. Messing, interview by the authors.

31. Karen Heller, "New Phila. Police Scandal, on Schedule," *Philadelphia Inquirer*, August 6, 2014, p. B1.

CHAPTER 13

1. National Legal Aid and Defender Association (NLADA), "Evaluation Report on the Defender Association of Philadelphia," September 1971, pp. 8–9 (in authors' possession).

2. Mike Leary, "Ex–Public Defender Files $100,000 Suit over Firing," *Philadelphia Inquirer*, October 31, 1974, p. 2-B.

3. NLADA, "Evaluation Report," 8–9.

4. "Rizzo Signs Pay Increases for 51 Top City Officials," *Philadelphia Inquirer*, December 15, 1973, p. 1-C.

5. Benjamin Lerner, interview by the authors, March 29, 2017, Philadelphia.

6. NLADA, "Evaluation Report," 10.

7. American Bar Association, "Ten Principles of a Public Defense Delivery System," February 2002, https://www.americanbar.org/content/dam/aba/administrative/legal_aid_indigent_defendants/ls_sclaid_def_tenprinciplesbooklet.pdf.

8. Lerner, interview by the authors.

9. Ibid.

10. Louis Natali, interview by the authors, June 4, 2017, Philadelphia.

11. Lerner, interview by the authors.

12. Jim Quinn, "Fighting for the Underdog," *Philadelphia Inquirer Magazine*, November 1, 1987, p. 14.

13. Lerner, interview by the authors.

14. Lorelei Laird, "Starved of Money for Too Long, Public Defender Offices Are Suing—and Starting to Win," *ABA Journal*, January 1, 2017, http://www.abajournal .com/magazine/article/the_gideon_revolution.

15. Teresa Wiltz, "Public Defenders Fight Back against Budget Cuts, Growing Caseloads," *Stateline*, November 21, 2017, https://www.pewtrusts.org/en/research -and-analysis/blogs/stateline/2017/11/21/public-defenders-fight-back-against-budget -cuts-growing-caseloads.

16. Fredric N. Tulsky, "Budget Pinch Spoils Public Defenders' 50th Anniversary," *Philadelphia Inquirer*, June 22, 1984, p. 1-B.

17. Ibid.

18. Fredric N. Tulsky, "Defender Association's Budget Ills May Cause Sharp Cutback in Services," *Philadelphia Inquirer*, July 1, 1984, p. 3-F.

19. Fredric N. Tulsky, "24 Lawyers Hired as Defenders," *Philadelphia Inquirer*, August 16, 1984, p. 1-B.

20. Henry Goldman, "Defenders' Shutdown Is Forecast," *Philadelphia Inquirer*, April 28, 1987, p. 1-B.

21. Ibid.

22. Lerner, interview by the authors.

CHAPTER 14

1. Fredric N. Tulsky, "Defender Association's Budget Ills May Cause Sharp Cutbacks in Service," *Philadelphia Inquirer*, July 1, 1984, p. 3-F.

2. For more on the award, see National Legal Aid and Defender Association, "Clara Shortridge Foltz Award (Biennial)," http://www.nlada.org/about-nlada/nlada -awards/clara-shortridge-foltz-award-biennial (accessed May 20, 2020).

3. Toni Locy, "Panel: Phila. Defense Best," *Philadelphia Daily News*, February 16, 1987, p. 10.

4. Jim Quinn, "Fighting for the Underdog," *Philadelphia Inquirer Magazine*, November 1, 1987, p. 12.

5. Ibid., 14.

6. John W. Packel, interview by the authors. January 26, 2018, Philadelphia.

7. Ibid. Lyrics used by permission of John W. Packel.

8. Defender Association of Philadelphia Board of Directors, *Defender Association of Philadelphia, 1934–1984: A Report on the First Fifty Years* (Philadelphia: Packard Press, 1984), 47.

9. Ibid., 47–48.

10. Ibid., 48.

11. Mary DeFusco, interview by the authors, April 11, 2018, Philadelphia.

12. Michael Kimmelman, "4 with Phila. Ties Are among Winners of 'Genius Awards,'" *Philadelphia Inquirer*, July 15, 1986, p. 1-A.

13. DeFusco, interview by the authors.

14. Fredric N. Tulsky, "Chief Public Defender in Phila. Steps Down; Will Join Private Firm," *Philadelphia Inquirer*, May 10, 1990, p. 7-B.

15. Fredric N. Tulsky, "Defender Association Appoints First Woman Chief in 56 Years," *Philadelphia Inquirer*, October 31, 1990, p. 4-B.

16. Ibid.

17. Ibid.

CHAPTER 15

1. Ellen Greenlee, interview by the authors, March 20, 2017, Philadelphia.
2. Ibid.
3. Ibid.
4. Mary DeFusco, interview by the authors, April 11, 2018, Philadelphia.
5. Edward Colimore and Fredric N. Tulsky, "Breaking Down Legal Bastions," *Philadelphia Inquirer*, December 6, 1986, p. 1-B.
6. Greenlee, interview by the authors.
7. Fredric N. Tulsky, "Defender Association Appoints First Woman Chief in 56 Years," *Philadelphia Inquirer*, October 31, 1990, p. 4-B.
8. Greenlee, interview by the authors.
9. Robert L. Listenbee and Ellen Greenlee, interview by the authors, February 1, 2018, Philadelphia.
10. Louis M. Natali Jr., interview by the authors, June 14, 2017, Philadelphia; Greenlee, interview by the authors.
11. Greenlee, interview by the authors.

CHAPTER 16

1. Fredric N. Tulsky, "A Step for Indigent Defense," *Philadelphia Inquirer*, April 12, 1993, p. B1.
2. Ellen Greenlee, interview by the authors, March 20, 2017, Philadelphia.
3. Fredric N. Tulsky, "Big-Time Trials, Small-Time Defenses," *Philadelphia Inquirer*, September 14, 1992, p. A1.
4. Henry Goldman, "Defenders Win Backing to Try Murder Cases," *Philadelphia Inquirer*, February 1, 1991, p. 4-B.
5. Tulsky, "Big-Time Trials, Small-Time Defenses," A1.
6. Fredric N. Tulsky, "Poor Defendants Pay the Costs as Courts Save on Murder Trials," *Philadelphia Inquirer*, September 13, 1992, p. A1.
7. Ibid.
8. Ibid.
9. Tulsky, "Big-Time Trials, Small-Time Defenses," A1.
10. Marc Bookman, interview by the authors, May 14, 2018, Philadelphia.
11. Tulsky, "Poor Defendants Pay the Costs," A1.
12. Bookman, interview by the authors.
13. Greenlee, interview by the authors.
14. Linda Loyd, "Chief Administrator Hired for Phila. Courts," *Philadelphia Inquirer*, September 5, 1991, p. 4-B.
15. L. Stuart Ditzen, "Judge Dismissed Ex–Court Official's Suit," *Philadelphia Inquirer*, November 10, 1998, p. B1.
16. Greenlee, interview by the authors.
17. Henry Goldman, "Bar Panel Shifts on Role of Defenders," *Philadelphia Inquirer*, February 1, 1991, p. 7-B.
18. Tulsky, "Big-Time Trials, Small-Time Defenses," A1.
19. Greenlee, interview by the authors.
20. American Bar Association, "Guidelines for the Appointment and Performance of Defense Counsel in Death Penalty Cases," rev. ed., *Hofstra Law Review* 31, no. 4 (2003): 952.
21. Greenlee, interview by the authors.

22. Fredric N. Tulsky, "Lawyers' Fees Get a New Look," *Philadelphia Inquirer*, December 9, 1992, p. A1.

23. Greenlee, interview by the authors.

24. Paul Conway, interview by the authors, September 11, 2018, Philadelphia.

25. Ibid.

26. Ibid.

27. Charles Cunningham, interview by the authors, April 30, 2018, Philadelphia.

28. Mary DeFusco, interview by the authors, April 10, 2018, Philadelphia.

29. Conway, interview by the authors.

30. Ibid.

31. Cunningham, interview by the authors.

32. Ibid.

33. James M. Anderson and Paul Heaton, "How Much Difference Does the Lawyer Make? The Effect of Defense Counsel on Murder Case Outcomes," *Yale Law Journal* 122, no. 1 (2012): 154–217.

34. Ibid., 179.

35. Ibid., 159.

36. Ibid., 188–200.

37. Joseph A. Slobodzian, "Pa. Justices Urged to Look at City Death-Penalty Pay," *Philadelphia Inquirer*, June 9, 2011, p. B5.

38. Nancy Phillips, "Mistakes in Life and Death Cases," *Philadelphia Inquirer*, October 23, 2011, p. A1.

39. Joseph A. Slobodzian, "Inquiry of Death Penalty Pay Rate," *Philadelphia Inquirer*, September 29, 2011, p. B1.

40. "Free Lawyers Defended," *Philadelphia Daily News*, February 22, 2012, p. 8.

41. Joseph A. Slobodzian, "Capital Defense Gets a Pay Boost," *Philadelphia Inquirer*, February 29, 2012, p. A1.

42. Anderson and Heaton, "How Much Difference Does the Lawyer Make?," 209.

43. Bookman, interview by the authors.

44. Ibid.

45. Ibid.

46. Ron Goldwyn, "Poor to Get 2nd Lawyer in Death Penalty Cases," *Philadelphia Daily News*, June 17, 2003, p. 6.

47. Anderson and Heaton, "How Much Difference Does the Lawyer Make?," 198.

48. Ibid., 196.

49. Bookman, interview by the authors.

50. Conway, interview by the authors.

51. Susan Phillips, "Lethal Direction," *Philadelphia City Paper*, July 22–28, 2004, https://mycitypaper.com/articles/2004-07-22/cover.shtml.

52. Bookman, interview by the authors.

53. Ibid.

54. Conway, interview by the authors.

55. Tina Rosenberg, "The Deadliest D.A.," *New York Times Magazine*, July 16, 1995, https://www.nytimes.com/1995/07/16/magazine/the-deadliest-da.html.

56. John Sullivan and Jennifer Moroz, "Rendell Willing to Review Death Row," *Philadelphia Inquirer*, January 15, 2003, p. A1.

57. Bookman, interview by the authors.

58. Cunningham, interview by the authors.

59. Jacqueline Soteropoulos, "Defenders Group Urged to Take on More Homicides," *Philadelphia Inquirer*, May 22, 2004, p. B2.

60. First Judicial District of Pennsylvania, "2005 Annual Report," 2005, p. 40, https://www.courts.phila.gov/pdf/report/2005-First-Judicial-District-Annual-Report.pdf.

61. Soteropoulos, "Defenders Group Urged to Take on More Homicides," B2.

62. Ibid.

63. Ibid.

64. Ibid.

65. Phillips, "Lethal Direction."

66. Greenlee, interview by the authors.

CHAPTER 17

1. Michael Isikoff and William Booth, "Miami 'Drug Court' Demonstrates Reno's Unorthodox Approach," *Washington Post*, February 20, 1993, https://www.washingtonpost.com/archive/politics/1993/02/20/miami-drug-court-demonstrates-renos-unorthodox-approach/67b7f5cc-d6ce-4dee-b5c1-105c2d470fe2.

2. Arthur J. Lurigio, "The First 20 Years of Drug Treatment Courts: A Brief Description of Their History and Impact," *Federal Probation: A Journal of Correctional Philosophy and Practice* 72, no. 1 (2008), https://www.uscourts.gov/sites/default/files/72_1_2_0.pdf; John S. Goldkamp and Doris Weiland, "Assessing the Impact of Dade County's Felony Drug Court," *National Institute of Justice Research in Brief*, December 1993, https://www.ncjrs.gov/pdffiles1/nij/145302.pdf.

3. "Rehabilitate, Don't Incarcerate," *Rap Sheet*, November 1989, p. 1.

4. Mary DeFusco, interview by the authors, April 11, 2018, Philadelphia.

5. Ibid.

6. Ibid.

7. Jacqueline Soteropoulos, "Funding Cuts Threaten Successful Drug Court," *Philadelphia Inquirer*, December 16, 2003, p. B4.

8. Philadelphia District Attorney's Office, "Pre-trial Diversion Programs," 2016, http://phlcouncil.com/wp-content/uploads/2016/04/Pre-Trial-Diversion.Philadelphia.pdf.

9. DeFusco, interview by the authors.

10. First Judicial District of Pennsylvania, "First Judicial District Testimony: Fiscal Year 2019 Operating Budget," April 24, 2018, p. 11, http://phlcouncil.com/wp-content/uploads/2018/04/FY19-Budget-Hearing-Testimony-FJD.pdf.

11. DeFusco, interview by the authors.

12. Ibid.

13. Ibid.

CHAPTER 18

1. Byron Cotter, interview by the authors, June 25, 2018, Philadelphia.

2. Ibid.

3. See discussion in Chapter 5.

4. Pernsley v. Harris, 474 U.S. 965 (1985).

5. Harris v. Pernsley, 654 F. Supp. 1042 (E.D. Pa. 1987).

6. John Woestendiek, "City Jail Moratorium Reinstated," *Philadelphia Inquirer*, June 8, 1988, p. 1-A.

7. Howard Goodman, "Consultants Urge Philadelphia to Build a New Prison," *Philadelphia Inquirer*, February 15, 1990, p. 13-B.

8. Howard Goodman, "Federal Judge Approves Agreement to Reduce Phila. Jail Overcrowding," *Philadelphia Inquirer*, March 12, 1991, p. B-1.

9. The remainder of the chapter is based largely on Cotter, interview by the authors. All quotations are from this source unless otherwise noted.

10. Linda Loyd, "City Names Jail System Coordinator," *Philadelphia Inquirer*, April 3, 1993, p. B3.

11. "Judge Gives Final Approval to End Oversight of Prisons," *Philadelphia Inquirer*, September 2, 2000, p. B2.

12. Melissa Dribben, "Graduation Scramble," *Philadelphia Inquirer*, May 9, 2013, p. A1.

13. Pennsylvania Horticultural Society, "Roots to Re-entry," https://phsonline.org/programs/roots-to-re-entry/ (accessed March 18, 2020).

14. West Philly Resource, "Legal Services—Community Based," https://westphillyresource.com/2018/11/05/legal-services-community-based/ (accessed March 18, 2020).

15. Philadelphia Prison System, "Inmate Handbook," p. 47, https://www.law.umich.edu/special/policyclearinghouse/Documents/Philadelphia%20Jail%20Inmate%20Handbook.pdf (accessed March 18, 2020).

16. Ibid., 48.

CHAPTER 19

1. Robert Listenbee Jr. and Ellen Greenlee, interview by the authors, February 1, 2018, Philadelphia.

2. In re Gault v. Arizona, 387 U.S. 1 (1967).

3. Rem Rieder, "Defender Group to Seek Set Terms for Phila. Women Inmates at Muncy: Unit Willing to Aid Poor Juveniles," *Philadelphia Inquirer*, July 9, 1968, p. 25.

4. "Juvenile Trials Threatened," *Philadelphia Inquirer*, June 23, 1968, p. 18.

5. "Law Unit Names Aide for Youths," *Philadelphia Inquirer*, April 7, 1968, p. 18.

6. Ellie Lingner, "Paula Gold: A Cacophony of Conflicts from Optimism to Despair," *Fort Lauderdale News*, October 28, 1981, p. 6 SL.

7. Acel Moore, "Juvenile Defender Unit Fights for Justice," *Philadelphia Inquirer*, March 22, 1970, p. 8.

8. Acel Moore, "Judges Are Hit on Treatment of Juveniles," *Philadelphia Inquirer*, December 31, 1969, p. 21.

9. Carlton E. Spitzer, "The Lawyer, the Judge and the Children," *Easton (Maryland) Star Democrat*, June 24, 2001, p. 5.

10. Benjamin Lerner, interview by the authors, November 12, 2018, Philadelphia.

11. Gayle Ronan Sims, "Alice 'Peg' O'Shea, 86, Juvenile Justice Pioneer," *Philadelphia Inquirer*, October 1, 2005, p. B6.

12. Martha Woodall, "Children's Legal Aid to Increase," *Philadelphia Inquirer*, April 18, 1990, p. 1-A.

13. Ellen Greenlee, interview by the authors, March 20, 2017, Philadelphia.

14. "Defender Association of Philadelphia: 37th Annual Report of the Board of Directors, for the Year July 1, 1970–June 30, 1971," pp. 14–15, Defender Association of Philadelphia Records, Special Collections Research Center, Temple University Libraries, Philadelphia.

15. "Public Defender Representation in Pennsylvania: A Report from Vincent J. Ziccardi, Esq., to the Honorable A. Evans Kephart, Court Administrator of Pennsylvania, Project Director," June 1974, p. 47 (in authors' possession).

16. Ibid., 35–36.

17. Ibid., 38.

18. "Public Defender Representation in Pennsylvania," 37; "Defender Association of Philadelphia: 37th Annual Report," 15.

19. "Public Defender Representation in Pennsylvania," 35.

20. Moore, "Juvenile Defender Unit Fights for Justice," 8.

21. Acel Moore and Michael Willmann, "Intensive Probation Unit Gives Juveniles Individual Aid," *Philadelphia Inquirer*, October 11,1970, p. 11; Mike Willman, "Inside City Hall," *Philadelphia Inquirer*, October 11, 1970, p. 36.

22. Lerner, interview by the authors.

23. Fredric N. Tulsky, Daniel R. Biddle, and Henry Goldman, "Casey Names 10 to City Court," *Philadelphia Inquirer*, February 25, 1987, p. 1-A.

24. Listenbee, interview by the authors.

25. Greenlee, interview by the authors.

26. Listenbee, interview by the authors.

27. Ibid.

28. Charles Cunningham, interview by the authors, April 30, 2018, Philadelphia.

29. Ibid.

30. Listenbee, interview by the authors.

31. Ibid.

32. Ibid.

33. Ibid.

34. Ibid

35. Ibid.

36. Ibid.

37. Ibid.

38. Ibid.

39. Ibid.

40. Greenlee, interview by the authors.

41. Listenbee, interview by the authors.

42. Ben Finley, "Court Strikes Pa. Juvenile Sex Offender List," *Philadelphia Inquirer*, January 5, 2015, p. A1.

43. Pennsylvania Department of Human Services, "Act 21," https://www.dhs.pa.gov/providers/Providers/Pages/Act-21.aspx (accessed May 20, 2020).

44. Listenbee, interview by the authors.

45. Ibid.

46. Ibid.

47. Ibid.

48. Juvenile Law Center, "Youth in the Justice System: An Overview," https://jlc.org/youth-justice-system-overview (accessed March 18, 2020).

49. Listenbee, interview by the authors.

50. Robert Swift, "Two More Named to Scandal Panel," *Times-Tribune* (Scranton, Pennsylvania), August 18, 2009, p. A4.

51. Darren Breslin, email interview by the authors, December 3, 2018.

52. Greenlee, interview by the authors.

53. John Kelly and Marion Mattingly, "Obama Administration to Name Bob Listenbee to Lead Juvenile Justice Agency," *Chronicle of Social Change*, January 31, 2013, https://chronicleofsocialchange.org/featured/administration-to-name-bob-listenbee-as-administrator-of-juvenile-justice-agency/1809.

54. Greenlee, interview by the authors.

CHAPTER 20

1. "Twelfth Annual Report of the Board of Directors of the Philadelphia Voluntary Defender Association, for the Year June 1, 1945, to May 31, 1946," p. 3, Defender Association of Philadelphia Records, Special Research Collections, Temple University Libraries, Philadelphia.

2. "Free Legal Defense Provided for 3002," *Philadelphia Inquirer,* October 22, 1951, p. 19.

3. "Defender Group Changes Name," *Philadelphia Inquirer,* March 30, 1958, p. 3.

4. U.S. Courts, "Criminal Justice Act: At 50 Years, a Landmark in the Right to Counsel," August 20, 2014, https://www.uscourts.gov/news/2014/08/20/criminal-justice-act-50-years-landmark-right-counsel.

5. The text of 18 U.S. Code §3006A, on adequate representation of defendants, is available at https://www.law.cornell.edu/uscode/text/18/3006A.

6. "38th Annual Report of the Directors, Defender Association of Philadelphia, for the Year July 1, 1971–June 30, 1972," p. 6, Defender Association of Philadelphia Records, Special Collections Research Center, Temple University Libraries.

7. U.S. Courts, "Defender Services," https://www.uscourts.gov/services-forms/defender-services (accessed March 18, 2020). The bill to amend the CJA was introduced by Senator Roman Hruska of Nebraska and cosponsored by Senators Barry Goldwater and Edward Kennedy.

8. "38th Annual Report," 7.

9. Ibid., 7.

10. Jim Smith, "Patio Payoff Costs Lawyer 2G Fine," *Philadelphia Daily News,* October 15, 1983, p. 4.

11. John F. Morrison, "Maureen Rowley, 57, Defender of Justice," *Philadelphia Inquirer,* October 20, 2011, https://www.inquirer.com/philly/obituaries/20111020_Maureen_Rowley__57__defender_of_justice.html.

12. Rompilla v. Beard, 545 U.S. 374 (2005).

13. Ibid.

14. Morrison, "Maureen Rowley."

15. Ibid.

16. L. Felipe Restrepo, interview by the authors, May 1, 2017, Philadelphia.

17. American Bar Association, "Impact of Federal Budget Cuts," December 1, 2013, https://www.americanbar.org/groups/committees/death_penalty_representation/project_press/2013/year-end/impact-of-federal-budget-cuts/.

18. John P. Martin, "Federal Cuts Hit Philadelphia Defenders," *Philadelphia Inquirer,* April 22, 2013, https://www.inquirer.com/philly/news/politics/congressional/20130422_Sequester_cuts_force_layoffs__furloughs_for_Philadelphia_s_federal_Public_Defender_s_Office.html.

19. Restrepo, interview by the authors.

20. 18 U.S. Code §3599(a)(2).

21. Debbie Garlicki, "Death Row Defenders Roil Legal Waters," *Morning Call* (Allentown, Pennsylvania), January 13, 2002, p. A1.

22. "Maureen K. Rowley '80 Named Temple Law Grad of the '80s," *Temple ESQ,* Fall 2005, p. 5; Morrison, "Maureen Rowley."

23. "Danny Glover Speaks for Inmates' Cause," *Philadelphia Daily News,* December 1, 2000, p. 62.

24. Federal Community Defender Office for the Eastern District of Pennsylvania, "Meet Our Staff," https://pae.fd.org/Our_Staff.html (accessed March 18, 2020).

25. Death Penalty Information Center, "Philadelphia District Attorney Asks Pennsylvania Supreme Court to Strike Down State's Death Penalty," July 18, 2019, https://deathpenaltyinfo.org/news/philadelphia-district-attorney-asks-pennsylvania -supreme-court-to-strike-down-states-death-penalty.

26. Commonwealth v. Spotz, 18 A.3d 244 (Pa. 2011).

27. Ibid.

28. In re Commonwealth's Motion to Appoint Counsel against or Directed to Defender Association of Philadelphia, 790 F. 3d 457 (3d Cir. 2015).

29. Ibid.

30. Ibid.

31. Ibid.

32. Ibid.

33. Leigh M. Skipper (chief federal defender), Helen Marino (first assistant federal defender), and Shawn Nolan (chief of Federal Community Defender Office for the Eastern District of Pennsylvania capital habeas unit), interview by Michael Schaffer and David Richman, September 6, 2018, Philadelphia.

CHAPTER 21

1. Joseph A. Slobodzian, "Agreement Ends Judge's Oversight of City Prisons," *Philadelphia Inquirer*, July 28, 2000, p. B1.

2. Pew Charitable Trusts, "Philadelphia's Crowded, Costly Jails: The Search for Safe Solutions," 2010, p. 6, https://www.pewtrusts.org/-/media/legacy/uploadedfiles/ wwwpewtrustsorg/reports/philadelphia_research_initiative/philadelphiascrowded costlyjailsrevpdf.pdf.

3. Ibid., 23–24.

4. Ibid., 25–26.

5. Samantha Melamed, "Turning the Prison Tide," *Philadelphia Inquirer*, May 22, 2016, p. A2.

6. Pew Charitable Trusts, "Philadelphia's Crowded, Costly Jails," 6.

7. Bowers v. Philadelphia, Civil Action No. 06-CV-3229 (E.D. Pa. September 28, 2006).

8. Vera Institute, "Incarceration Trends: Philadelphia County, PA," http:// trends.vera.org/rates/philadelphia-county-pa (accessed May 21, 2020).

9. Maura Ewing, "A Reckoning in Philadelphia," *The Atlantic*, March 3, 2016, https://www.theatlantic.com/politics/archive/2016/03/a-reckoning-in-philadelphia/ 472092/.

10. Bowers v. Philadelphia.

11. Pew Charitable Trusts, "Philadelphia's Crowded, Costly Jails," 17.

12. Bowers v. Philadelphia.

13. Vera Institute, "Incarceration Trends"; Pew Charitable Trusts, "Philadelphia's Crowded, Costly Jails," 1.

14. Williams v. Philadelphia, 2:08-cv-01979-RBS (E.D. Pa. 2008); David Rudovsky, telephone interview by the authors, July 23, 2019.

15. Pew Charitable Trusts, "Philadelphia's Crowded, Costly Jails," 20.

16. Dylan Purcell, Craig R. McCoy, and Nancy Phillips, "Violent Criminals Flout Broken Bail System," *Philadelphia Inquirer*, December 15, 2009, p. A1; Samantha Melamed, "Turning the Prison Tide," *Philadelphia Inquirer*, May 22, 2016, p. A1.

17. Craig R. McCoy, "New Court Cracks Down on Fugitives," *Philadelphia Inquirer*, May 6, 2012, p. A1.

18. Rudovsky, interview by the authors.

19. Pew Charitable Trusts, "Philadelphia's Crowded, Costly Jails," 6.

20. Ibid.

21. Ibid., 22, 24.

22. Erik Eckholm, "'Smart on Crime' Mantra of Philadelphia Prosecutor," *New York Times*, June 19, 2010, https://www.nytimes.com/2010/06/20/us/20philly.html.

23. Pew Charitable Trusts, "Philadelphia's Crowded, Costly Jails," 29.

24. Sarah Smith and Mark Fazlollah, "Officer Arrested in FBI Sting," *Philadelphia Inquirer*, May 23, 2013, p. B1.

25. Mensah M. Dean, "Judge Tosses 53 Drug Cases amid Cop Probe," *Philadelphia Daily News*, November 10, 2013, p. 6.

26. David Gambacorta, "12 of Ex-cop's Cases Tossed," *Philadelphia Daily News*, December 8, 2013, p. 16.

27. Jeremy Roebuck, "6 on Narcotics Squad Acquitted," *Philadelphia Inquirer*, May 15, 2015, p. A1; Matt Gelb, "Former Philly Narcotics Cop Jeffrey Walker Sentenced to 3½ Years," *Philadelphia Inquirer*, July 29, 2015, https://www.inquirer.com/philly/news/20150730_Former_Philly_narcotics_cop_Jeffrey_Walker_sentenced_to_31_2_years_in_prison.html; Bobby Allyn, "Cleared of Corruption, 6 Philly Cops Get Jobs Back through Arbitration," *WHYY*, July 13, 2015, https://whyy.org/articles/cleared-of-corruption-6-philly-cops-get-jobs-back-through-arbitration.

28. Mark Fazlollah, "More Tainted Drug Cases Tossed," *Philadelphia Inquirer*, February 6, 2016, p. B2.

29. Chris Palmer, Samantha Melamed, and Mark Fazlollah, "Costs Could Be Huge in Police Cases," *Philadelphia Inquirer*, November 26, 2017, p. A1.

30. Chris Hepp, "Phila. Wins $3.5 Million Grant to Cut Inmate Numbers," *Philadelphia Inquirer*, April 13, 2016, p. A1.

31. MacArthur Foundation, "About Us," https://www.macfound.org/about/ (accessed March 18, 2020).

32. Tricia L. Nadolny, "City Will Study Ways to Cut Jail Crowding," *Philadelphia Inquirer*, May 28, 2015, p. B7.

33. Hepp, "Phila. Wins $3.5 Million Grant."

34. Katie Colaneri, "$3.5 Million Grant to Help Philly Cut Inmate Population, Launch Other Prison Reforms," *WHYY*, April 13, 2016, https://whyy.org/articles/35-million-grant-to-help-philly-cut-inmate-population-launch-other-reforms/.

35. Miller v. Alabama, 567 U.S. 460 (2012).

36. Montgomery v. Louisiana, 577 U.S. ___ (2016).

37. Defender Association of Philadelphia, "Juvenile Life without Parole," https://www.philadefender.org/practice-units/juvenile-life/ (accessed March 18, 2020); Samantha Melamed, "For Juvenile Lifers, Philly Courts Set a Tough Path Forward," *Philadelphia Inquirer*, April 20, 2017, https://www.inquirer.com/philly/news/Philly-juvenile-lifers-contested-hearings-Philadelphia.html.

38. Bradley S. Bridge, interview by the authors, April 25, 2018, Philadelphia.

39. Paul Conway, interview by the authors, October 5, 2018, Philadelphia.

40. Ibid.

41. Pennsylvania Department of Corrections, "Juvenile Lifers Information," https://www.cor.pa.gov/About%20Us/Initiatives/Pages/Juvenile-Lifers-Information.aspx (accessed March 18, 2020).

42. Conway, interview by the authors.

43. Bridge, interview by the authors.

44. Ibid.

45. Rudovsky, interview by the authors.

46. Miriam Hill, "New Public Safety Czar's Broad Role," *Philadelphia Inquirer*, March 25, 2008, p. B1.

47. Rudovsky, interview by the authors.

48. Ibid.

49. Defender Association of Philadelphia, untitled PowerPoint presentation, 2017, http://phlcouncil.com/wp-content/uploads/2017/05/Defender-Association -Power-Point-May-2017.pdf.

50. Bridge, interview by the authors.

51. Craig R. McCoy, "Association Seeks to Close Pay Gaps for Public Defenders," *Philadelphia Inquirer*, June 24, 2012, https://www.inquirer.com/philly/news/politics/ city/20120624_Association_seeks_to_close_pay_gaps_for_public_defenders.html.

52. Keir Bradford-Grey, interview by the authors, May 1, 2017, Philadelphia.

53. Chris Mondics, "Defender Association's Greenlee to Leave in March," *Philadelphia Inquirer*, December 10, 2014, p. A13.

54. Max Mitchell, "Phila.'s Longtime Chief Public Defender Retiring," *Legal Intelligencer*, December 10, 2014, https://www.law.com/thelegalintelligencer/almID/ 1202678457150/.

EPILOGUE

1. Tricia L. Nadolny, "Council Tackles Criminal Justice Reform," *Philadelphia Inquirer*, February 4, 2016, https://www.inquirer.com/philly/news/politics/ 20160205_Council_names_panel_to_study_justice_system.html.

2. City of Philadelphia, "City Awarded $4 Million by MacArthur Safety and Justice Challenge," October 24, 2018, https://www.phila.gov/2018-10-24-city-awarded -4-million-by-macarthur-safety-and-justice-challenge/.

3. Keir Bradford-Grey, interview by the authors, April 26, 2017, Philadelphia.

4. Defender Association of Philadelphia, "Three Years of Positive Change at the Defender Association," September 2018, p. 6 (in authors' possession).

5. Jeremy Roebuck, "Philly DA Seth Williams Pleads Guilty, Goes to Prison," *Philadelphia Inquirer*, June 29, 2017, https://www.inquirer.com/philly/news/crime/ philly-da-seth-williams-xxxxxxxx-20170629.html.

6. David Rudovsky, interview by the authors, July 5, 2017, Philadelphia.

7. Ibid.

8. Ibid.

9. Chris Palmer, "Larry Krasner's First Year as Philly DA: Staff Turnover, Fewer Cases, Plenty of Controversy," *Philadelphia Inquirer*, January 6, 2019, https://www .inquirer.com/news/larry-krasner-philadelphia-district-attorney-staff-reform-cases -first-year-20190106.html.

INDEX

Edward W. Madeira Jr. (1928–2020) practiced law in Philadelphia for more than 60 years and was the Retired Chair Emeritus of Pepper Hamilton. As a young lawyer, he worked as a volunteer public defender, on loan from Pepper Hamilton to the Defender Association of Philadelphia. He was a member of the Defender's Board of Directors from 1958 to 2016 and was Chairman of the Board from 1973 to 1998.

Michael D. Schaffer held a variety of reporting and editing posts at the *Philadelphia Inquirer*, including Book Review Editor, before retiring from the newspaper at the end of 2014. He has a Ph.D. in American history from Yale University and worked at the National Portrait Gallery of the Smithsonian Institution before becoming a journalist. He is the coauthor of two books, *"The Dye Is Now Cast": The Road to American Independence, 1774–1776*, published by the Smithsonian Institution as part of its Bicentennial observance, and *1787: Inventing America—A Day-by-Day Account of the Constitutional Convention*.